Film Stars in Indian Politics

Film Stars in Indian Politics

RAM AWATAR AGNIHOTRI

COMMONWEALTH PUBLISHERS
NEW DELHI (INDIA)
1998

Film Stars in Indian Politics

1st Edition : 1998

ISBN : 81-7169-506-X

Published by :
AJAY VERMA
for **Commonwealth Publishers**
4831/24, Prahlad Street,
Ansari Road, Darya Ganj,
New Delhi-110002.
Phone : 3272541
Fax : 91-11-3257835

Laser Typesetting by :
Stylish Laser Typesetter, Delhi-53.

Printed at :
Efficient Offset Press, Shahzada Bagh, Delhi.

Dedicated to

MY ELDEST BROTHER
MASTER RAMESH AGNIHOTRI
WHO LEFT US IN 1942

Preface

During the preparation on "Film Stars in Indian Politics", I visited Film Archives, Poona and many universities, libraries of the country. In respect of this research work, Professor S.K. Chaturvedi, Head, Department of Political Science, Institute of Advanced Studies, Ch. Charan Singh University, Meerut provided me invaluable co-operation and guidance. I owe high gratitude for him. I also owe high gratitude to Prof. I.N. Tewary and Dr. Archana Sharma of this Department for their invaluable co-operation.

At this solemn occasion, to remember my grand father Late Pandit Anant Prasad Agnihotri, grand mother Late Mrs. Gomati Agnihotri, parents Late Pandit Shiv Nandan Agnihotri and Late Mrs. Shakuntala Agnihotri and also my late brothers and sisters, Baby Premvati Agnihotri, Master Ramesh Agnihotri, Master Mahesh Agnihotri, Master Mania Agnihotri, Baby Shiela Agnihotri, Baby Pushpa Agnihotri, and Baby Rajni Agnihotri is my duty. Again, I dedicate my younger brother late Master Bhupendra Agnihotri (Bhappu) who left us a day before of the Basant Panchami's Saraswati Pooja (Worship of Goddess of Knowledge) in 1958. My true remembrance of my late younger brother is to keep continue the worship of goddess Saraswati as learning, reading, writing and revealing truth through research.

At the time of publication of this work, I am thankful to my family members Pandit Jagdish Prasad Agnihotri (elder brother), Mrs. Taramati Dixit, Mrs. Saroj Tiwari (elder sisters), Mrs. Prem Lata Tiwari, Mrs. Krishna Sharma (younger sisters), Mrs. Swatantra Bala Agnihotri (wife) and Miss Meenakshi Agnihotri, Mr. Lavkush Agnihotri and Master Lavkesh Agnihotri (children), whose motivation made possible to bring this research work in book form.

I am also thankful to Mr. B.R. Verma, Commonwealth Publishers, New Delhi, for his co-operation.

Ram Awatar Agnihotri

Contents

Preface .... *(vii)*

List of Tables .... *(xi)*

List of Diagrams .... *(xiii)*

Chapter *Pages*

PART I

1. Introduction : 1
   - I. Morality in Films and Box office Position of 1996 Released Hindi Films
   - II. Television in India
   - III. Impact of Satellite Channels in India
   - IV. Censorship loses meaning with video, cable boom
   - V. Cable TV Ordinance Disappointed Film Industry
   - VI. Asia produces over 50% of Total World Film output

PART II

2. Surveyed Political Study of Sunil Dutt 47
3. Surveyed Political Study of Shabana Azmi : M.P. (Nominated Rajya Sabha Member) 63

Chapter *Pages*

4. Surveyed Political Study of Raj Babbar : M.P. 'Rajya Sabha Member) 74

PART II

5. Surveyed Political Study of Rajesh Khanna 90
6. Surveyed Political Study of Shatrughna Sinha : M.P. (Rajya Sabha Member) 111
7. I. Amitabh Bachchan and Politics 125
   II. Late Smita Patil : Interest in Social Activities and Politics through Her Films

PART III

8. Surveyed Political Study of Shivaji Ganesan 143
9. Surveyed Political Study of Late N.T. Rama Rao 160
10. I. J. Jayalalitha
    II. V.N. Janaki Ramchandran
    III. Late Utpal Dutt

PART IV

11. Conclusion 195
    I. Ronald Wilson Reagon
    II. Great Charlie Chaplin

Bibliography 235

List of Tables

Table No.	Title	Pages
1.1	Box Office Position of Hindi Films Released in 1996	8
1.2	Music Directors of Hindi Films Released in 1996	16
1.3	New Transmitters during 1986-87	21
2.1	Detailed Study of Sunil Dutt's One Hundred Surveyed Political Supporters in Delhi in August, 1997	51
3.1	Detailed Study of Shabana Azmi's One Hundred Surveyed Political Supporters in Delhi in July, 1996	64
4.1	Raj Babbar's Films, Leading Heroines and Directors upto present period	78
4.2	Detailed Study of Raj Babbar's One Hundred Surveyed Political Supporters in Delhi in January, 1996	83
5.1	Rajesh Khanna's films, Leading Heroines and Directors upto present period	98
5.2	Detailed Study of Rajesh Khanna's One Hundred Surveyed Political Supporters in Delhi in September, 1997	103

Table No.	Title	Pages
6.1	Detailed Study of Shatrughna Sinha's One Hundred Surveyed Political Supporters in Delhi in March, 1997	118
8.1	Detailed Study of Shivaji Ganesan's One Hundred Surveyed Political Supporters in Delhi in July, 1997	148
9.1	Detailed Study of Late N.T. Rama Rao's One Hundred Surveyed Political Supporters in Delhi in September, 1993	170
11.1	Ronald Reagon—Star Politico; Reagon's Films of Socio-Political Background in which he Acted	213
11.2	Writers and Musicians of Ronald Reagon's Socio-Political Background Films	224

List of Diagrams

No.	Title	Pages
2.1	Views-Wise Number of Sunil Dutt's One Hundred Surveyed Political Supporters in Delhi in August 1997 (Views about his Political Future)	56
2.2	Income Group-Wise Number of Sunil Dutt's One Hundred Surveyed Political Supporters in Delhi in August 1997	57
2.3	Education-Wise Number of Sunil Dutt's One Hundred Surveyed Political Supporters in Delhi in August 1997	58
2.4	Religion-Wise Number of Sunil Dutt's One Hundred Surveyed Political Supporters in Delhi in August 1997	59
2.5	His Watched Political Films Group-Wise Number of Sunil Dutt's One Hundred Surveyed Political Supporters in Delhi in August 1997	60
2.6	Age Group-Wise Number of Sunil Dutt's One Hundred Surveyed Political Supporters in Delhi in August 1997	61
2.7	Occupation-Wise Number of Sunil Dutt's One Hundred Surveyed Political Supporters in Delhi in August 1997	62

No.	Title	Pages
3.1	Religion-Wise Number of Shabana Azmi's One Hundred Surveyed Political Supporters in Delhi in July 1996	69
3.2	Education-Wise Number of Shabana Azmi's One Hundred Surveyed Political Supporters in Delhi in July 1996	70
3.3	Age Group-Wise Number of Shabana Azmi's One Hundred Surveyed Political Supporters in Delhi in July 1996	71
3.4	Views-Wise Number of Shabana Azmi's One Hundred Surveyed Political Supporters in Delhi in July 1996 (Views about Her Political Future)	72
3.5	Occupation-Wise Number of Shabana Azmi's One Hundred Surveyed Political Supporters in Delhi in July 1996	73
5.1	1952-1991 Electoral Performance in New Delhi Lok Sabha Constituency	108
8.1	His Watched Political Films Group-Wise Number of Shivaji Ganesan's One Hundred Surveyed Political Supporters in Delhi in July 1997	153
8.2	Views-Wise Number of Shivaji Ganesan's One Hundred Surveyed Political Supporters in Delhi in July 1997 (Views about His Political Future)	154
8.3	Income Group-Wise Number of Shivaji Ganesan's One Hundred Surveyed Political Supporters in Delhi in July 1997	155
8.4	Age Group-Wise Number of Shivaji Ganesan's One Hundred Surveyed Political Supporters in Delhi in July 1997	156

No.	*Title*	*Pages*
8.5	Education-Wise Number of Shivaji Ganesan's One Hundred Surveyed Political Supporters in Delhi in July 1997	157
8.6	Occupation-Wise Number of Shivaji Ganesan's One Hundred Surveyed Political Supporters in Delhi in July 1997	158
8.7	Religion-Wise Number of Shivaji Ganesan's One Hundred Surveyed Political Supporters in Delhi in July 1997	159

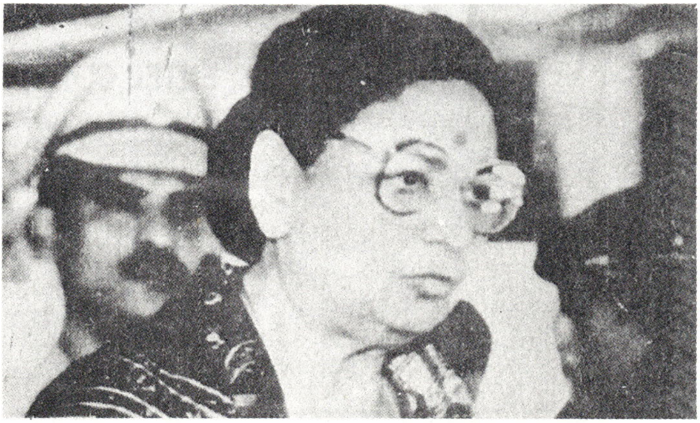

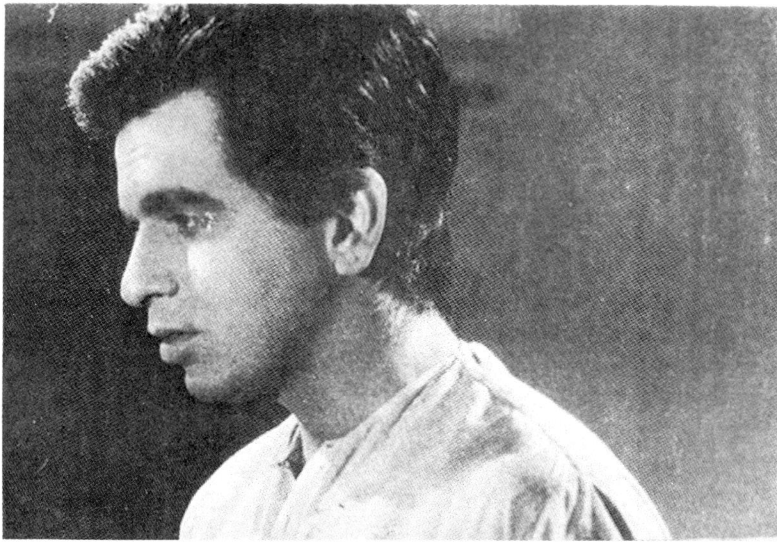

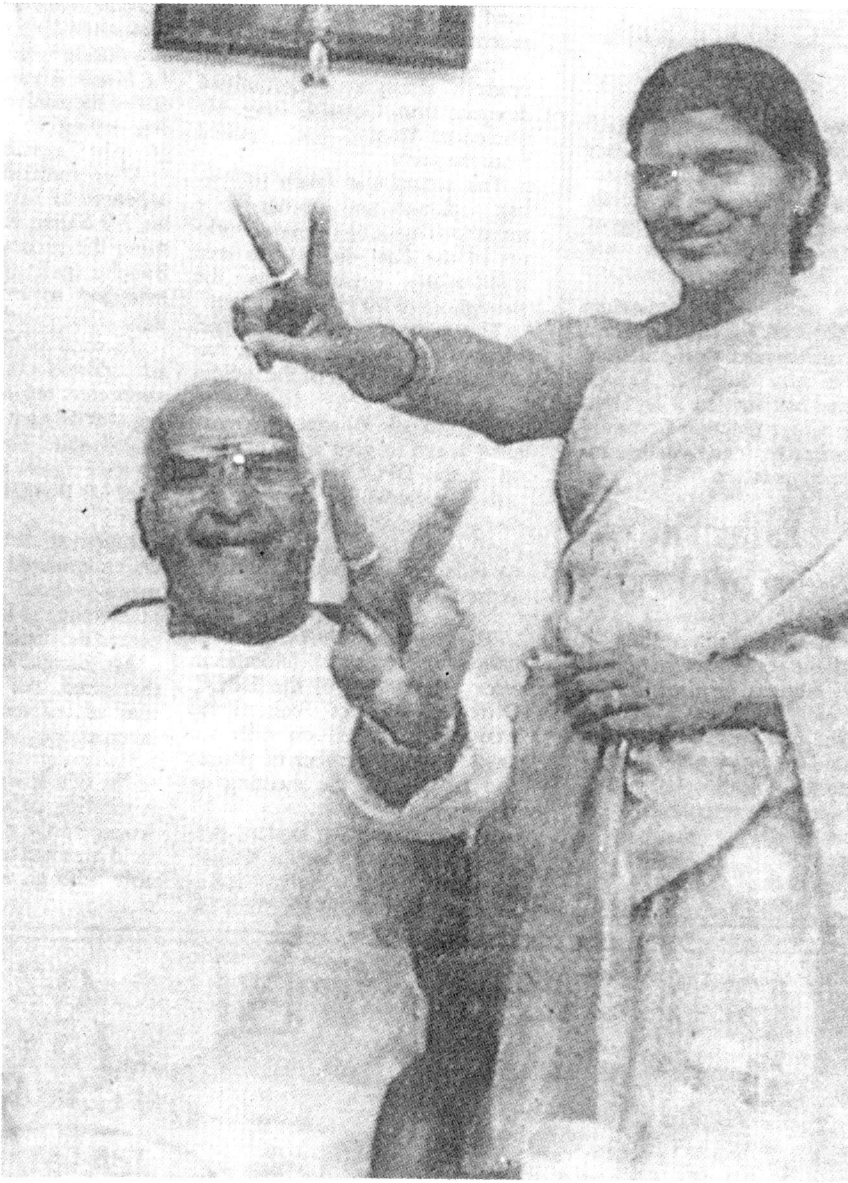

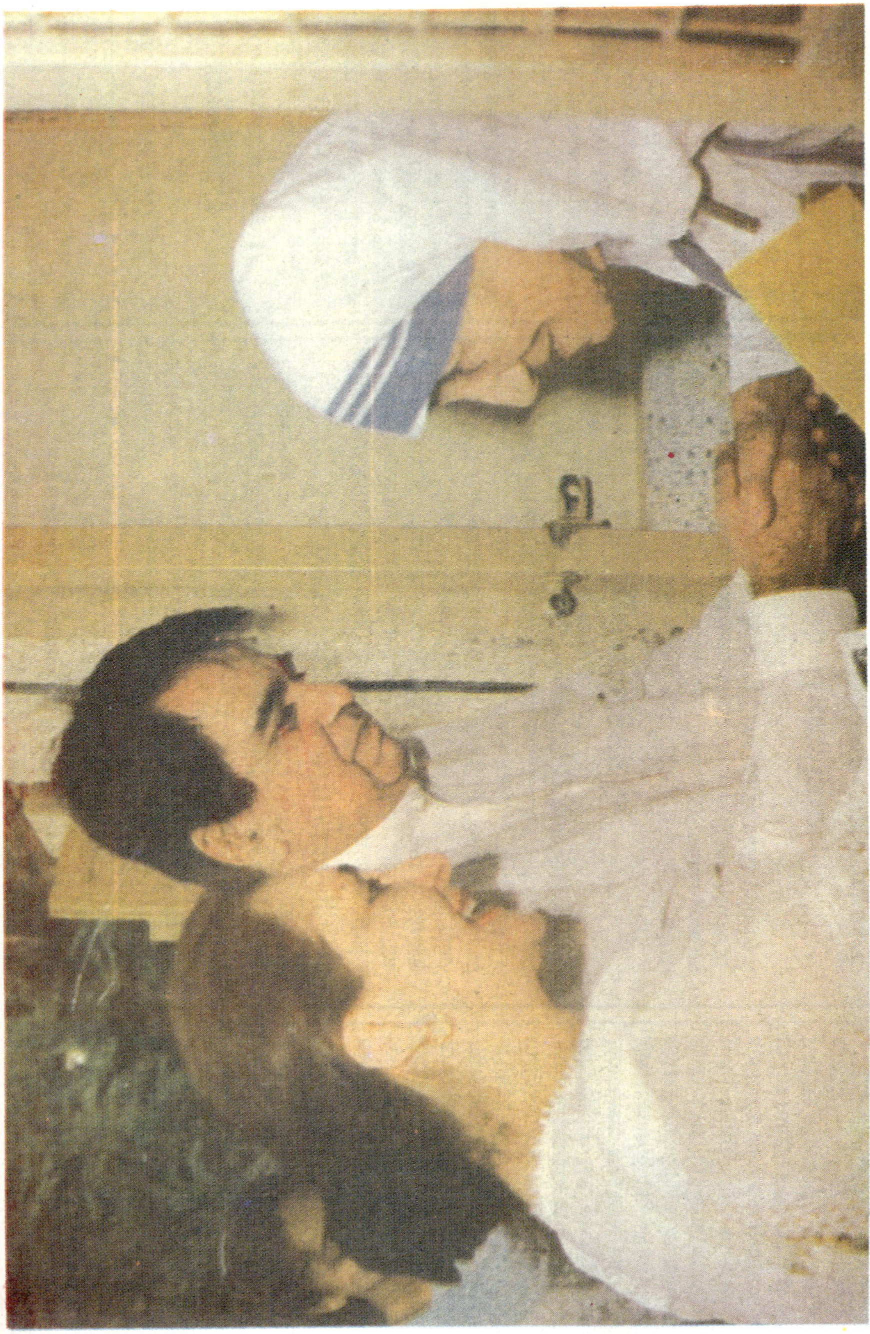

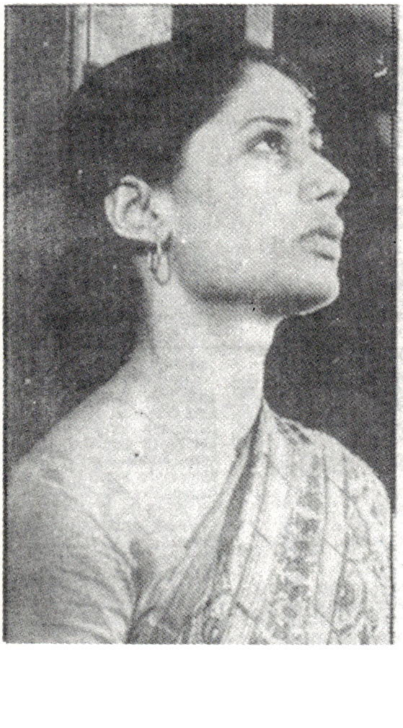

TAKE TWO: Sarada is fighting hard to retain her Tenali seat

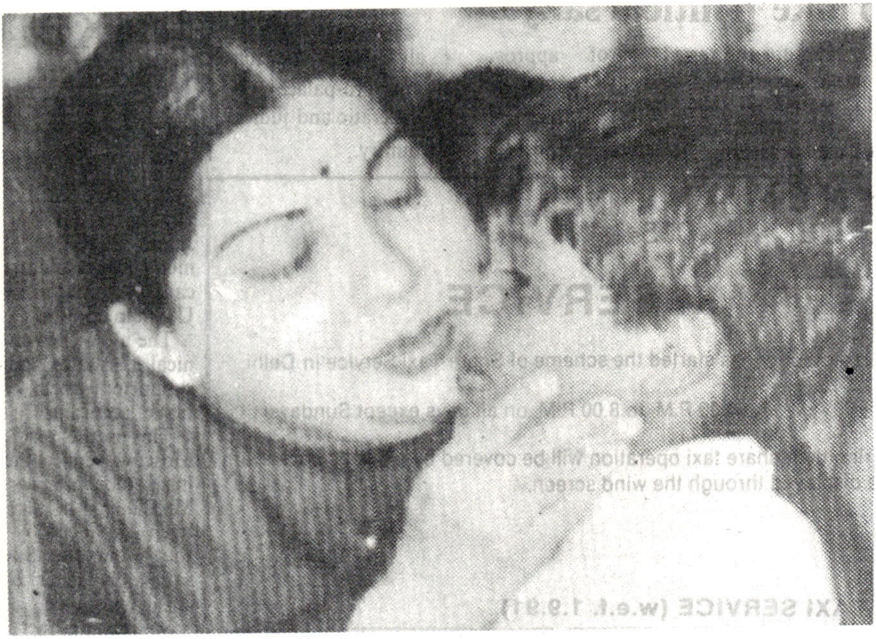

PART I

Chapter 1
Introduction

I. MORALITY IN FILMS

The film 'Basic Instinct' was a great hit at 1993 film festival of India though for the wrong reasons. On the face of it the film had some scenes to please the voyeur but it carried a lot more that would not come home so easily to a male chauvinist sensibility used to seeing Hindi films where, besides the visual, the linguistic aspect has reached the rock bottom obscenity. Morally superior as we claim to be to the spiritually bankrupt west, we cannot accept naked facts even though we take liberties without compunction with the suggestive. According to a school of thought, portrayal of pornography is a violation of civil rights. It is considered as active in creating and maintaining the civil inequality of the sexes. Though 'Basic Instinct' despite some bold, brash shots escapes the charge, a majority of our own Indian films are doing a far more notorious job, rather a systematic one of exploitation and subordination based on sex which differentially harms women. Rape scenes are the biggest bane of a standard Hindi film. The scenes are not there as part of the portrayal of violence against women but often added to please the prurient among the audience. One remembers one such film when men in droves flocked to cinema halls to see a particular film for a particular rape scene. The VCRs were not in vogue then. The most enthusiastic age group was 50 and above some with a medical history of by-pass surgery, others showing early signs of palsy but all of them holding respectable positions including vocations where one is supposed to be the arbiter of morals. Rape scenes on the screen often mirror an even uglier reality that knows no borders.

On the occasion of International Women's Day on March 8, 1993, UN Secretary-General Boutros Boutros-Ghali said in a message, "Rape is the most despicable crime against women",—a time to celebrate what women have achieved in their struggle for equal rights, social progress and peace but also a time, according to him, to speak honestly about the continuing oppression of women in many areas of the world and in various aspects of daily life. Women's rights are high on the agencies of the UN Commission on human rights especially after reports of sexual violence as a form of warfare in Bosnia where such acts have passed from the imagistic to the real. It's no film story that poor women including young girls forced to migrate to other States in India become helpless victims of sexual exploitation by khatedars, contractors, gang leaders and others of that ilk. Women form about 25 percent of the total labour force that migrates to other states. This is only a short clip from a newspaper published on a particular day. Cans full of such clips could be had for the asking. Gender bias, a cause that concerned a seminar in New Delhi to commemorate the International Women's Day, could be tackled only after first attacking the commercial medium that reinforces such prejudice. Women in most of our formula films are shown as totally passive beings—shy, sexy and dependent. They are dominated either by the strong male image of a powerful father or a lover who might even be a criminal but is acceptable once he is past the subjective barrier of sentiment.

By contrast, Miss Catherine Tramell (played by Sharon Stone in 'Basic Instinct') is an economically independent writer. A woman in complete command of herself. Falsity of the risque and bold notwithstanding, Miss Tramell, in a very special way, supports the illusion of a complete person. Attractive, child-like vulnerable and lethal at the same time. The whole purpose of the film, it seems, is to confuse the priorities of the viewer. Whether or not she is the murderess becomes irrelevant once the full impact of her projected personality makes itself felt. Here at last is the persona of D.H. Lawrence's prophecy. An outline of the dominating image of woman whose coming is expected in the 21st century. As a matter of incidental detail, Sharon Stone has moved to instant stardom with 'Basic Instinct'. She had starred earlier in 'Irreconciliable differences' and 'Total Recall'. She is today the much sought after actress in Hollywood. A steep climb from B and C Movies.

According to an author Surinder K. Datta, wittingly or unwittingly, the film forces us to think. Whatever our protestations and concerns about pornography, the sobering fact remains that the sexual content of the film that pushed boundaries of sorts earned dollar 115 million. So much for morality! Paradoxically, the sexual content is the only falsification (in the sense of remoteness from reality) in the film. Pornography, in the words of Susan Sontag, serves to drive a wedge between one's existence as a full human being and one's existence as a sexual being. A good work of art reconciles the dichotomy. Despite a rather heavy does of one aspect at the beginning, the fullness of being of Miss Tramell stands out in the end. A question valid in some permissive societies between public morality and individual liberty may become poignant in the years to come in India too. We have had pioneers like the late Raj Kapoor who used the erotic to very authentic effect in films despite very rigid rules of censorship in Post-Independence India. The laws as before Independence concerned mainly with obscenity among other things. Drinking was not permitted in the films. Kissing and embracing were forbidden too. One would find to incredible today in the face of complete reversal of values that in the early fifties film songs were considered 'cheap and vulgar' and their broadcasting over AIR was as such drastically reduced. We have today a tribe of film-makers who defy all rules of decency for the sake of a quick buck. Ours is a society in transition and not used to living by norms. The question of opinion being polarized between the conservatives and civil libertarians would take time to crystallize in a free-for-all laissez faire that affects all aspects of our life. Meanwhile, someone has to catch the rapist while still in a state of reverie the overactively imaginative who plays on the suggestive that results in acts of aggression against women both on the screen and in real life.

Those who exploit freedom to take us to unfreedom are also transgressing on the rights of those who would not like to be red-faced in the presence of family members by an unexpected exposure to overt sex whether in the service of family planning or cheap entertainment. Equally sinful and damaging to the wholeness of the entire community would be the brute repressions of facts in the name of decency, an euphemism for hypocrisy. Doordarshan reportedly took a year and half to decide on the telecasting of a film on rape awarded the North Indian Film Association's award of excellence while continuing at peak time with its propaganda on family planning in explicit detail. What attracts us to Miss Tramell is her courage and candidness. A basic truth about herself that she openly accepts and that throws out of gear even a lie detector. Miss Tramell has crossed the region of moral uncertainty and as such confronts her tormentors with altogether new facts. Facts for which their own stereotypal morality is not ready. The film could be rechristened 'Basic Facts' towards which we both as individuals and as a community have to move and individuate. In all aspects of our life whether cultural or political, we are still short of the moral either/or of real freedom but rest rather complacently on moral overlaps that are either confusion or hypocrisy. Poet Kabir came closest to chiding us out of this self-deception. While he offers equal alternatives in Kailash and Kaba, he urges a bit of soul searching before the highest value is born in us. There is a road to Being and there is a road to Nothingness and never the twain shall meet.

Rudyard Kipling completes the introduction to 'The Ballad of East and West' with the line "But there is neither East nor West, Boarder nor Breed, nor Birth/when two strong men stand face to face, though they come from the ends of the earth?" Face to face could be our own split self lost in the mist of unmorality and awaiting a rare act of will or grace for the veil of ignorance to lift itself. 'Gunghat ke pat khol re, tohe piya mil geye," goes a popular song immortalised by the voice of late Geeta Dutt. Sado-masochistic relations befuddle both sexes. Such drives are born in a bid to escape from the aloneness of self. It is usually the case that women are on the receiving end of such compulsive behaviour. Miss Tarmell reverses the role and puts men on the defensive instead. What neurotic manifestations she is suspected of, fall in place as she is overpowered by genuine love.

Michael Douglas who is the lead actor helps the suspected psychotic killer find herself. Though supposedly in a string of Hollywood films with similar theme, 'Basic Instinct', despite the controversy it generated, has a cold, rational message with Sharon Stone at her red-hot best. One had once heard at a seminar respectable academic voices suggesting a ministry of morality for India. With the experience of Emergency in 1975 behind us, would we like the government to

Table 1.1
Box Office Position of Hindi Films Released in 1996

Sl. No.	Name of the Film	Month of Release	Producer	Director	Main Artistes	Box Office's Position
1	2	3	4	5	6	7
1.	Himmat	January 1996	Dinesh Gandhi	Sunil Sharma	Sunny Deol, Tabbu, Shilpa Shetty, Mukesh Khanna, Nasiruddin Shah	Flop
2.	Jurmana	January 1996	Man Singh Deep	T.L.V. Prasad	Mithun Chakravarty, Rambha, Ronit Ray	Flop
3.	Smugglar	January 1996	Buta Singh Shad	Ajay Kashyap	Dharmendra, Reena Roy, Ayub Khan, Karina Grover, Mukesh Khanna	Flop
4.	Bekabu	January 1996	N. Chandra	N. Chandra	Sanjay Kapoor, Mamta Kulkarni	Flop
5.	Ek Tha Raja	January 1996	R. J. Sharma	Dayal Nihalani	Sunil Shetty, Saif Ali Khan, Aditya Pancholi, Pratibha Sinha, Neelam	Flop
6.	Dushmani	January 1996	Karim Morani/ Ali Morani/ Banti Soorama	Shekhar Kapoor/ Banti Soorama	Jacky Shroff, Maneesha Koirala, Sunny Deol, Dipti Nawal	Flop
7.	Vishvasghat	January 1996	Pradip Shirodkar	Himanshu Brahmbhutt	Sunil Shetti, Anjali Jathar, Kiran Kumar, Anupam Kher	Flop
8.	English Babu Desi Mem	January 1996	Pravin Nishchal	Pravin Nishchal	Shahrukh Khan, Sonali Bendre, Kiran Kumar, Master Sunny Singh	Flop
9.	Vijeta	January 1996	Anil Rathi	K. Murliomohan Rao	Sanjay Dutt, Raveena Tandan, Paresh Rawal, Amrish Puri	Flop

(Contd.)

1	2	3	4	5	6	7
10.	Bandit Queen	January 1996	Sandeep Singh Bedi	Shekhar Kapoor	Seema Bisvas, Nirmal Pandey, Raghuvir Yadav, Manoj Vajpayee	Hit
11.	Jagannath	February 1996	Shibu Mitra	Shibu Mitra	Shatrughna Sinha, Sangeeta Bijlani, Ronit Ray	Flop
12.	Papi Gudiya	February 1996	Amar Chchabada	Lawrence D'suja	Avinash Vadhavan, Karijma Kapoor	Flop
13.	Aatank	February 1996	M.S. Lalwani	O.P. Kohali	Dharmendra, Hema Malini, Kader Khan, Ravi Kishan	Flop
14.	Bandish	February 1996	Prakash Jha	Prakash Jha	Jackie Shroff, Juhi Chawla, Shilpa Shirodkar	Flop
15.	Nirbhay	February 1996	T.C. Diwan	Vinod Diwan	Mithun Chakravarti, Sangeeta Bjlani, Arbaj Khan	Flop
16.	Pyasa Shaitan	February 1996	Jogindra	Jogindra	Kamal Haasan, Jogindra	Flop
17.	Divine Lovers (Dubbed)	February 1996	B. Subhash	B. Subhash	Mark Juber, Saied Jaferi, Hement Birje	Flop
18.	Miyan, Bibi Aur Saali (Dubbed)	March 1996	J. Raghunath Reddy	A.K. Reddy	Nagarjun, Ramaiya, Nagma	Flop
19.	Apne Dam Par	March 1996	Manisha Bimal	Arshad Khan	Mithun Chakravarti, Shilpa Shirodkar, Shakti Kapoor, Reema Lagoo	Flop
20.	Bombay Ka Babu	March 1996	Ravi Vachchani	Vikram Bhatt	Saif Ali Khan, Kajol, Atul Agnihotri, Vaishnavi	Flop
21.	Raaj Kumar	March 1996	Tutu Sharma	Pankaj Parashar	Anil Kapoor, Madhuri Dixit, Reena Roy, Naseeruddin Shah	Flop

(Contd.)

1	2	3	4	5	6	7
22.	Agnisakshi	March 1996	Binda Thakarey	Partho Ghosh	Jackie Shroff, Maneesha Koirala, Nana Patekar	Super Hit
23.	Ye Manjhadhar	March 1996	Pravin Thakkar	Ismail Shroff	Salman Khan, Maneesha Koirala, Raj Babbar, Rahu Ray	Flop
24.	Megha	March 1996	B.K. Jaiyaswal	Mohan G. Prasad	Karijma Kapoor, Rahul Ray, Ronit Ray	Flop
25.	Saajan Chale Sasural	April 1996	Nansoor Ahmad Siddiqi	David Dhawan	Govinda, Karijma Kapoor, Tabbu, Kader Khan	Hit
26.	Jang	April 1996	Rajiv Kumar	T. Rama Rao	Mithun Chakravarti, Ajay Devgan, Rambha, Sujata, Aditya Pancholi	Average
27.	Ek Anadi Do Khiladi	April 1996	Dinesh Salgiya	Ravi Raja	Raveena Tandan, Ramaiya,	Flop
28.	Chhaila	May 1996	Time Magnetics/ Rajan Lal	R. Kanan	Prabhu Deva and Others	Flop
29.	Easi Bhi Kya Jaldi Hai	May 1996	Sachin	Sachin	Sachin, Vivek Mushran, Srashti Bahal	Flop
30.	Duniya Jhukti Hai	May 1996	Yash Chauhan	Yash Chauhan	Anupam Kher, Sadashiv	Flop
31.	Tu Chor Main Sipahi	May 1996	Namrata Dehal	Guddu Dhanoa	Akshya Kumar, Tabbu, Saif Ali Khan, Pratibha Sinha	Flop
32.	Jaan	May 1996	Ashok Ghai	Raj Kanwar	Ajay Devgan, Twinkle Khanna, Suresh Oberay, Amrish Puri	Hit
33.	Suhag Raat Se Pahale	May 1996	Meena Sharma	S. Ravi Kumar	South Indian Artistes	Flop

(Contd.)

1	2	3	4	5	6	7
34.	Papa Kahate Hain	May 1996	Plus Films	Mahesh Bhatt	Jugal Hansraj, Mayuri Kango, Anupam Kher	Flop
35.	Maafia	May 1996	Pran Lal Mehta	Ajij Sajwal	Dharmendra, Jay Mehta, Somi Ali	Flop
36.	Prem Granth	May 1996	Randhir Kapoor/ Rishi Kapoor/ Rajiv Kapoor	Rajiv Kapoor	Rishi Kapoor, Madhuri Dixit, Shammi Kapoor, Om Puri	Flop
37.	Masoom	May 1996	Sanjay Bali/ Lokesh Bali	Mahesh Kothare	Ayasha Julka, Indra Kumar, Renuka Shahane	Average
38.	Lofar	June 1996	Surendra Kapoor/ Boni Kapoor	David Dhawan	Anil Kapoor, Juhi Chawla, Shakti Kapoor, Mukesh Rishi	Hit
39.	Ias Raat Ki Subah Nahin	June 1996	Plus Films	Sudhir Mishra	Nirmal Pandey, Tara Deshpandey, Ashish Vidhyarthi	Flop
40.	Khiladion Ka Khiladi	June 1996	Keshu	Umesh Mehra	Rekha, Akshay Kumar, Raveena Tandan, Gulshan Grover	Hit
41.	Himmatvar	June 1996	Shakeel Chishti	Talat Jaani	Dharmendra, Mukesh Khanna, Hitesh, Rubena	Flop
42.	Aur Ek Prem Kahani	June 1996	Plus Films	Balu Mahendra	Ramesh Arvind, Revti, Hira Raj Gopal	Flop
43.	Chahat	June 1996	Robin Bhatt	Mahesh Bhatt	Shahrukh Khan, Puja Bhatt, Ramaiya, Anupam Kher, Nasiruddin Shah	Average
44.	Army	June 1996	Nitin Manmohan/ Mukul Anand	Ram Shetty	Shri Devi, Shahrukh Khan, Dainy, Sudesh Beri, Mohnish Bahal	Average

(Contd.)

1	2	3	4	5	6	7
45.	Fareb	June 1996	Mukesh Bhatt	Vikram Bhatt	Milind Gunaji, Farhaj Khan, Suman Ranganathan	Hit
46.	Darar	July 1996	Sujit Kumar	Abbas Mastan	Rishi Kapoor, Juhi Chawla, Arbaj Khan	Flop
47.	Muqaddar	July 1996	Rajiv Babbar	T.L.V. Prasad	Mithun Chakravarti, Ayasha Julka	Flop
48.	Mahir	July 1996	Pratap Barot	Lawrence D'suja	Hema Malini, Govinda, Farha	Flop
49.	Muqaddama	July 1996	K.C. Bokadia	K.C. Bokadia	Vinod Khanna, Zeba, Varsha Usganvkar, Harish, Aditya Pancholi	Flop
50.	Bhishma	July 1996	Jagdish A. Sharma	Jagdish A. Sharma	Mithun Chakravarti, Vani Vishvanath, Anjali Jathar, Harish	Flop
51.	Great Robbery (Dubt ..l)	July 1996	Ram Gopal Verma	Ram Gopal Verma	Shri Devi, Nagarjun	Flop
52.	Krishna	August 1996	Dhiraj Lal Shah	S. Deepak	Sunil Shetti, Karijma Kapoor, Shakti Kapoor,	Flop
53.	Khamoshi the Musical	August 1996	Sanjay Lila Bhansali	Sanjay Lila Bhansali	Nana Patekar, Salman Khan, Manisha Koirala, Sima Biswas	Flop
54.	Dil Tera Diwana	August 1996	Pahlaj Nihlani	Lawrence D'suja	Saif Ali Khan, Twinkle Khanna, Shatrughna Sinha, Shakti Kapoor	Flop
55.	Hindustani	August 1996	A.M. Ratnam	Shankar	Kamal Hasan, Manisha Koirala, Aruna Irani, Urmila	Super Hit
56.	Jeet	August 1996	Sajid Nadiyadwala	Raj Kanwar	Sunny Deol, Salman Khan, Karijma Kapoor, Tabbu	Hit
57.	Shoharat	August 1996	Sakshi Thakur	Satish Rajan	Avinash Vadhavan, Madhu, Sudesh Beri	Flop

(Contd.)

1	2	3	4	5	6	7
58.	Jai Dakshineshwar Kali Maan	August 1996	Anuradha Paudval	Shanti Lal Soni	Hema Malini and Others	Flop
59.	Bhairvi	August 1996	Plus Films	Aruna Raje	Ashvini Bhave, Shridhar	Flop
60.	Lalchi	August 1996	Plus Films	Raj Sippi	Rohit Ray, Karina Grover, Pran, Anil Dhawan	Flop
61.	Mr. Bechara	August 1996	Nandu Ji Tolani	K. Bhagyaraj	Anil Kapoor, Shri Devi, Nagarjun, Anupam Kher, Hira Raj Gopal	Flop
62.	Saja-E-Kalapani	August 1996	R. Mohan/ Mohan Lal	Priyadarshan	Mohan Lal, Tabbu, Amrish Puri	Flop
63.	Yash	August 1996	Sushil Kumar Agarwal	Sharad Saran	Bijoy Anand, Kartika Rane, Sonu Valiya	Flop
64.	Bal Brahmchari	September 1996	Prakash Mehra	Prakash Mehra	Puru Raj Kumar, Karijma Kapoor, Simran, Deepak Tijori	Flop
65.	Angara	September 1996	Anil Ganguli	Anil Ganguli	Mithun Chakravarti, Rupali Ganguli, Kamal Sadana	Flop
66.	Farar Qaidi (Dubbed)	September 1996	South Indian	South Indian	Jayaprada, Chiranjivi	Flop
67.	Daanvir	September 1996	D.N. Joshi/ Vijyendra Ahuja	T.L.V. Prasad	Mithun Chakravarti, Rambha, Ronit Ray	Flop
68.	Diljale	September 1996	Paramjit Baveja	Hairi Baveja	Ajay Devgan, Sonali Bendre, Amrish Puri, Madhu	Average
69.	Shastra	October 1996	Nadir Irani	Sanjay Khanna	Sunil Shetti, Anjali Jathar	Flop
70.	Bhayanak Panja	October 1996	R. Mittal	R. Mittal	South Indian Artistes	Flop

(Contd.)

1	2	3	4	5	6	7
71.	Aashiq Mastane	October 1996	K.C. Bokadiya	Ajay Kashyap		Flop
72.	Jordaar	October 1996	Abbu Malik	Ajay Kashyap	Govinda, Neelam, Aditya Pancholi, Mandakini	Flop
73.	Return of Jwel Thief	October 1996	T.P. Agarwal	Ashok Tyagi	Devanand, Dharmendra, Madhu, Jackie Shroff, Shilpa Shirodker	Flop
74.	Raja Ki Aayegi Baraat	October 1996	Salim Akhtar	Ashok Gayakwad	Rani Mukherji, Shadab Khan, Divya Dutta	Flop
75.	Rangbaj	October 1996	P.L. Ahuja/ Kanti Shah	Kanti Shah	Mithun Chakravarti, Gayatri, Shilpa Shirodkar, Vijaya, Kader Khan, Kiran Kumar	Flop
76.	Phool Bane Patthar	October 1996	Vinod Talwar	Ambarish Sangal	Avinash Vadhawan, Indrani Banerji	Flop
77.	Rangila Raja	October 1996	Dinesh Salgiya	K. Raghvendra Rao	Nagarjun, Ramaiya	Flop
78.	Maachis	October 1996	R.B. Pandit	Guljar	Chandra Chud Singh, Tabbu, Raj Jutshi, Kanwaljit, Om Puri	Hit
79.	Sapoot	November 1996	Rajan Sharma/ Satyen Sharma	Jagdish A. Sharma	Akshya Kumar, Karijma Kapoor, Sunil Shetti, Sonali Bendre	Average
80.	Ghaatak	November 1996	Raj Kumar Santoshi	Raj Kumar Santoshi	Sunny Deol, Meenakshi Sheshadri, Amrish Puri, Dainy, Mamta Kulkarni	Hit
81.	Raja Hindustani	November 1996	Karim Morani/ Ali Morani/ Banti Soorama	Dharmesh Darshan	Amir Khan, Karijma Kapoor, Suresh Obray, Navnit Nishan	Super Hit

(Contd.)

1	2	3	4	5	6	7
82.	Chhote Sarkar	November 1996	Vimal Kumar	Vimal Kumar	Govinda, Shilpa Shetti, Divya Dutta	Flop
83.	Rakshak	November 1996	Ashok Honda	Ashok Honda	Sunil Shetti, Karijma Kapoor, Sonali Bendre	Flop
84.	Dastak	November 1996	Mukesh Bhatt	Mahesh Bhatt	Sushmita Sen, Sharad Kapoor, Manoj Vajpayee, Makul Dev	Flop
85.	Tere Mere Sapne	December 1996	A.B. Corporation Ltd.	Joy Agastin	Chandra Chud Singh, Arshad Varsi, Priya Gill, Simran	Average
86.	Uf-Ye Mohabbat	December 1996	Vipin Handa	Vipin Handa	Twinkle Khanna, Abhishek, Sadiya Siddiqi, Anupam Kher	Flop
87.	Khilauna	December 1996	Mukesh Duggal	Mukesh Duggal	Monika Bedi, Ayub Khan, Shakti Kapoor, Aditya Pancholi	Hit
88.	Namak	December 1996	Kawal Sharma	Kawal Sharma	Sanjay Dutt, Farha, Shakti Kapoor	Hit
89.	Judwan	December 1996	Sajid Nadiyadwala	David Dhawan	Salman Khan, Karijma Kapoor, Rambha, Anupam Kher	Average
90.	Ram Aur Shyam	December 1996	Raju Mavani	Raju Mavani	Samrat Mukharji, Manik Bedi, Kanchan, Divya Dutta	Average

Table 1.2

Music Directors of Hindi Films Released in 1996

Sl. No.	*Name of the Film*	*Music Director*
1	2	3
1.	Himmat	Anand Milind
2.	Jurmana	Dilip Sen/Samir Sen
3.	Smugglar	Bhappi Lahari
4.	Bekabu	Anu Malik
5.	Ek Tha Raja	Anand Milind
6.	Dushmani	Anand Milind
7	Vishvasghat	Shyam Surendra
8.	English Babu Desi Mem	Nikhil Vinay
9.	Vijeta	Anand Milind
10.	Bandit Queen	Nusarat Fateh Ali Khan
11.	Jagannath	Sonik Omi
12.	Papi Gudiya	Naresh Sharma
13.	Aatank	Laxmikant-Pyarelal
14.	Bandish	Anand Milind
15.	Nirbhay	Ram Laxman
16.	Pyasa Shaitan	Sonik Omi
17.	Divine Lovers (Dubbed)	Bhappi Lahri
18.	Miyan, Biwi Aur Sali (Dubbed)	M.M. Karim

(Contd.)

1	2	3
19.	Apne Dam Par	Aadesh Shrivastav
20.	Bombay Ka Babu	Anand Milind
21.	Raaj Kumar	Laxmi Kant-Pyare Lal
22.	Agni Sakshi	Nadim Shravan
23.	Ye Manjhadhar	Nadim Shravan
24.	Megha	Ram Laxman
25.	Saajan Chale Sasural	Nadim Shravan
26.	Jang	Nadim Shravan
27.	Ek Anadi Do Khiladi	Raj Koti
28.	Chhaila	Ialya Raja
29.	Easi Bhi Kya Jaldi Hai	Gauri Shankar
30	Duniya Jhukti Hai	Not Available
31.	Tu Chor Main Shipahi	Dilip Sen—Samir Sen
32.	Jaan	Anand Milind
33.	Suhag Raat Se Pahale	Anu Malik
34.	Papa Kahate Hain	Rajesh Roshan
35.	Maafia	Anand Milind
36.	Prem Granth	Laxmi Kant—Pyare Lal
37.	Masoom	Anand Raj Anand
38.	Lofar	Anand Milind
39.	Ias Raat Ki Subah Nahin	M.M. Karim

(Contd.)

1	2	3
40.	Khiladion Ka Khiladi	Anu Malik
41.	Himmatvar	Nadim Shravan
42.	Aur Ek Prem Kahani	Ialya Raja
43.	Chahat	Anu Malik
44.	Army	Anand Milind
45.	Fareb	Jatin Lalit
46.	Darar	Anu Malik
47.	Muqaddar	Anand Milind
48.	Mahir	Bhappi Lahri
49.	Muqaddama	Bhappi Lahri
50	Bhishma	Dilip Sen—Samir Sen
51.	Great Robbery (Dubbed)	Raj Koti
52.	Krishna	Anu Malik
53.	Khamoshi The Musical	Jatin Lalit
54.	Dil Tera Diwana	Adesh Shrivastva
55.	Hindustani	A.R. Rehman
56.	Jeet	Nadim Shravan
57.	Shoharat	Nikhil Vinay
58.	Jai Dakshineshwar Kali Maan	Aditya Podwal
59.	Bhairvi	Laxmi Kant—Pyare Lal
60.	Lalchi	Laxmi Kant—Pyare Lal
61.	Mr. Bechara	Anand Milind
62.	Saja-E-Kala-Pani	Ialya Raja
63.	Yash	Tabun

(Contd.)

1	2	3
64.	Baal Brahmchari	Bhappi Lahri
65.	Angara	Dilip Sen—Samir Sen
66.	Farar Qaidi (Dubbed)	Sonik Omi
67.	Daanvir	Anand Milind
68.	Diljale	Anu Malik
69.	Shastra	Anand Milind
70.	Bhayanak Panja	Vijay Ajit
71.	Aashiq Mastane	Bhappi Lahri
72.	Jordaar	Anu Malik
73.	Return of Jewel Thief	Jatin Lalit
74.	Raja Ki Aayegi Baraat	Adesh Shrivastva
75.	Rangbaj	Bhappi Lahri
76.	Phool Bane Patthar	Shyam Surendra
77	Rangila Raja	M.M. Karim
78.	Maachis	Vishal Bhardwaj
79.	Sapoot	Anu Malik
80.	Ghaatak	R.D. Burman/Anu Malik
81.	Raja Hindustani	Nadim Shravan
82.	Chhote Sarkar	Anand Milind
83.	Rakshak	Anand Milind
84.	Dastak	Rajesh Roshan
85.	Tere Mere Sapne	Viju Shah
86.	Uf-Ye-Mohabbat	Nikhil Vinay
87.	Khilauna	Naresh Sharma
88.	Namak	Not Available
89.	Judwan	Anu Malik
90.	Ram Aur Shyam	Anu Malik

regulate people's morality? Perversely enough, we have instances of some cable operators unilaterally censoring films but then they are doing it out of fear of displeasing conservative subscribers and losing money. Governments themselves reeling under allegations of scams, lose the right to become arbiters of public morality.

II. TELEVISION IN INDIA

Television (Doordarshan) was introduced in India in September 1959 with the establishment of a centre at Delhi as a pilot project. Over the years, it acquired its Indian name DOORDARSHAN and expanded its reach and area of activities in the spheres of information, education and entertainment to achieve the following main objectives[1]—

(i) to act as a catalyst for social change;

(ii) to promote national integration;

(iii) to stimulate scientific temper among the people;

(iv) to disseminate the message of family planning as a means of population control and family welfare;

(v) to stimulate greater agricultural production by providing essential information and knowledge;

(vi) to promote and help in preservation of environmental and ecological balance;

(vii) to highlight the social welfare measures including welfare of women and children and the less privileged;

(viii) to promote interest in games and sports; and

(ix) to stimulate appreciation of country's artistic and cultural heritage.

Expansion and Consolidation of Services and Indian National Satellite (INSAT)

Table 1.3
New Transmitters during 1986-87

Sl. No.	*Transmitter's Centre*	*State*
1.	Proddutur	Andhra Pradesh
2.	Betiah	Bihar
3.	Jagdalpur	Madhya Pradesh
4.	Damoh	Madhya Pradesh
5.	Satara	Maharashtra
6.	Bhuj	Gujarat
7.	Ballia	Uttar Pradesh
8.	Hassan	Karnataka
9.	Madikeri	Karnataka
10.	Udipi	Karnataka
11.	Mandi	Himachal Pradesh
12.	Darjilling	West Bengal

During 1986-87, total number of transmitters in the country were 192. Indian Television achieved a break-through in designing and setting an unmanned solar remote centre at Rawatbhata (Rajasthan) on January 4, 1987 with indigenous expertise.

Srinagar, Jalandhar, Lucknow, Calcutta, Madras, Bangalore, Bombay and Delhi are already linked on a microwave system for simultaneously receiving and telecasting TV signals. It is also proposed to link Hyderabad and Trivendrum during 1986-87.

Indian National Satellite (INSAT) multiple service project has been made use of by Doordarshan (Indian Television) for direct telecast of the programmes and for the national networking of the existing terrestial transmitters through the use of microwave system. The INSAT-based TV service continued to provide educational programmes for the primary school children as also telecast area specific programmes on agriculture, adult education, rural development, health and hygiene, family welfare etc. for the rural viewers in selected clusters in six states, namely; Andhra Pradesh, Bihar, Gujarat, Maharashtra, Orissa and Uttar Pradesh. The educational TV programmes in Hindi for Uttar Pradesh and Bihar were relayed by all transmitters in these states as well as the transmitters in four other states *i.e.*, Madhya Pradesh, Rajasthan, Haryana and Himachal Pradesh. Similarly, the area-specific programmes for Uttar Pradesh, Bihar, Andhra Pradesh and Orissa, uplinked from Delhi via INSAT-1B, were rediffused by all these transmitters in these states.

Telecasts of higher education programmes which commenced on August 15, 1984 via INSAT-1B continued successfully. A one-hour programme on higher education provided by the University Grants Commission continued to be telecast in the afternoon and repeated in the evening. The INSAT plan includes the provision of 2,000 direct reception sets and 2,000 very high frequency sets for community viewing in six INSAT states. Out of these 1,869 had been installed by the end of September 1986.

Through the use of a transportable uplink hired from the Department of Telecommunications, regional service of transmitting programmes introduced from Bombay has been started for Bombay and other transmitters in Maharashtra with effect from August 9, 1986.[2] This has enabled all the transmitters located in the State of Maharashtra to share programmes of Doordarshan Kendra (TV centre), Bombay from the start upto 8.40 p.m. daily, when they switch over to national programmes of from Delhi Centre. Nagpur Centre, however, continues to relay area-specific programmes from 7.30 p.m. to 8.05 p.m. which is uplinked from Delhi. Uplink facility has also been set up at Hyderabad and the regional service in the state of Andhra Pradesh was started on January 13, 1987. All the TV transmitters in Andhra Pradesh now relay programmes produced and telecast by TV Centre, Hyderabad, in addition to the national programmes telecast from Delhi.

National Programmes and Programme Activities etc.

Upto the year 1982, the Centres at Delhi, Calcutta, Madras, Bombay, Srinagar, Jalandhar and Lucknow continued to telecast largely locally produced programmes. On August 15, 1982 a daily national programme of 90 minutes for a simultaneous telecast throughout the country by all the transmitters was introduced to foster social, economic and cultural unity, to promote the spirit of national integration and to project progress being made by the country in various fields. The duration of the national programme was increased in subsequent years. The programme is currently telecast for a minimum of 155 minutes daily from 8.40 p.m. to 11.15 p.m. and also extended if necessary. It consists of two news bulletins of 20 minutes duration each one in Hindi and one in English. Other items telecast in the national programme include art, music, dance and programmes based on literary works in various Indian languages and important issues of current affairs and social relevance. In addition, a number of entertaining sponsored programmes produced by eminent private producers are also telecast.[3]

Some of the notable programmes produced for Doordarshan (TV) and telecast as national programmes during the year (1986-87) included a series entitled "Beyond Tomorrow" and a news and current affairs programme entitled "Roving Eye". Notable sponsored programmes privately produced included "Buniyaad", "Malgudi Days", "Karamchand" etc. Doordarshan assigned to private producers" programmes like "Sach ki Parchhaian" to enable the viewers to come to an independent judgement on issues and events. "Janwani" an audience participation programme, wherein a Union Minister replied to questions and doubts of the people, invited from all parts of the country, concerning his department was very popular and received excellent response from the people.

A morning transmission of national programme has been started with effect from February 23, 1987. It is of 45 minutes' duration from 7.30 in the morning. It contains two news bulletins of ten minutes duration each one in Hindi and the other in English.

Doordarshan (TV) telecast in the national network a number of programmes on national integration and communal harmony. Programmes on this theme were also telecast by the various programme-originating centres in the concerned languages. The programmes were under various formats including discussions, interviews, mushairas, qawalis, news items, feature films, documentaries, quiz programmes, songs under the community singing programme as well as patriotic songs.

Keeping in view the Prime Minister's 15 point directive about welfare of minorities, the electronic media (both Doordarshan and AIR) put out programmes in relevant formats aimed at restoring confidence and peace in areas affected by communal trouble.

To provide adequate and authentic information, Doordarshan continued to telecast news and current affairs programmes. In the national programme, two bulletins, one each in English and Hindi, of 20 minutes' duration were telecast every day simultaneously by all the transmitters (except Madras, which did not telecast the news bulletin in Hindi). These bulletins received visual stories from outside agencies apart from Doordarshan's own sources. The outside agencies included PTI and UNI in India and international news services like the Visnews and Asiavision.[4]

To cater to the interests and needs of the local population, the centres at Delhi, Calcutta, Madras, Bombay, Jalandhar, Srinagar, Lucknow, Guwahati, Hyderabad, Ahmedabad, Bangalore and Trivendrum continued to telecast a 10-minute daily news bulletin in the local regional language.

TV also continued to telecast from Delhi Centre Parliament news in Hindi and English for ten minutes daily on all the days Parliament was in session. Regional centres, however, arranged telecast of news based on Parliament proceedings for ten minutes every week in the respective languages. Doordarshan, Delhi organised telecast of news headlines in brief at the end of the transmission everyday.

In view of the tremendous importance and topicality of the Non-Aligned Summit held in Harare, Doordarshan organised live-telecast of its proceedings. Its inaugural session, the closing session and the press conference addressed by the Indian Prime Minister were telecast live. Similarly, the SAARC Conference of Bangalore in November, 1986 was covered live in its inaugural session, closing session and the Prime Minister's press conference. The visit of Mr. Mikhail Gorbachev, General Secretary of Communist Party of the Soviet Union in November 1986 was covered extensively. His arrival, banquet ceremony at the Hyderabad House, New Delhi, address to the joint session of the Parliament and the press conference were covered live. "Apna Utsav", a major national event of cultural importance involving about six thousand artistes from all over the country, was covered live.

Indian television (Doordarshan) organised Indo-Australia Hi-Tech Conference between Indian and Australian experts in Australia which was recorded via satellite from various locations. The medical conference known as Medicon held at Delhi was also recorded in a similar manner and telecast from Doordarshan. The experts from India sitting in the Doordarshan Studio at Delhi and American experts sitting in New York discussed various aspects of Cardiac problems for the benefit of viewers.[5] Another landmark was Doordarshan and BBC co-production—a sixteen-nation "Space Bridge" programme on wild life wherein live-video sources from Old Fort, Delhi and from the studios of Doordarshan, Delhi were made use of for an interview with the Prime Minister.

To promote the welfare of African children, Door–darshan participated in a twenty-six nation 'Sports Aid' programme via the satellite. The participate of Indian sportsmen at Jawaharlal Nehru Stadium and the Indira Gandhi Indoor Stadium, New Delhi was significantly reflected. Other important live-telecast programmes included Ganga-Cleaning Project at Varanasi, Indepen–dence Day celebration on 15th August, Republic Day celebrations on 26th January and 29th January.

Programme Activities

A number of new, interesting, thought-provoking and investigative programmes have been developed by Doordarshan. These are—

(a) "Roving Eye"

The programme aimed at bringing in indepth stories from the socio-economic life of the people, their problems and possible solutions.

(b) "Beyond Tomorrow"

The programme presented a futuristic overview of today's problems that were being tackled in an interesting and confident way. It aimed to involving the people in the national ventures of development and growth.

(c) "Baton Baton Mein"

This programme has been introduced to bring to the viewers the lighter moments and interesting aspects of life of the celebrated national figures. The personalities having features so far in various episodes include Anup Jalota, Gurdas Mann, Amrita Pritam, Amjad Ali Khan, Bishan Singh Bedi, Sonal Mansingh and Mrs. Kiran Bedi. People's response to this programme has been encouraging.

(d) "Tasvir Ka Doosra Rukh"

The serial aimed at presenting in a humourous way the functioning of Doordarshan. The dramatic presentation based on actualities has brought the viewers very close to Doordarshan in its functioning.

(e) "Andhi Galian"

In conformity with its over-all objectives Doordarshan developed this serial for educating the Youth in the country about the ill effects of drug addiction.

(f) "Sanrakshan Upbhokta Ka"

The programme was introduced to project the interest of consumers.

(g) "Janvani"

Doordarshan continued to telecast programmes like "Janvani" and "Sach Ki Parchhaian". In "Janvani" the first round of programme participated by Union Ministers incharge of various departments has completed.

(h) "Sach Ki Parchhaian"

In various episodes of "Sach Ki Parchhaian", the procedures and methods of working of different organisations which do not fit into the present democratic functioning have been brought out to create a more favourable climate for the people seeking services and redressal of their grievances.

(i) "Focus"

Doordarshan involved some of the private producers to produce a programme entitled "Focus" wherein the filming, interviews and programme sequences are entirely decided by the outside producers. Doordarshan in such cases has offered its facilities for completing and telecasting the programme.

Sponsored Programmes

Sponsored programmes continued to take pride of place due to their variety and popularity in the overall programme pattern of Doordarshan. The scheme was initially introduced in the year 1984 when a couple of programmes produced by eminent producers were telecast with the help of sponsors/advertisers in the country. The scheme broadly has aimed at enriching the programme fare.

Doordarshan (TV) has also brought to the viewers literary masterpieces.[6] These include "Malgudi Days" a serial based on R.K. Narayan's stories and "Srikant", a serial based on Sarat Chandra's Bengali novel of the same name. Some of the world classic short stories were adopted to produce TV programmes like "Katha Sagar" and "Khazana" serials directed by leading film directors such as Satyajit Ray, Mrinal Sen, Sai Paranjape, Yash Chopra, Amol Palekar, G.B. Iyer, etc., were also telecast as sponsored programmes.

During the year 1986-87 Doordarshan revised the scheme of sponsorship to make it more rational. The revision also aimed at widening opportunities for creative producers. Doordarshan has also rationalised its rate structure for spot advertisements and sponsorship-fee with a view to attracting a wider range of advertisers. It is expected that these measures will result in improvement in quality of programming, variety in content as well as increase in commercial revenue. The procedure for the selection of serials has been streamlined and eminent non-officials from various fields have been co-opted on the selection committee.

Films and Film based Programmes

Doordarshan (TV) continued to telecast films and film-based programmes. The selection of the films was made on broad criteria including their national/international award status, thematic, cinematic and entertainment value, year of production and suitability for family viewing. The selection of the Hindi feature films telecast on Sundays were made by a duly appointed committee including non-officials at the centre. In the case of regional language films, the selection was made at the regional centres by the regional selection committees appointed for the purpose. Foreign feature films were obtained through the National Film Development Corporation and Sovexport for telecast. A few selected serials were purchased from BBC and other organisations.[7]

Doordarshan continued to telecast a programme on the national hook-up entitled "World of Sports" every Sunday. This programme offered a wide variety of sports activities taking place within the country and abroad. The major TV centres also continued to telecast similar programmes in the regional languages to suit the interest and requirements of the viewers.

Doordarshan continued to organise direct live telecasts via satellite or 'after the event' telecasts of important international and national sports events. Among the important sports events telecast were super soccer series; India vs. Bochum (West Germany) soccer matches at Delhi, Madras, Calcutta and Bangalore, National Hockey Championship at Bangalore, Beighton Cup Hockey final at Calcutta, 11th All India Gold Cup Hockey final at Srinagar, Subroto Cup Football final at Delhi, Federation Cup Football final at Srinagar, Durand Cup Football final at Delhi and Sanjay Gandhi Hockey final at Delhi. Live coverage of the India-Sri Lanka Cricket series and the India-Pakistan Cricket series 1986-87 was arranged on the national net-work. Doordarshan is making arrangements to provide international picture signals and sound for foreign organisations regarding World Cup Cricket 1987. It is expected that seventeen matches will be played at 14 different locations. Doordarshan arranged live telecast of matches with the help of ten colour OB vans, with six to eight camera coverage. Arrangements were made for the live coverage of important matches in the 39th World Table Tennis in Delhi.

Commercial Service

The Commercial Service of Indian Television made a modest beginning in January 1976. The service has been extended through more centres resulting in substantial increase in revenues as is evident from the following figures—

1982-83	Rs. 15.89 crores
1983-84	Rs. 19.79 crores
1984-85	Rs. 31.43 crores
1985-86	Rs. 60.23 crores
1986-87	Rs. 53.23 crores (upto 31-10-1986)

With the expansion of Doordarshan network, the Commercials of Doordarshan have become an important medium for marketing of products and services. During the year 1986-87, over 600 advertising agencies played commercial advertisements and sponsored programmes with Doordarshan. Doordarshan has provided the facilities of direct booking of commercial advertisements to public sector undertakings, small-scale industries, government departments, co-operative societies, etc.

Programme Exchange and Rural Programmes

Since 1982, when Doordarshan started production of programmes in colour, there has been a substantial increase in the number of bilateral cultural agreements with different countries providing for exchange of TV programmes. Doordarshan has also signed protocols for exchange of programmes with some foreign TV organisations.[8] Doordarshan continued to produce a one hour weekly programme "India Magazine" for circulation in India missions abroad and selected TV organisations.

All programme originating centres continued to telecast programmes on agriculture, animal husbandry, rural health and sanitation and small scale industries for the rural viewers in their respective languages. The programmes in addition included items on folk songs and folk dances. On days of national importance and festivals, programmes were suitably enriched by proper comparing to highlight the relevance of occasions.

Advisory Committees and Audience Research

Doordarshan gets the benefit of advice of eminent non-officials and experts by associating them in various advisory committees. These committees include Media Advisory Committee, Programme Advisory Committees at the centres, Advisory Committees on Family Welfare Programmes at the centres, the Selection Committees for serials, Selection Committee for Hindi Feature Films/ Regional Language Films. Programme Advisory Committees at Delhi, Bombay, Calcutta, Madras, Lucknow, Srinagar, Jalandhar, Cuttack and Hyderabad have been reconstituted.

Doordarshan has developed an inbuilt mechanism to gauge the reaction and opinion of the viewers about the telecast programmes. A large number of letters are received by the centres. Comments of the pres critics are taken note of. To bring the audience and the organisation closer, programmes like "Aap Aur Hum" are produced by the TV centres. In addition, Audience Research Units have been attached to various Centres where in feed-back and feed-forward studies, formative research including pre-testing of proto-type programmes and summative evaluation are conducted. The findings of these studies are made use of in planning and designing the programmes. Recently a system of concurrent evaluation has also been introduced by developing viewers panels in twelve cities, *i.e.*, Delhi, Calcutta, Madras, Bombay, Srinagar, Nagpur, Jalandhar, Lucknow, Hyderabad, Cuttack, Jaipur and Rajkot.[9] Here, hundred respondents belonging to different categories of TV owners living in different areas of the city were supplied weekly diaries to record their comments and opinions on programmes on a daily basis. These diaries were thereafter collected by mail through pre-paid business envelopes. To assess the performance of newscasters news panels have also been setup recently.

Periodic researches conducted by private agencies are made use of by Doordarshan. Services of expert agencies are also commissioned for required studies.

Doordarshan Awards

The Doordarshan Awards for TV programmes are given annually for the best programmes produced and telecast by Doordarshan during each calender year.[10] The aim of these awards is to promote the art of TV as a medium of communication and means of self-expression and to raise the standards of Doordarshan production. The awards are of two types, namely, *(a)* Best Production

Awards, and *(b)* Individual Excellence Award. The entries for these awards are judged by a Central Jury.

III. IMPACT OF SATELLITE CHANNELS IN INDIA

There are a couple of telling one-liners that sum-up the way satellite channels are invading Indians homes, and emerging as a force for advertisers to stay with the young, educated, upscale types who are coming up through the ranks and consuming like crazy as they climb. They have lots of bucks, are more mainstream and in the thick of things—which makes them a hell of a big potential audience to make money from. No wonder, cable channels are continuing to dish out entertainment, much of which targets this audience; and a considerable share of ad revenue, which, till now, remained loyal to Doordarshan, has started pouring in. The invasion from the sky is complete. "Doordarshan is the medium that really reaches consumers and cable has scarcely been a competition". Mandi House counters cable claims, only to be pooh-poohed by majority of viewers. Even DD, in its own loomy way, spilled the beans. All news bulletins on January 24, 1993, carried a story about the 'ill-effects of cable TV watching'. The contents of the story supported by two medical experts which meant to 'de-cable' viewers actually endorsed the fact that people were preferring cable to Doordarshan. For many ad agencies and advertisers the news bulletin worked as a survey on TV watching behaviour of people. Thanks to DD, the reluctance of advertisers and ad agencies to take the cable into their media plans has been erased. This is expected to change the balance of media plans drastically in the not too distant future.

What determines the state of advertising switch to cable? Is it household income? Is it attitude? Is it just a passing phase? Answers are not hard to find. A study on the buying tendency of people has it all. No doubt, rapid market penetration, burgeoning numbers of affluent viewers and creative advertising opportunities are turning cable networks into a sure—sell medium where planning upmarket media. Extra-long spots, info-commercials and image-screamers are on the increase on the cable where upscale demographics have become quite strong and in just a year and a half of growth, major market penetration has surpassed 5 percent of the country's population. And that 5 percent penetration represents the cream of country's affluent consumers viewers with upper-bracket incomes, better education and greater buying power. Latest figures place total cable subscribership in the country at 3.5 million in December 1992, up from two million from July 1992. Demographic studies show that cable subscribers are 50 percent more likely than the average Indian household to have incomes of Rs. 50,000 or more—the same figure holds for those with an annual income of Rs. 40,000 or more and are 71 percent more likely to be employed in executive, managerial or administrative positions.

Findings reveal cable subscribers are more likely to surpass the national average in ownership of: a music system by 21 percent, Automobile by 14 percent, other luxury goods by 27 percent; further they are 29 percent more likely to invest in mutual funds and share market. The interpretation of studies, however, does not go uncontested by other media where millions of rupees are spent every year as advertising budget. For instance, the print media managers counter that despite the generous demographic descriptions of the cable audiences, the statistics reflect an audience only a fraction the size of the market in print media. Or cable figures reflect just a fraction the size of Doordarshan audience. DD is still the medium of choice for advertisers seeking an all category audience. Consumable targeting middle class homes, are still considered a DD monopoly. But advertisers have come to believe that DD is gradually losing upscale audience to cable. There is yet another school of thought contesting cable descriptions opining that people who have cable TV, subscribe for one of the two reasons. Either they are upscale consumers who buy the additional service because it is part of an affluent lifestyle,. or because they are very much into electronic entertainment and television. But subscribing for cable TV does not necessarily mean that people watch cable more or respond more strongly to cable TV. The truly affluent watch very little television in general and the audience that is very interested in electronic entertainment listens to radio or turn to VCR etc. Even household income measures, that support cable claims, do not go unquestioned. According to 'Hate Cable Club' members, today an income of Rs. 50,000 can hardly be considered affluent unless other factors are evaluated. In a place like Delhi Rs. 50,000 is just getting by, and even in other markets, a family with household income of Rs. 50,000 may not be termed as affluent. On the other hand, HCC members opine, Doordarshan "provides a single broad-based audience without much opportunity for target marketing and segmentation. Chitrahaar, Films, Sport-based programmes, music programmes etc. are all designed to reach out to young, upscale viewers."

But the ad world dismisses this targeting to un-segmented audience as anti-advertising. According to them cable's strength is in its ability to provide segmented audiences and flexibility in techniques for reaching those audiences. For instance, STAR TV's Santa Barbara, The Bold and The Beautiful, Donahue etc. in Star Plus, Prime Sports and BBC news bulletins and current affairs programmes; Zee TV's Hindi telecast; and MTV's music bonanza draw a select affluent audience. Other satellite channels like CNN and ATN have their share of viewers which even some of the 'highly seen' serials of DD have not been able to pull over. According to studies on DD viewership, DD's current affairs programme 'Focus' and the popular 'The World This Week' carry a viewship of a maximum of 1 and 12 percent respectively. The most viewed programme, 'Samachar' (8.30 p.m. bulletin) has never gone beyond 38 percent. On cable, the audience for Star Plus, 'The Bold and The Beautiful' is 76 percent more likely to have an household income of more than Rs. 60,000 compared with the nation at large, 'Snakes and Ladders' is 59 percent more likely, and MTV 71 percent. Product studies show that 32 percent of MTV's 15 to 23 year old viewers bought Jackson's 'Dangerous', while 6 percent of the viewers did the same after getting to know about the cassette from other sources. The upscale demographics led successful pitches by big ticket advertisers. Some of cable's biggest successes have been with automobiles and cosmetics.

Small agencies seem to be, of late, more receptive to cable claims. To encourage business from small agencies, some cable channels plan to expand production facilities to India to produce some programmes and feature films in order to attract more buyers for spots and sponsorships. Which also brings DD tariff into focus. No doubt DD boasts of a far larger audience, but a prime time spot buy on satellite channel is just 10 percent of DD's super 'A' special category spot buy.

IV. CENSORSHIP LOSES MEANING WITH VIDEO, CABLE BOOM

Censorship today has lost much of its meaning with the video and cable boom coercing films out of theatres and into the drawing room. The censor board has lost its bite and cable operators have a field day beaming previews of objectionable songs before the censor board gets into action. They almost always wake up too late, feel experts and commoners alike. They tried it with the 'Choli' phenomenon and the gyrating numbers of Govinda and Karishma, but the songs were on top of the charts much before the moral awakening to their vulgarity. Even as the scissors of the censor officials lie idle film-makers are making a habit of targeting audiences with footage that is getting spicier by the day. Even if the censor board does get into the act the ensuing controversy serves to excite the imagination but fuelling curiosity.

Film makers have been quick to point out that films mirror society and cater to what they term 'popular tastes'. Says Ms. Neha Bisht, Lucknow based freelance journalist, "violence and vulgarity on screen is, to an extent, a reflection of the same already prevalent in society". "The flip side of the coin, however, is that violence on screen, inspires the same in society too." Aruna Vasudev, editor of 'Cinemaya' and a member of the censor board, said "it is a two way traffic where the question of real life and real life influencing each is concerned". Films echo degradation in society, and society draws inspiration from films leading to a vicious cycle, she added. College student Ramneek Samir does not blame film makers for the 'Garish fare'. "Today average cine-goer is from the lower class and cannot afford a video so they throng theatres to extract three hours of cheap thrills after a hard days work."

Film making being an expensive affair, the movie moghuls cannot be blamed for catering to 'popular tastes' to make a hit film, he says, hammering home his point. Is censorship then the answer? Perhaps not, feels academic Deborah Perry, "with objectionable songs being aired before the release of the film, the purpose of censorship is .defeated". And with senseless violence being eugolised as a trend, its impact on impressionable minds is irreversible and may prove devastating with children being radically exposed at a relatively young age. Retribution comes too late, with the censor board becoming active long after the damage in done, she added. In this context, it would appear that just a particular section of society is being targeted for censorship, feels journalist Nadeem Ahmed.

Double standards may crop up leading to an imbalance in society, if the affluent get to view uncensored versions on video, in contrast to the less affluent who would suffer censored versions in theatres. Mr. Shakti, an autorikshaw driver, is more vocal when he decries censorship. He feels the general public does not really need cuts imposed by the 'more intellectual' member of society, and doubts whether the standard of society would improve if such cuts are engineered and vulgar songs banned. "Will men cease to ogle at women or stop treating them as sex objects?," he queries. Likewise Mr. Ratan Singh—a ticket checker at a Delhi theatre feels people should be allowed the freedom to view what they wish without being dictated to by a censor board using its own 'peculiar yardstick'. Collegian Ankit Agnihotri feels cinema is not only a major source of entertainment but also of awareness. Both the film makers and the censor board have to be collectively aware of the responsibility they shoulder, he says. Repeated depiction of corrupt police officials and politicians on the silver screen has lent social justification to the situation, he says, adding, "resultantly the masses instead of shunning corruption have come to accept it". Psychologist Ashish Nandy says though people are influenced by what they see, the impact differs relatively. Urbanites are more susceptable to violence and sex on screen than to rural populace because of the partial uprooting from native culture of people living in cities.

Banning or censoring a particular song or sequence tends to focus attention on the song leading to an added interest being generated over the issue. "People tend to speak more of the song that has been censored than about the film itself, says housewife Mrs. Tajender Kaur of Delhi. Mr. Nandy feels the same, "Censorship provides no solution and tends to ignite curiosity by spotlighting the issue". A rating system which would deter children from objectionable viewing would be more effective, he adds. The censors themselves, however, have their task cut out. "With themes dealing with violence, it is possible only to make cosmetic cuts without detracting from the spirit of the film," says Aruna Vasudev. The solution, she feels, lies in upgrading the quality of cinema halls. She recommends the western concept of a cluster of cinema halls housed together under a single roof. It would, include shopping arcades restaurants and recreation places where people could come with families to shop and stay over to watch a film. "Once families are drawn to the theatre again, film-makers would be in a position to cater to family-oriented entertainment leading to a natural cut in screen violence and vulgarity", she says. The point is pertinent and could mark a return to the good, clean entertainment of yesteryear.

V. CABLE TV ORDINANCE DISAPPOINTED FILM INDUSTRY

Although after much dilly-dallying the union government has issued an ordinance in October 1994, making it mandatory for the cable operators of India to register themselves forthwith, instead of generating hopes, many of the articles in it have only raised hackles in the affected quarters. These articles are so binding that doubts have already been expressed as to whether the ordinance will serve its purpose and help standardise the cable TV operation in India. While on the one hand, the cable operators are unhappy over the fact that the ordinance has been issued not so much to allow for the growth of the cable network as to forestall the entry of the foreign satellite networks into the country and to promote the pre-eminence of the government-owned

Doordarshan, on the other, the film industry is resenting it as it has not taken any cognizance of its demand of stopping the reckless growth of the network, which has long been felt to be the hot-bed of piracy of pre recorded films.

It may be recalled that the film industry was the first to cry halt to the haphazard growth of the cable TV operation just when it had become popular in the country. While the industry has no grouse against the advent and popularity of the cable network, it is the network's clandestine operation of showing unauthorised films which it had wanted the government to stop and for this purpose it had submitted to the government a model cable legislation a long time back. Much water has flowed down the bridge since then and now when the government has issued an ordinance to regulate the cable TV operation in the country, it has completely overlooked the film industry's demands. Because there is no article in the ordinance which says that the cable operators will have to take prior permission from the regulatory body before showing a film through the network. The film industry demand has been that the cable operators must submit the list of films they have in their pipeline to the regulatory body at least before a week of their actual exhibition through the network to enable the producers to know whether the cable rights for those films have been passed on to the network or not. Although, ever since the film industry devised its own in house measures with a view to minimising piracy, it has been able to stop the unauthorised showing of newly released films through the cable network to some extent, it is not in a position to monitor the nearly 25,000 cable operators in the country.

It is in view of this the film industry demanded a cable TV Act passed with a provision to stop the illegal cable operation, which mostly thrived on films. But the ordinance issued to this effect has disappointed the industry as there are no provisions in it to make the unauthorised exhibition of films through the network a cognizable offence. But, on the other hand, the government takes all the precaution that the cable operators comply with the articles introduced in the Ordinance, foremost among which is the one which makes it mandatory on the operators to run two channels of Doordarshan. "If the government can adopt measures to protect its own Doordarshan network, a move which we do not disapprove in principle, but why must it turn a Nelson's eye to protect the film industry's interests?" asked K.D. Shorey, who has been campaigning for a Cable Bill for a long time and who had voiced the film industry's concern in this respect in the Joint Parliamentary Committee not long ago. According to him, since it will take another six months to ratify the Ordinance in the Parliament and make it into an Act, the film industry still has the time at its disposal to move the government and urge it to introduce adequate measures in the Bill to protect the film industry's interest insofar as cable TV operation is concerned.

VI. ASIA PRODUCES OVER 50% OF TOTAL WORLD FILM OUTPUT

Out of about 4,000 feature films being made annually throughout the world, Asian countries including India and Pakistan, contribute to over 50 per cent of the total output. The remaining amount is produced by other countries. In term of annual average production during the last three years. India stands first with 900, Japan and United States of America come second and third with 310 and 260 feature films per year respectively. Pakistan is one of the twelve major film producing countries of the world with an annual average of 100 pictures. The following are the annual output of the other major eight film producing countries of the world. Hong

Kong—210, Taiwan—190, Philippines—160, Turkey—160, France—155, China—120, Italy—110, Mexico—102. There are over 100 countries on the map of the world which do not produce a single film.

The above figures show that India produces the highest number of feature films. It has produced the largest number of feature films, a total of 26,003 from 1913 to 1992 in over 30 languages. As compared to this, Pakistan's total output during the last 45 years, from 1948 to December 31, 1992 is 2,946, a little over 11 percent of the Indian total. But the production of Pakistan is higher, if compared with the cinema houses of both the countries. For instance, therc are 13,312 cinemas in India, whereas the total number of cinema houses in Pakistan is hardly 650, or less than 5 percent of the Indian figure. As far as the total number of films is concerned, Pakistan has produced 2,946 pictures, a little ovcr 11 percent of the Indian output, but it took India 80 long years, from 1913 to 1992 to reach the existing figures, while Pakistan made 11 percent of the Indian total in just 45 years, from 1948 to 1992. 'Raja Harish Chandra' (silent), made in 1913 was the first feature film of India, while Pakistan's first film, 'Teri Yaad' was made in 1948 with Asha Posley and Nasir Khan (younger brother of Dilip Kumar) in the romantic lead. Since then India has made a number of big-budgeted films, but the titles of 'Pukar' (1939), 'Mughal-e-Azam' and 'Sholay' will be written in gold in the history of Indian films, for not only their cost and cast and box-office collections, but to their craftsmanship as well. Pakistan makes movies in eight languages—Urdu, Punjabi, Pushtu, Sindhi, Balochi, Bengali, Gujarati and English. It made and released 142 pictures, the highest during the last 45 years in 1970, when Pakistan was united. Following the separation of the eastern wing (now Bangladesh), film production had dropped to 82. But with the passage of time it has again reached to about 100. The average cost of production in Pakistan has increased many times over during the last 45 years. In the late 40s, the cost of production of a black and white film was a mere Rs. 25,000. Now after over 45 years, the cost of an average colour picture (with 20 prints) is not less than Rs. 4 million. Similarly, the business has also increased, but not to that extent, because of a number of alternate entertainments like TV, video, theatre and, above all, illegal exhibition of the latest Indian films on the video circuit.

The highest grossing film to date is 'Moula Jutt' (Punjabi) with Sultan Rahi playing the title role. It was released in 1979. One of the main reasons for its colossal success was its repeated ban by the Censor Board, because of excessive violence. However, the Urdu film 'Aina' (1977) takes the credit of the longest run—401 combined weeks in Karachi. Nadeem and Shabnam had played the romantic lead in the film, directed by Nazrul Islam. The most successful foreign film released in Pakistan to date is 'Noorjehan', an Indian film, which was allowed special permission by the then President General Mohammed Zia-ul-Huq in 1980 to producer-distributor Sheikh Mukhtar, who unfortunately, could not live to see the extraordinary success of his starrer. The film is reported to have grossed a sum of Rs. 40 million at the box-office during its first screening. It had Meena Kumari, Pradeep Kumar, Sohrab Modi and Sheikh Mukhtar in its cast. The most expensive film produced in Pakistan was 'Qasam Us Waqt Ki' (1969). Based on the 1965 war between Pakistan and India, it has Shabanam, Tariq Aziz and Swarnalata in its main cast. But it was a big flop for a number of reasons, the main being the excessive deletion of action scenes, following the Tashkent agreement between the two countries. A number of other films, including 'Anndata' were made in the following years with bigger budgets, but in terms of real cost (inflation adjusted) 'Qasam Us Waqt Ki' remained the most expensive movie ever made in

Pakistan. The lowest budgeted Pakistani film to win international recognition was 'Jago Huwa Savera' (The Day Shall Dawn), the first Urdu film of East Pakistan. Made in Dhaka (now the capital of Bangladesh), it was made in 1959. It was based on the lives of the fishermen of East Pakistan.

References

1. Ministry of Information and Broadcasting: Annual Report 1986-87, Published by Government of India, 1987, page 24.
2. *Ibid.*, page 25.
3. *Ibid.*
4. *Ibid.*, page 26.
5. *Ibid.*
6. *Ibid.*, page 27.
7. "Selected song and dance sequences from Hindi films and regional language films were telecast on the net-work/national programme as also locally by different centres in the country. Doordarshan continued to produce programmes reflecting talents and achievements of different film personalities in the interview-based programmes like "Phool Khilen Han Gulshan Gulshan" and "Aarohi"."
   —*Ibid.*
8. *Ibid.*, page 28.
9. *Ibid.*
10. *Ibid.*, page 29.

PART II

Chapter 2

Surveyed Political Study of Sunil Dutt

Mumbai, North-West Parliamentary constituency having 12.24 lakh odd voters, including film stars, cine workers, merchants, rich and poor alike witnessed a keen tussle between Mr. Sunil Dutt (Cong.-I) and former Bombay Mayor Dr. Ramesh Prabhoo (Shiv Sena). The constituency has a cosmopolitan complexion with a population comprising Punjabis, Sindhis, Gujaratis, Uttar Bharatiyas, Kannadigas alongwith Maharashtrians—sons of the soil who constitute about 45 percent of the total electorate. Mr. Dutt himself has been residing in Bombay for over four decades now and for all practical purposes a Maharashtrian. This is the constituency which had sent Ram Jethmalani to Lok Sabha twice. The same constituency also saw to it that he was defeated by Mr. Dutt in 1984 in the wake of Rajiv wave.

The contest had become significant as Mr. Dutt was seeking third term. He won in 1984 due to the Rajiv wave, in 1989 despite Hindutva movement, he won with a handsome margin defeating the BJP candidate. Now he took on Dr. Prabhoo, the Sena's firebrand MLA, who was known for his 'never say die' qualities. Dr. Prabhoo was the first Sena MLA who faced an election petition challenging Hindutva.

Sunil Dutt's Son Sanjay Dutt and TADA Case on him

The senior counsel for Central Bureau of Investigation, N. Natarajan, appearing in the serial blast case on June 28, 1994, surprised everyone present in the special designated TADA court by making a submission that seemed like coming from a defence counsel. He submitted that though he was opposing the bail application filed by accused Sanjay Dutt on the merits of the matter, he had instructions from the CBI to conduct the trial in as fair a manner as possible. He submitted an interpretation of section 20(8) of Terrorists and Disruptive Activities (Prevention) Act, 1987, which deals with provisions of bail. The section is like a blanket section denying bail to accused under TADA, sub-clause eight of section 20 lays down that no accused charged under the Act, if in custody, shall be granted bail without the public prosecutor having been heard and unless the court is convinced that there is no basis to invoke the provisions of the act.

Natarajan said the section was applicable to an accused who is in custody. This part of the section obviously did not apply to this accused, he submitted. The continuance of bail granted by Bombay High Court in September, 1993, revealed that the High Court had also applied the same interpretation, he said. The other submissions made by Natarajan were that the circumstances of Dutt's case were not ordinary, that the case was about a diabolical conspiracy, abetted by a foreign country and that lethal weapons had been acquired by the accused applicant.

Efforts for Bail

A Division Bench of the Supreme Court declined bail to film actor Sanjay Dutt, who has been detained in Thane Jail in Maharashtra since July 4, 1994, when the TADA Judge, Mr. J.N. Patel, denied bail to him. In a short order read out at the apex court on September 23, 1994, Justice Jeevan Reddy on behalf of Justices G.N. Ray and N.P. Singh said that they were not inclined to enlarge the petitioner on bail at this juncture They added that, therefore, the petition was accordingly rejected.

The three judges said that it was open to the petitioner to renew his request for bail before the designated court after his defence evidence is adduced at the trial. According to the charge-sheet, Dutt procured three AK 56 rifles, a 9 mm pistol, 25 hand grenades and cartridges on January 16, 1993, when riots were taking place in Bombay. He later returned two AK 56 rifles and some of the cartridges to those who supplied it to him. As a distraught Sunil Dutt, father of Sanjay Dutt and Congress MP from Bombay, looked on, the bench said in view of its decision to reject the bail plea of the accused it did not find it appropriate to give any reasons. On August 18, 1994, the Division Bench, comprising justices Jeevan Reddy and N.P. Singh, had referred the petition of Sanjay Dutt against TADA Judge Patel's order to a Constitution Bench for interpretation of several sections of TADA.

The Constitution Bench, comprising Justices A.M. Ahmadi, J.S. Verma, P.B. Sawant and N.P. Singh, diluted Section 5 by holding that an accused was entitled to prove by adducing evidence that the reason for possession of unauthorised arms was wholly unrelated to any terrorist activity and referred Sanjay Dutt's bail plea to a Division Bench. Before Justices Reddy, Ray and Singh, Dutt's counsel argued that the weapons were acquired by him for self-defence. CBI's counsel N. Natarajan considered the defence story unbelievable as the actor already possessed three licensed weapons.

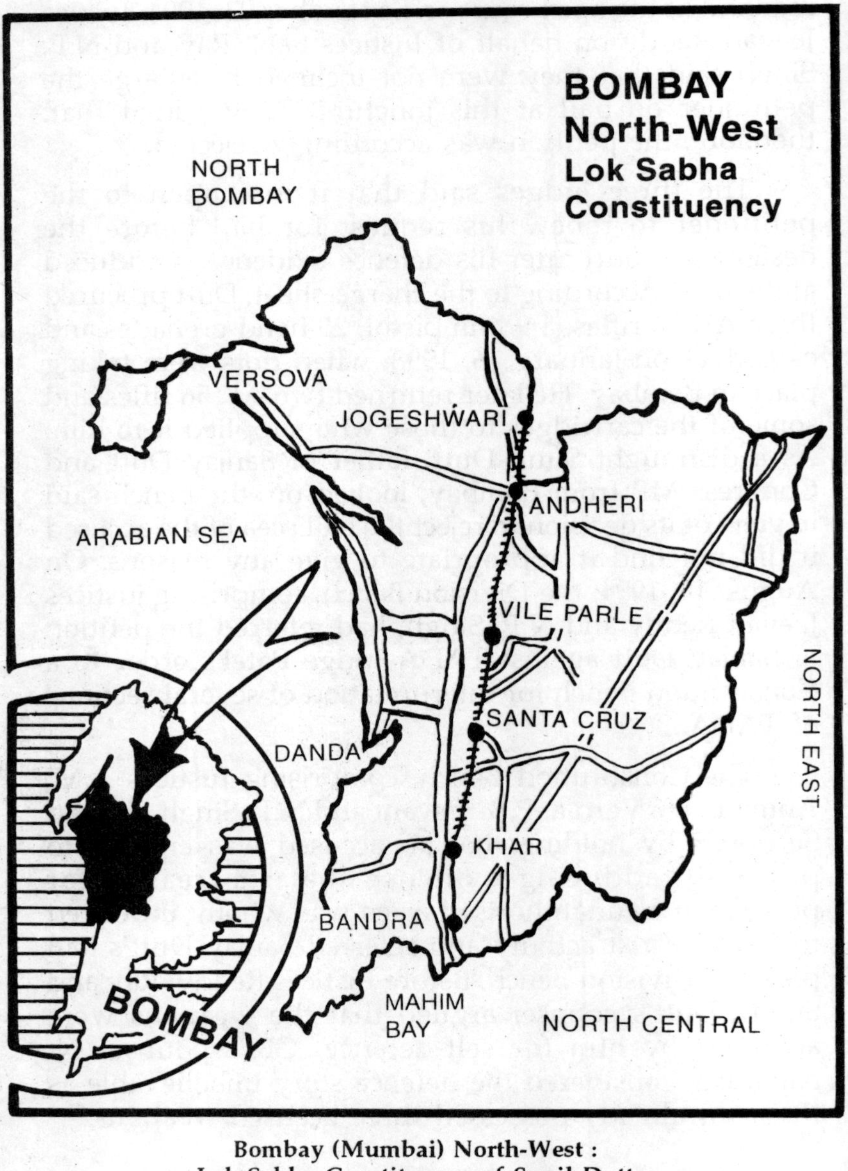

Bombay (Mumbai) North-West :
Lok Sabha Constituency of Sunil Dutt

Table 2.1

Detailed Study of Sunil Dutt's One Hundred Surveyed Political Supporters in Delhi in August 1997

S. No.	*Name of the Person*	*Sex*	*Age (in years)*	*Urban/ Rural*	*Religion*	*Whether SC/ST*	*Family's income P.M. (in Rs.)*	*Education*	*Occupation*	*No. of His watched Political Films*	*View about His Political Future*
1	*2*	*3*	*4*	*5*	*6*	*7*	*8*	*9*	*10*	*11*	*12*
1.	Parmesh Dikshit	Male	27	Urban	Hindu	Nil	2800.00	M.A.	Service	09	May be Minister
2.	Saroj Sharma	Female	28	Rural	Hindu	Nil	2400.00	B.A.	Housewife	07	Very Good
3.	Aruna Kumari	Female	21	Rural	Hindu	SC	2200.00	Matric	Housewife	12	May be Re-elected
4.	Taiyab Hussain	Male	32	Urban	Muslim	Nil	2400.00	Inter	Business	11	More popular in future
5.	Gyan Devi	Female	31	Rural	Hindu	Nil	2700.00	B.A.	Service	14	Brighter as a Ex-M.P.
6.	Farooq Hussain	Male	45	Urban	Muslim	Nil	1800.00	Matric	Business	10	Very Good
7.	Madhuri Sharma	Female	34	Urban	Hindu	Nil	2500.00	B.A.	Business	09	May be Re-elected
8.	Geeta Saxena	Female	29	Urban	Hindu	Nil	3600.00	M.A.	Service	07	More popular in future
9.	Shashi Saxena	Female	34	Urban	Hindu	Nil	3500.00	Matric	Housewife	15	May be Minister
10.	Ibrahim Khan	Male	24	Rural	Muslim	Nil	3000.00	Inter	Business	11	Brighter as a Ex-M.P.
11.	Sonakshi Gupta	Female	25	Rural	Hindu	Nil	2800.00	B.A.	Student	14	Very Good
12.	Rukma Devi	Female	24	Rural	Buddhist	SC	1800.00	Matric	Housewife	09	Good
13.	Laxman Das	Male	25	Rural	Buddhist	SC	1500.00	Matric	Business	13	May be Minister
14.	R.K. Tiwari	Male	28	Urban	Hindu	Nil	1900.00	M.Sc.	Service	15	May be Re-elected
15.	Sukh Ram	Male	34	Urban	Hindu	SC	2300.00	B.A.	Service	12	Brighter as a politician

(Contd.)

1	2	3	4	5	6	7	8	9	10	11	12
16.	Shrikrishna Saxena	Male	25	Urban	Hindu	Nil	2700.00	M.A.	Business	15	Should be President of India
17.	Vimlesh Kaur	Female	27	Urban	Sikh	Nil	1800.00	Inter	Housewife	11	More popular in future
18.	Sudesh Sharma	Female	29	Rural	Hindu	Nil	2100.00	B.A.	Service	12	Very Good
19.	Maharaj Singh	Male	27	Rural	Hindu	Nil	3500.00	M.Sc.	Business	15	May be Re-elected
20.	Madhubala	Female	31	Urban	Hindu	SC	2600.00	Inter	Housewife	09	May be Minister
21.	Ummed Singh	Male	24	Urban	Hindu	SC	2200.00	B.A.	Student	11	Brighter as a Ex-M.P.
22.	Raj Narain Verma	Male	33	Rural	Hindu	Nil	3000.00	M.Com.	Service	10	May be Re-elected
23.	Kanta Devi	Female	31	Rural	Hindu	SC	2100.00	Matric	Housewife	09	More popular in future
24.	Vibha Pandey	Female	24	Urban	Hindu	Nil	2900.00	B.A.	Housewife	08	More popular in future
25.	Prempal Kaushik	Male	29	Urban	Hindu	Nil	3300.00	M.A.	Service	11	May be Re-elected
26.	A.K. Dubey	Male	25	Rural	Hindu	Nil	2700.00	B.A.	Business	15	Should be President of India
27.	Lalit Kumar	Male	27	Rural	Hindu	SC	1800.00	Inter	Service	09	Very Good
28.	Sone Lal Shukla	Male	40	Urban	Hindu	Nil	2500.00	M.Com.	Business	14	Good
29.	Taramati Chaube	Female	31	Rural	Hindu	Nil	2100.00	B.A.	Housewife	13	Brighter as a Ex-M.P.
30.	Maurine Fermandes	Female	29	Urban	Christian	Nil	3100.00	M.A.	Service	09	Brighter as a Politician
31.	Peter Victor	Male	32	Urban	Christian	Nil	2200.00	M.Sc.	Service	11	May be Re-elected
32.	S. S. Pandey	Male	30	Urban	Hindu	Nil	2400.00	B.A.	Business	07	May be Re-elected
33.	Khajan Singh	Male	31	Rural	Hindu	SC	2100.00	Inter	Business	09	More popular in future
34.	Amba Prasad	Male	27	Urban	Hindu	Nil	2500.00	M.A.	Service	08	Brighter as a Ex-M.P.
35.	Mujaffar Hussain	Male	26	Rural	Muslim	Nil	2600.00	B.A.	Service	15	Brighter as a politician
36.	Waheeda Khatoon	Female	27	Urban	Muslim	Nil	2900.00	Inter	Housewife	13	May be Re-elected

(Contd.)

1	2	3	4	5	6	7	8	9	10	11	12
37.	Sudarshan Kaur	Female	32	Rural	Sikh	SC	2400.00	Inter	Housewife	11	Very Good
38.	Kusum Lata	Female	31	Rural	Hindu	Nil	2200.00	Matric	Service	08	Brighter as a politician
39.	Chhote Lala	Male	45	Urban	Hindu	SC	1800.00	Matric	Business	11	More popular in future
40.	Kapuri Devi	Female	36	Urban	Hindu	Nil	2700.00	B.A.	Housewife	09	May be Re-elected
41.	H.R. Gupta	Male	34	Urban	Hindu	Nil	3300.00	M.Com.	Business	11	More popular in future
42.	Pritam Singh	Male	31	Rural	Sikh	SC	2200.00	Matric	Service	15	Brighter as a Ex-M.P.
43.	Om Prakash	Male	22	Rural	Hindu	SC	1900.00	B.A.	Student	10	Very Good
44.	J.N. Juneja	Male	24	Urban	Hindu	Nil	2600.00	M.A.	Service	13	Good
45.	S.S. Talwar	Male	39	Urban	Hindu	Nil	3700.00	M.Com.	Business	12	Brighter as a politician
46.	Ramesh Chand	Male	34	Rural	Hindu	Nil	3200.00	B.A.	Service	11.	More popular in future
47.	Laxmi Devi	Female	31	Urban	Hindu	SC	1900.00	Matric	Housewife	09	Should be President of India
48.	Durgeshwari Kalra	Female	31	Urban	Hindu	Nil	2500.00	B.A.	Housewife	10	More popular in future
49.	Kavita Jain	Female	24	Urban	Jain	Nil	2900.00	M.A.	Student	15	May be Re-elected
50.	Kanhaiya Lal	Male	26	Rural	Hindu	SC	1900.00	Inter	Service	14	Very Good
51.	Bharati Joshi	Female	27	Urban	Hindu	Nil	2600.00	Matric	Housewife	12	Brighter as a politician
52.	Ashok Kumar	Male	29	Rural	Hindu	SC	2200.00	Inter	Service	08	Brighter as a Ex-M.P.
53.	Pradip Kumar	Male	34	Urban	Hindu	Nil	2300.00	B.A.	Business	14	More popular in future
54.	Radha Raman Sharma	Male	43	Urban	Hindu	Nil	2600.00	M.Com.	Business	13	Should be President of India
55.	Kanwaljit	Male	26	Rural	Hindu	Nil	2900.00	M.Sc.	Business	12	More popular in future

(Contd.)

1	2	3	4	5	6	7	8	9	10	11	12
56.	Mukesh Kumar	Male	32	Urban	Hindu	Nil	2800.00	B.A.	Service	06	May be Re-elected
57.	Kishan Chand	Male	29	Rural	Hindu	SC	1900.00	Inter	Service	09	Brighter as a Ex-M.P.
58.	R.L. Kapoor	Male	36	Urban	Hindu	Nil	2500.00	M.A.	Business	12	More popular in future
59.	Prakash Singh	Male	32	Rural	Sikh	Nil	4000.00	B.Sc.	Business	05	Very Good
60.	Bhole Nath Chaturvedi	Male	42	Urban	Hindu	Nil	4500.00	M.A.	Business	09	Brighter as a politician
61.	Hanuman Prasad	Male	40	Rural	Hindu	Nil	2700.00	M.Com.	Business	11	Brighter as a Ex-M.P.
62.	Hansa Jain	Female	29	Urban	Jain	Nil	2900.00	M.A.	Housewife	09	More popular in future
63.	Asim Kumar Jain	Male	24	Urban	Jain	Nil	3400.00	B.A.	Student	15	May be Re-elected
64.	Romila Nagar	Female	23	Urban	Hindu	Nil	3600.00	B.Sc.	Student	09	May be Re-elected
65.	Hukum Singh	Male	22	Rural	Sikh	Nil	3400.00	B.A.	Student	17	More popular in future
66.	Kalu Ram	Male	36	Rural	Hindu	SC	1400.00	Martic	Service	12	Brighter as a politician
67.	Anjali Devi	Female	32	Urban	Hindu	SC	1200.00	Inter	Housewife	09	Brighter as a Ex-M.P.
68.	Roopesh Kumar	Male	21	Rural	Hindu	Nil	2400.00	B.A.	Student	15	Very Good
69.	Gurcharan Singh	Male	19	Urban	Sikh	Nil	4500.00	Inter	Student	14	Should be President of India
70.	Gurmit Kaur	Female	22	Urban	Sikh	Nil	3300.00	B.A.	Student	16	Good
71.	Badruddin Khan	Male	44	Urban	Muslim	Nil	4500.00	M.A.	Business	14	More popular in future
72.	Basanti Deyi	Female	24	Rural	Hindu	SC	1200.00	Matric	Housewife	09	More popular in future
73.	Surjit Singh	Male	26	Urban	Sikh	Nil	3500.00	B.A.	Business	17	May be Re-elected
74.	S.S. Sharma	Male	29	Urban	Hindu	Nil	3200.00	M.A.	Service	10	More popular in future
75.	Hanumant Singh	Male	27	Rural	Hindu	SC	2400.00	M.Sc.	Service	07	Brighter as a politician
76.	Divya Sharma	Female	24	Urban	Hindu	Nil	2600.00	M.A.	Student	15	Brighter as a Ex-M.P.
77.	Devdoot Barua	Male	26	Urban	Hindu	Nil	3600.00	B.Sc.	Business	14	More popular in future

(Contd.)

1	2	3	4	5	6	7	8	9	10	11	12
78.	Harkishan Singh	Male	35	Rural	Sikh	Nil	3800.00	M.A.	Business	10	Should be President of India
79.	Balram Singh	Male	39	Urban	Sikh	Nil	3400.00	B.A.	Service	23	May be Re-elected
80.	Mona Mathur	Female	26	Urban	Hindu	Nil	2400.00	M.Sc.	Service	13	May be Minister
81.	Poonam Kukreja	Female	36	Urban	Hindu	Nil	3500.00	B.A.	Housewife	15	Brighter as a Ex-M.P.
82.	Geetta Ray	Female	28	Rural	Hindu	Nil	4500.00	M.A.	Business	14	Brighter as a politician
83.	Anita Rani	Female	27	Rural	Hindu	SC	1800.00	B.A.	Housewife	12	May be Re-elected
84.	Parmesh Kumar	Male	25	Urban	Hindu	SC	2300.00	M.A.	Service	13	More popular in future
85.	Ajmer Singh	Male	27	Urban	Sikh	Nil	4200.00	B.A.	Business	16	Very Good
86.	Sundar Lal Jain	Male	33	Urban	Jain	Nil	4000.00	M.A.	Business	14	Brighter as a Ex-M.P.
87.	Milkiyat Singh	Male	39	Urban	Sikh	Nil	4300.00	B.A.	Business	11	Brighter as a politician
88.	Manorama Ray	Female	26	Urban	Hindu	Nil	2700.00	M.A.	Service	12	May be Re-elected
89.	Mayur Tiwari	Male	24	Urban	Hindu	Nil	3400.00	B.A.	Student	15	More popular in future
90.	Manjula Parekh	Female	23	Rural	Hindu	Nil	3600.00	B.Com.	Student	08	May be Minister
91.	R.K. Singh	Male	26	Rural	Hindu	SC	2700.00	M.A.	Business	12	Should be President of India
92.	Zagir Singh	Male	29	Urban	Sikh	Nil	3500.00	M.Sc.	Service	09	Brighter as a Ex-M.P.
93.	M.L. Sharma	Male	36	Urban	Hindu	Nil	3600.00	M.A.	Business	21	More popular in future
94.	S.K. Tewari	Male	29	Rural	Hindu	Nil	4300.00	M.Com.	Service	15	Good
95.	Kuldip Singh	Male	36	Rural	Sikh	Nil	4000.00	B.A.	Business	11	May be Minister
96.	S.L. Purohit	Male	29	Urban	Hindu	Nil	2700.00	M.A.	Service	13	May be Minister
97.	R.A. Sharma	Male	24	Rural	Hindu	Nil	3300.00	B.A.	Business	12	May be Re-elected
98.	Ratan Lal	Male	26	Rural	Hindu	SC	2500.00	B.A.	Student	13	More popular in future
99.	Naina Devi	Female	29	Urban	Hindu	Nil	3600.00	M.A.	Housewife	15	Brighter as a Ex-M.P.
100.	Gurdayal Singh	Male	36	Urban	Sikh	Nil	4500.00	Inter	Business	14	May be Re-elected

Findings of the research are shown in diagrams.

(Contd.)

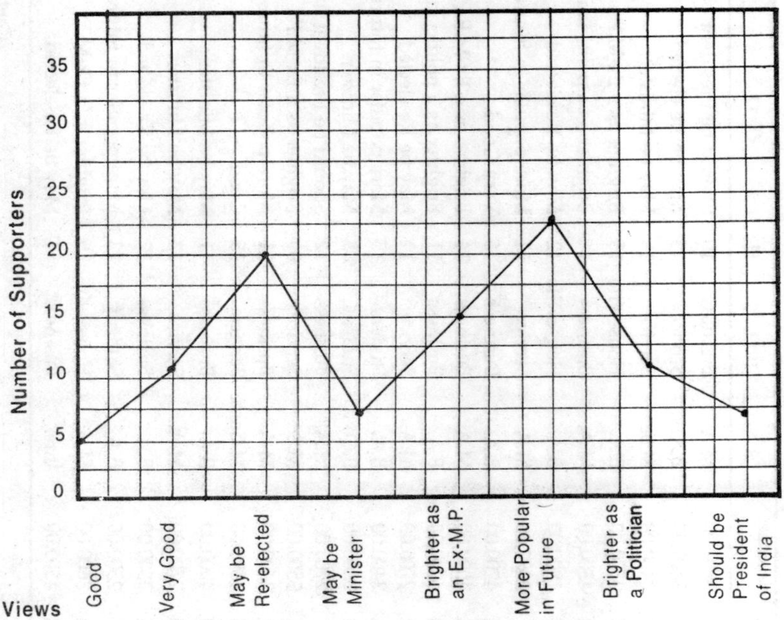

Diagram 2.1
Views-wise Number of Sunil Dutt's One Hundred Surveyed Political Supporters in Delhi in August 1997 (Views about his Political Future).

Out of one hundred surveyed political supporters of Sunil Dutt in Delhi; according to five supporters, his political future is 'Good'; according to eleven supporters, his political future is 'Very Good'; according to twenty supporters, he 'may be re-elected' in future; according to eight supporters, he 'may be minister in future'; according to fifteen supporters his political future is 'brighter as Ex-M.P.'; according to twenty-three supporters, he may be 'more popular in future' according to eleven supporters, his political future is 'brighter as a politician'; according to seven supporters, he should be President of India in future.

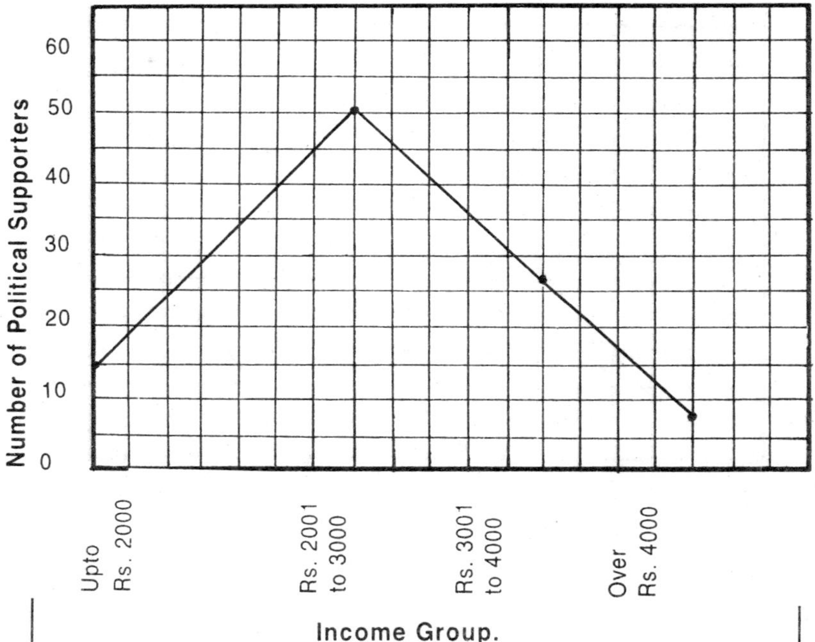

Diagram 2.2

Income-group-wise Number of Sunil Dutt's One Hundred Surveyed Political Supporters in Delhi in August 1997.

Out of one hundred surveyed political supporters of Sunil Dutt in Delhi, fifteen supporters are in upto Rs. 2000 income-group, fifty supporters are in from Rs. 2001 to Rs. 3000 income-group, twenty-seven supporters are in from Rs. 3001 to Rs. 4000 income group and only eight supporters are in over Rs. 4000 income-group.

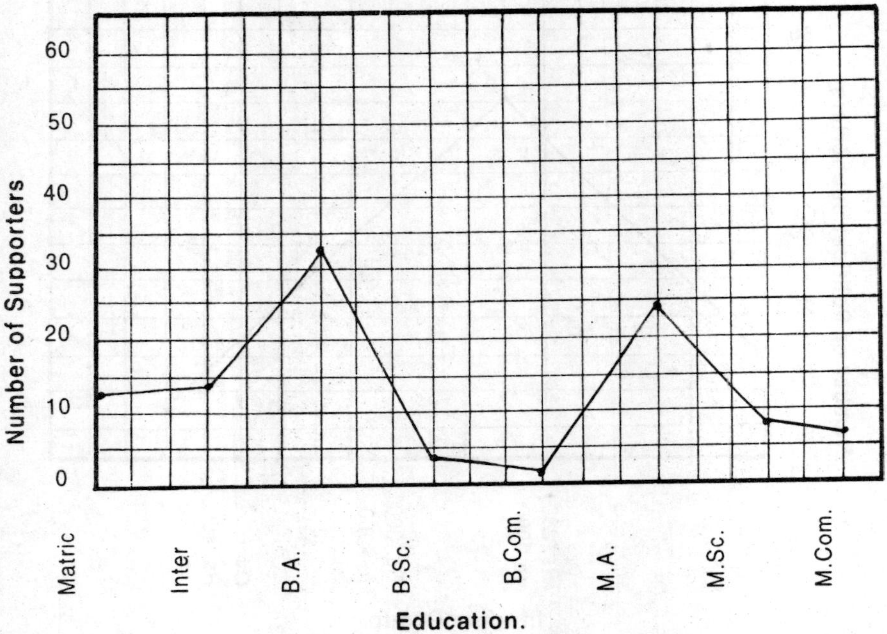

Diagram 2.3

Education-wise Number of Sunil Dutt's One Hundred Surveyed Political Supporters in Delhi in August 1997.

Out of one hundred surveyed political supporters of Sunil Dutt in Delhi, thirteen supporters are only Matric passed, fourteen supporters are Inter examination passed, thirty-two are B.A., three are B.Sc., only one is B.Com., twenty-three are M.A., seven are M.Sc. and seven also supporters are M.Com.

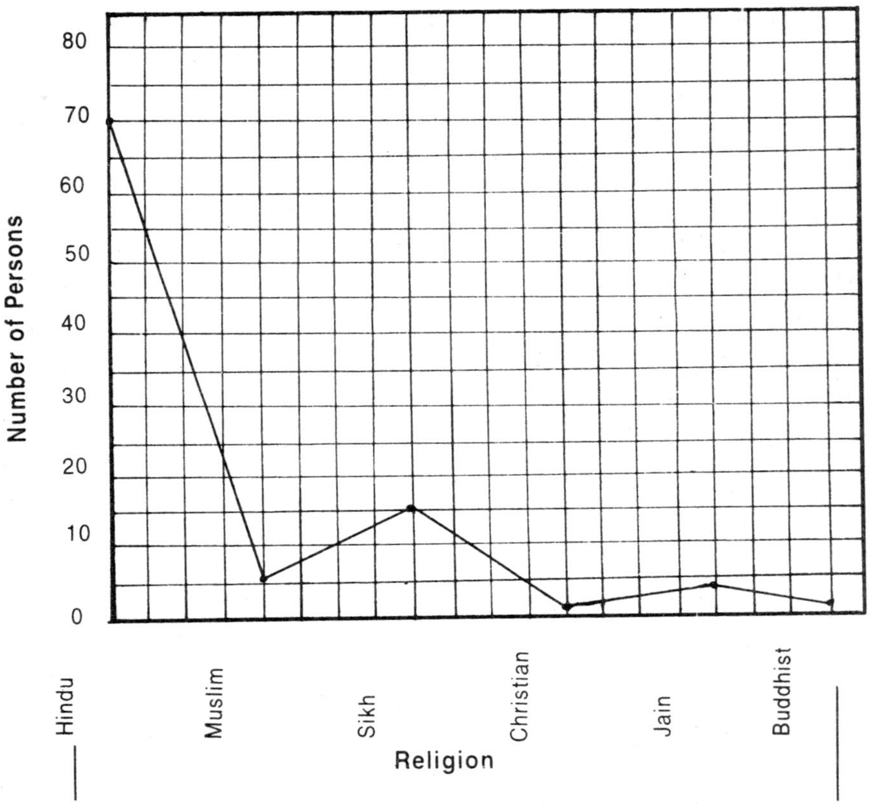

Diagram 2.4

Religion-wise Number of Sunil Dutt's One Hundred Surveyed Political Supporters in Delhi in 1997.

Out of one hundred surveyed political supporters of Sunil Dutt in Delhi, seventy-one supporters are Hindus, six supporters are Muslims, fifteen supporters are Sikhs, two supporters are Christians, four supporters are Jains and two supporters are Buddhists.

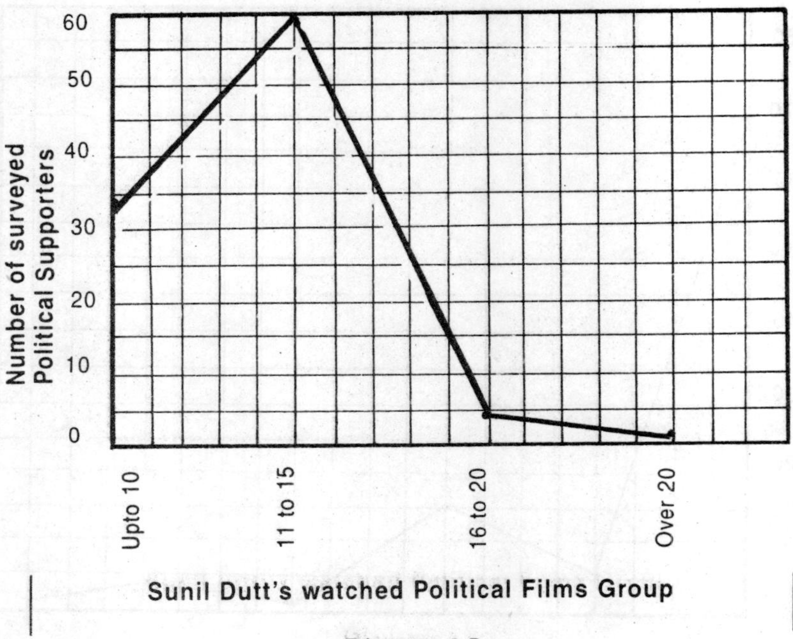

Diagram 2.5

His Watched Political Films Group-wise number of Sunil Dutt's One Hundred Surveyed Political Supporters in Delhi in August 1997.

Out of one hundred surveyed political supporters of Sunil Dutt in Delhi, thirty-four supporters are in upto 10 watched political films-group, sixty supporters are in 11 to 15 watched political films-group, four supporters are in 16 to 20 watched political films-group and only two supporters are in over 20 watched political films-group.

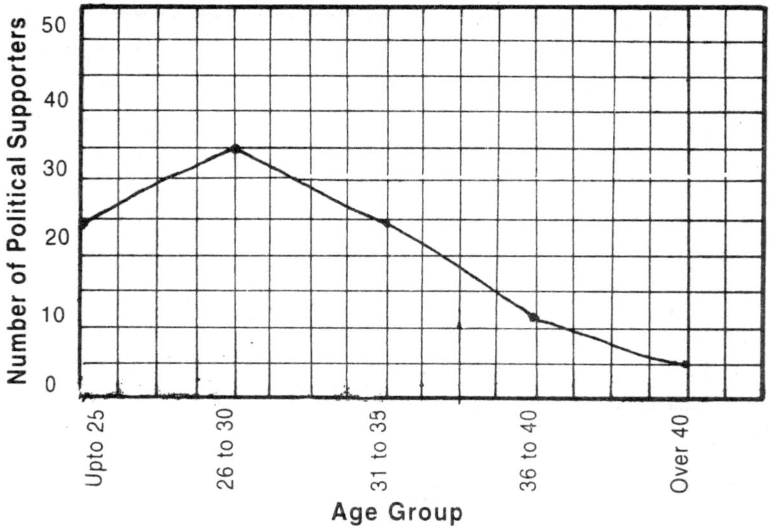

Diagram 2.6

Age Group-wise Number of Sunil Dutt's One Hundred Surveyed Political Supporters in Delhi in August 1997.

Out of one hundred surveyed political supporters of Sunil Dutt in Delhi, twenty-four are in upto 25 age-group, thirty-five are in 26-30 age-group, twenty-four are in 31 to 35 age-group, twelve are in 36 to 40 age-group and only five are in over 40 age-group.

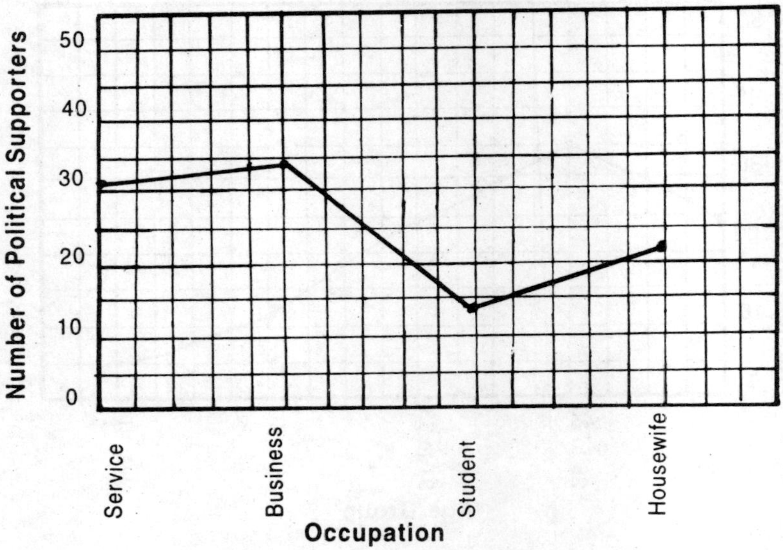

Diagram 2.7
Occupation-wise Number of Sunil Dutt's One Hundred Surveyed Political Supporters in Delhi in August 1997.

Out of one hundred surveyed political supporters of Sunil Dutt in Delhi, thirty-one are in service, thirty-four are in business, fourteen are as students and twenty-one are as housewives.

Chapter 3

Surveyed Political Study of Shabana Azmi : M.P.

(Nominated Rajya Sabha Member)

Shabana Azmi is a nominated member of Rajya Sabha. She is an international fame film actress. She is also a dedicated social worker. She has worked for welfare the people of slum areas of Mumbai.

Shabana Azmi is daughter of Kaifi Azmi, noted poet of Urdu. Her husband Zaved Khan is also a famous Urdu poet.

Here, in present study, I am presenting a survey study about her socio-political career. This study shows her popularity in public also. As a social worker and reformer, her future is definitely brighter.

Here is a table that shows detailed study of Shabana Azmi's one hundred surveyed political supporters in Delhi in July 1996.

Table 3.1

Detailed Study of Shabana Ajmi's One Hundred Surveyed Political Supporters in Delhi in July 1996

S. No.	*Name of the Person*	*Sex*	*Age (in years)*	*Urban/ Rural*	*Religion*	*Whether SC/ST*	*Family's income P.M. (in Rs.)*	*Edu- cation*	*Occup- ation*	*No. of Her watched Political Films*	*View about Her Political Future*
1	*2*	*3*	*4*	*5*	*6*	*7*	*8*	*9*	*10*	*11*	*12*
1.	Baldev Dutt	Male	29	Urban	Hindu	Nil	3000.00	B.A.	Service	07	Brighter as a politician
2.	Kabul Singh	Male	33	Rural	Sikh	Nil	4500.00	M.A.	Business	09	Brighter as a reformist
3.	Pooja Ahuja	Female	23	Urban	Sikh	Nil	4000.00	B.A.	Student	05	May be elected as M.P.
4.	Pragat Singh	Male	26	Rural	Sikh	Nil	3600.00	M.Sc.	Business	06	More popular in future
5.	Mohan Das	Male	29	Rural	Hindu	SC	2400.00	Inter	Service	02	Brighter as a reformist
6.	Alka Jain	Female	23	Urban	Jain	Nil	2600.00	B.A.	Student	04	May be elected as M.P.
7.	Sadiq Hussain	male	26	Rural	Muslim	Nil	3200.00	M.A.	Business	03	May be elected as M.P.
8.	Parvez Ahmad	Male	25	Urban	Muslim	Nil	2700.00	M.A.	Student	04	More popular in future
9.	Hemlata Jain	Female	27	Urban	Jain	Nil	2900.00	B.A.	Housewife	10	May be elected as M.P.
10.	Sohan Lal	Male	24	Rural	Buddhist	SC	2500.00	B.A.	Student	07	Brighter as a reformist
11.	Puspa Rani	Female	29	Rural	Buddhist	SC	2100.00	Matric	Housewife	09	Brighter as a politician
12.	A.K. Saxena	Male	27	Urban	Hindu	Nil	3300.00	Inter	Service	06	More popular in future
13.	Dazy Narula	Female	34	Urban	Hindu	Nil	3100.00	B.Sc.	Business	10	May be elected as M.P.
14.	Sonia Sharma	Female	22	Rural	Hindu	Nil	2600.00	B.Com.	Student	09	Brighter as a politician
15.	Kuldip Sharma	Male	22	Rural	Hindu	Nil	2400.00	B.Com.	Student	09	More popular in future

(Contd.)

1	2	3	4	5	6	7	8	9	10	11	12
16.	Brahm Prakash	Male	23	Rural	Hindu	SC	2300.00	B.A.	Student	04	May be elected as M.P.
17.	Prem Chand Verma	Male	33	Urban	Hindu	Nil	2700.00	M.A.	Service	06	Brighter as a reformist
18.	P.L. Dubey	Male	45	Urban	Hindu	Nil	4000.00	Inter	Business	03	Brighter as a politician
19.	S. Vasudev	Male	41	Rural	Hindu	Nil	3100.00	M.A.	Service	08	May be elected as M.P.
20.	Satwant Singh	Male	39	Urban	Sikh	Nil	3500.00	Matric	Business	08	More popular in future
21.	Kamlesh Kumari	Female	36	Rural	Hindu	SC	2300.00	Matric	Housewife	04	May be elected as M.P.
22.	Kartari Devi	Female	32	Urban	Hindu	SC	1800.00	Inter	Service	08	More popular in future
23.	Pradip Mishra	Male	23	Rural	Hindu	Nil	2600.00	B.A.	Student	10	Brighter as a politician
24.	S.L. Thapa	Male	26	Urban	Hindu	Nil	2100.00	Inter	Service	07	Brighter as a reformist
25.	Munni Devi	Female	31	Rural	Hindu	SC	1800.00	Matric	Service	05	May be elected as M.P.
26.	R.N. Vats	Male	27	Rural	Hindu	Nil	2300.00	Inter	Business	04	More popular in future
27.	Harjinder Kaur	Female	25	Urban	Sikh	Nil	2100.00	B.A.	Student	05	Brighter as a reformist
28.	Harprit Singh	Male	26	Rural	Sikh	Nil	3600.00	M.A.	Business	07	Brighter as a politician
29.	Wilson Thomas	Male	25	Urban	Christian	Nil	3100.00	Inter	Business	09	May be elected as M.P.
30.	Harminder Kaur	Female	33	Urban	Sikh	Nil	2600.00	B.A.	Housewife	08	More popular in future
31.	Jaswant Singh	Male	24	Urban	Hindu	SC	1800.00	B.A.	Student	03	Brighter as a reformist
32.	Achla Verma	Female	22	Urban	Hindu	Nil	2600.00	Inter	Housewife	05	May be elected as M.P
33.	Darshan Singh	Male	34	Rural	Sikh	Nil	3400.00	B.Sc.	Service	07	Brighter as a politician
34.	M.B. Shah	Male	25	Urban	Jain	Nil	4500.00	M.A.	Business	10	May be elected as M.P.
35.	Dipika Gupta	Female	42	Rural	Hindu	Nil	4100.00	M.A.	Housewife	08	May be elected as M.P.
36.	Harcharan Singh	Male	45	Urban	Sikh	Nil	4400.00	B.A.	Business	02	More popular in future

(Contd.)

1	2	3	4	5	6	7	8	9	10	11	12
37.	M.S. Solanki	Male	34	Urban	Hindu	Nil	3400.00	M.Sc.	Service	04	May be elected as M.P.
38.	Bhikha Ram	Male	29	Urban	Hindu	SC	2400.00	Matric	Service	06	More popular in future
39.	Vimlesh Kaur	Female	25	Urban	Sikh	SC	2400.00	Matric	Housewife	08	May be elected as M.P.
40.	V.S. Saxena	Male	29	Urban	Hindu	Nil	2700,00	B.A.	Service	20	May be elected as M.P.
41.	Rameshwar Prasad	Male	25	Urban	Hindu	SC	2400.00	Matric	Business	17	More popular in future
42.	Prem Singh Tomar	Male	22	Urban	Hindu	Nil	2300.00	B.A.	Student	10	May be elected as M.P.
43.	S.S. Prit	Male	28	Rural	Hindu	Nil	2600.00	Inter	Service	04	Brighter as a reformist
44.	Dipti Garg	Female	34	Urban	Hindu	Nil	2400.00	B.A.	Business	06	May be elected as M.P.
45.	Arjun Singh	Male	32	Urban	Sikh	Nil	4500.00	M.A.	Business	09	May be elected as M.P.
46.	Purushottam Das	Male	29	Urban	Hindu	Nil	4000.00	M.Sc.	Service	12	Brighter as a politician
47.	Har Prakash	Male	27	Urban	Hindu	SC	1900.00	Matric	Service	04	May be elected as M.P.
48.	V.P. Yadav	Male	31	Urban	Hindu	Nil	2300.00	Inter	Service	06	More popular in future
49.	Devi Lal	Male	39	Rural	Hindu	Nil	4300.00	M.A.	Business	08	May be elected as M.P.
50.	Om Prakash Sharma	Male	26	Rural	Hindu	Nil	1900.00	B.A.	Business	04	Brighter as a reformist
51.	Sunita Arora	Female	23	Urban	Hindu	Nil	2700.00	B.Com.	Student	09	May be elected as M.P.
52.	Raj Kalra	Male	27	Urban	Hindu	Nil	3600.00	M.A.	Business	13	Brighter as a politician
53.	Ram Shankar Tewari	Male	29	Urban	Hindu	Nil	3100.00	B.A.	Service	07	May be elected as M.P.
54.	Ram Nath	Male	36	Rural	Hindu	SC	2200.00	Matric	Service	09	More popular in future
55.	Shakuntala Devi	Female	26	Urban	Hindu	Nil	2900.00	B.A.	Housewife	06	May be elected as M.P.
56.	B.S. Rawat	Male	34	Urban	Hindu	Nil	3600.00	M.A.	Service	09	More popular in future
57.	Puran Singh	Male	29	Rural	Hindu	SC	2200.00	Inter	Service	07	May be elected as M.P.

(Contd.)

1	2	3	4	5	6	7	8	9	10	11	12
58.	Narain Singh	Male	27	Rural	Hindu	Nil	2600.00	Matric	Service	06	Brighter as a reformist
59.	Naresh Yadav	Male	37	Rural	Hindu	Nil	3100.00	M.Com.	Business	10	Brighter as a reformist
60.	Raj Bahadur	Male	26	Urban	Hindu	SC	2300.00	Inter	Service	06	May be elected as M.P.
61.	R. Masiah	Male	43	Urban	Christian	Nil	2500.00	B.A.	Service	09	May be elected as M.P.
62.	Hemant Kumar	Male	37	Urban	Hindu	Nil	2600.00	M.A.	Business	05	More popular in future
63.	Ram Naresh Sharma	Male	24	Urban	Hindu	Nil	3100.00	B.A.	Student	09	May be elected as M.P.
64.	Rajinder Kaur	Female	26	Urban	Sikh	Nil	4400.00	M.Sc.	Student	06	Brighter as a reformist
65.	Shiv Prasad	Male	25	Rural	Hindu	SC	3600.00	M.A.	Service	04	May be elected as M.P.
66.	Sumit Jain	Male	29	Rural	Jain	Nil	3900.00	M.Com.	Business	06	May be elected as M.P.
67.	Sunder Kaur	Female	36	Urban	Sikh	SC	2400.00	Matric	Housewife	05	More popular in future
68.	Chandrika Prasad	Male	33	Rural	Hindu	Nil	3200.00	Inter	Service	10	May be elected as M.P.
69.	Archana Sharma	Female	26	Urban	Hindu	Nil	3400.00	B.A.	Business	09	Brighter as a reformist
70.	Anant Prasad	Male	29	Urban	Hindu	Nil	2900.00	M.A.	Housewife	04	May be elected as M.P.
71.	Milap Singh	Male	26	Urban	Hindu	Nil	2700.00	Inter	Service	05	More popular in future
72.	Gurnam Singh	Male	39	Urban	Sikh	Nil	2900.00	B.A.	Service	07	May be elected as M.P.
73.	Rajani Pathak	Female	34	Urban	Hindu	Nil	3900.00	M.A.	Housewife	09	Brighter as a politician
74.	Iqbal Narain	Male	45	Rural	Hindu	Nil	3600.00	B.A.	Business	03	Brighter as a reformist
75.	Bharat Singh	Male	36	Urban	Hindu	SC	3500.00	M.A.	Service	06	May be elected as M.P.
76.	Vimal Jain	Male	27	Urban	Jain	Nil	4500.00	M.Com.	Business	08	More popular in future
77.	Vishnu Prasad	Male	35	Urban	Hindu	Nil	3400.00	Inter	Business	20	May be elected as M.P.
78.	Tirath Ram	Male	31	Rural	Hindu	SC	2900.00	B.A.	Service	09	More popular in future

(Contd.)

1	2	3	4	5	6	7	8	9	10	11	12
79.	Bala Sharma	Female	24	Urban	Hindu	Nil	3400.00	B.A.	Housewife	07	May be elected as M.P.
80.	Balwan Singh	Male	27	Urban	Hindu	SC	3100.00	M.A.	Student	09	More popular in future
81.	Rama Devi	Female	36	Urban	Hindu	Nil	3200.00	Inter	Housewife	06	Brighter as a reformist
82.	Bharat Sinha	Male	34	Rural	Hindu	Nil	3600.00	M.Com.	Business	08	May be elected as M.P.
83.	Mahavir Jain	Male	31	Urban	Jain	Nil	4500.00	M.Sc.	Service	03	May be elected as M.P.
84.	Kalpana Vyas	Female	22	Urban	Hindu	Nil	4100.00	B.Sc.	Student	20	Brighter as a reformist
85.	Mansa Ram	Male	24	Urban	Hindu	Nil	3600.00	B.Com.	Student	04	More popular in future
86.	Jwala Prasad Sharma	Male	26	Rural	Hindu	Nil	4000.00	M.A.	Business	07	May be elected as M.P.
87.	M.L. Goswami	Male	29	Urban	Hindu	Nil	2700.00	M.A.	Service	07	Brighter as a politician
88.	Jyoti Vyas	Female	32	Urban	Hindu	Nil	3600.00	B.A.	Housewife	20	Brighter as a reformist
89.	Yashwant Kale	Male	26	Urban	Hindu	Nil	4500.00	M.A.	Business	09	May be elected as M.P.
90.	Ram Kumar	Male	34	Rural	Hindu	SC	2600.00	B.A.	Service	04	More popular in future
91.	Rajiv Jain	Male	22	Rural	Jain	Nil	4000.00	B.Com.	Student	03	May be elected as M.P.
92.	J.S. Vadhawa	Male	45	Urban	Sikh	Nil	4500.00	M.A.	Business	08	More popular in future
93.	Gyan Chand	Male	41	Urban	Hindu	SC	4100.00	B.A.	Service	06	May be elected as M.P.
94.	J.P. Sharma	Male	39	Urban	Hindu	Nil	3400.00	M.A.	Service	07	May be elected as M.P.
95.	Nayantara Mishra	Female	29	Urban	Hindu	Nil	3200.00	M.A.	Service	07	More popular in future
96.	K.K. Sharma	Male	34	Rural	Hindu	Nil	4500.00	M.Com.	Business	10	May be elected as M.P.
97.	Santosh Kumar	Male	31	Rural	Hindu	SC	2100.00	B.A.	Service	06	Brighter as a reformist
98.	Rakhee Jain	Female	24	Rural	Jain	Nil	3900.00	M.A.	Student	08	May be elected as M.P.
99.	D.K. Vats	Male	29	Urban	Hindu	Nil	3600.00	M.Com.	Business	02	Brighter as a politician
100.	L.N. Jha	Male	36	Urban	Hindu	Nil	3400.00	M.A.	Service	06	May be elected as M.P.

Findings of the research are shown in the diagrams.

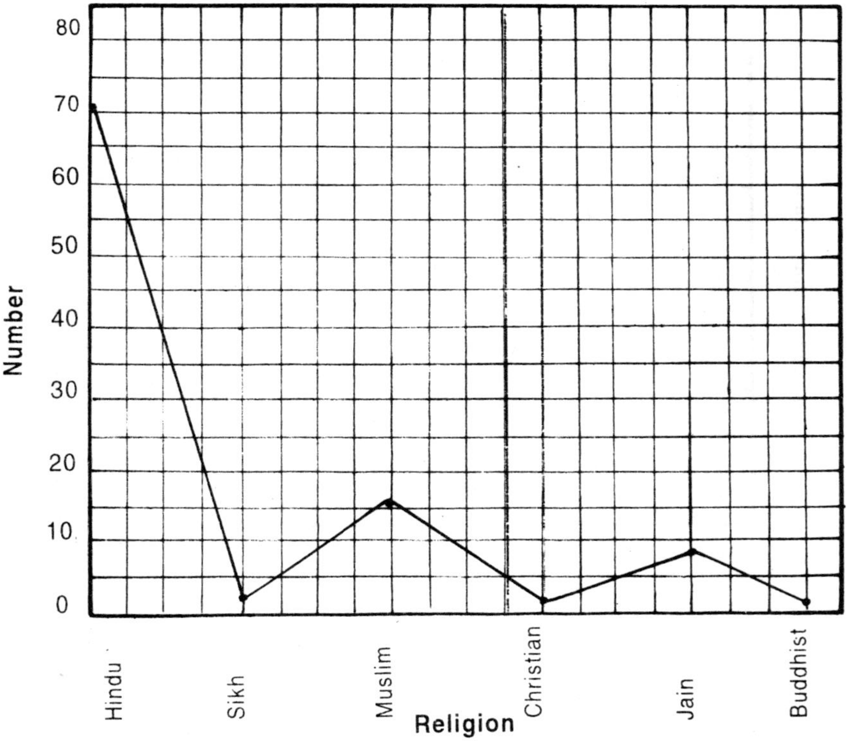

Diagram 3.1

Religion-wise Number of Shabana Azmi's One Hundred Surveyed Political Supporters in Delhi in July 1996.

Out of one hundred surveyed political supporters of Shabana Azmi in Delhi, seventy-one are Hindus, two are Muslims, fifteen are Sikhs, eight are Jains and two are Buddhists.

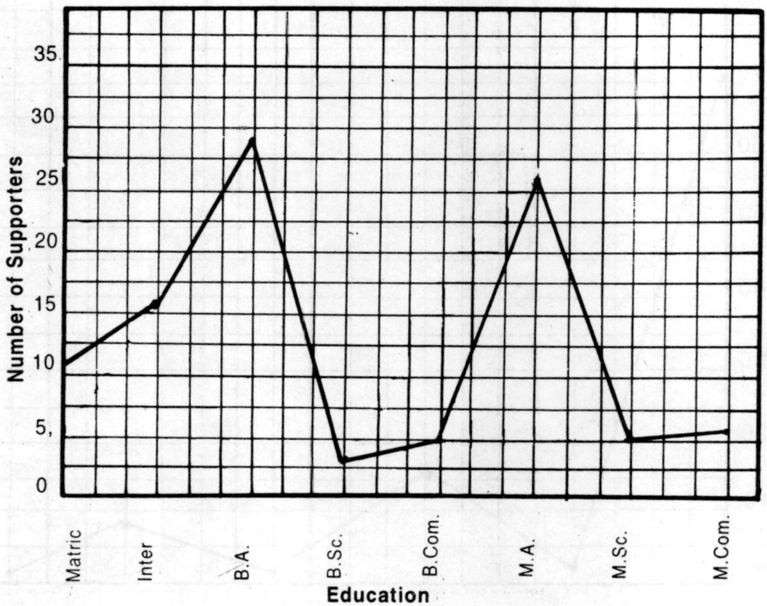

Diagram 3.2

Education-wise Number of Shabana Azmi's One Hundred Surveyed Political Supporters in Delhi in July 1996.

Out of one hundred surveyed political supporters of Shabana Azmi in Delhi, eleven supporters are only Matric passed, sixteen are Inter examination passed, twenty-eight are B.A., three are B.Sc., five are B.Com., twenty-six are M.A., five are M.Sc., and six are M.Com.

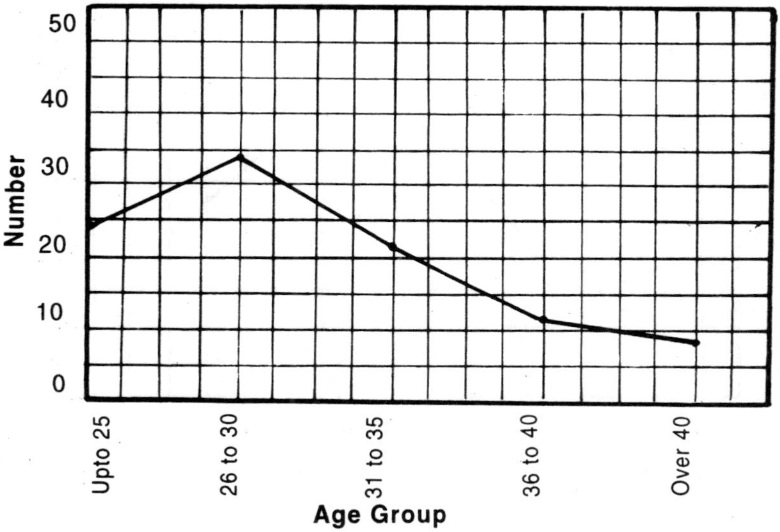

Diagram 3.3

Age Group-wise Number of Shabana Azmi's One Hundred Surveyed Political Supporters in Delhi in July 1996.

Out of one hundred surveyed political supporters of Shabana Azmi in Delhi, twenty-four are in upto 25 age-group, thirty-four are in 26 to 30 age-group, twenty-two are in 31 to 35 age-group, twelve in 36 to 40 age-group and eight in over 40 age-group.

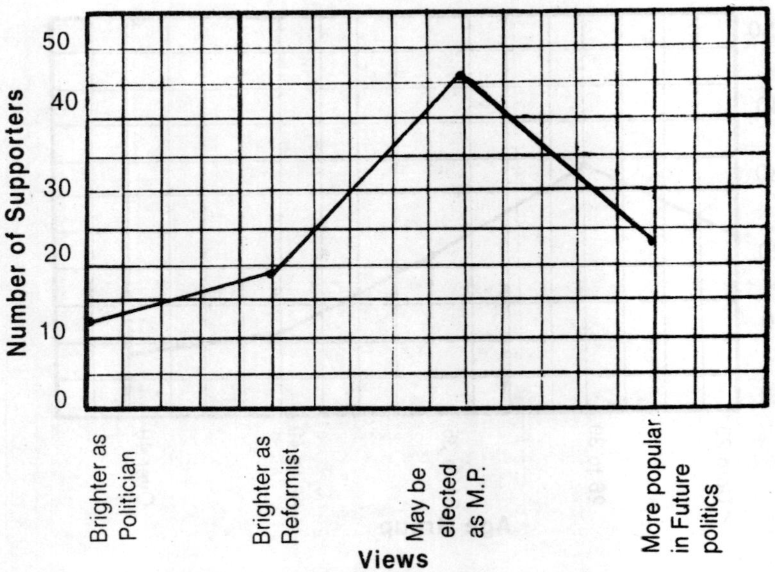

Diagram 3.4

Views-wise Number of Shabana Azmi's One Hundred Surveyed Political Supporters in Delhi in July 1996. (Views about her Political Future)

Out of one hundred surveyed political supporters of Shabana Azmi in Delhi, according to twelve persons, her political future is 'Brighter as a politician'; according to eighteen persons, her political future is 'brighter as a reformist'; according to forty-six persons, in future 'she may be elected as M.P.'; and according to twenty-four persons, she may be 'more popular in future politics'.

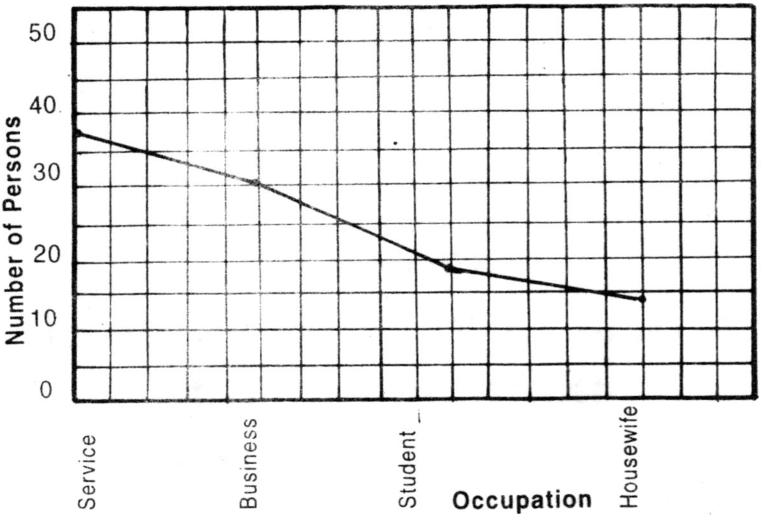

Diagram 3.5

Occupation-wise Number of Shabana Azmi's One Hundred Surveyed Political Supporters in Delhi in July 1996.

Out of one hundred surveyed political supporters of Shabana Azmi in Delhi, thirty-seven are in service, thirty are in business, nineteen are as students, and fourteen are as housewives.

Chapter 4

Surveyed Political Study of Raj Babbar : M.P.

(Rajya Sabha Member)

Raj Babbar has completed twenty years in films. It is not a short period in a man's life, and in the ephemeral life of an actor it is considered to be a long career span in which to ride the crest of success as Raj Babbar has done with seemingly effortless ease. From 'Dulha Bikta Hai' to 'Insaaf Ka Tarazu' through 'Bheegi Palken' and 'Aaj ki Awaj' and a host of other films Raj has come a long way, covering a formidable gamut of characters which few actors of his calibre have done during one and half decade long career in films. Today he is in the enviable position of stardom in which he is firmly ensconced. What galvanizes Raj's staying power which is so steadfast as to be indefatigable? What helps him survive unscathed in this dog-eat-dog world of films where the ascent of one actor takes the toll of two others?

Raj Babbar believes it is his sincerity which in the main has seen him through. "Sincerity, you know, always pays in the end. In the beginning you may feel that people are taking advantage of it. Because there is no dearth of people who take your sincerity to be your weakness. But in the end after having sown the seeds of your sincerity you begin to reap the harvest. Your alleged weakness turns out to be your asset. I do not know about the other fields of profession but in our professron, in films, in this industry of ours we have people who are basically emotional, who tend not to forget a favour shown, a good turn done. Gratitude has not yet lost its meaning. If one has done a good service to another the latter is too willing to reciprocate. It is true that here in this industry we get carried away by the warmth of emotions too soon and in consequence get easily hoodwinked by one or the other smart-alecks whose very presence in the film industry is a blot on its fair name. But by and large the people around here are nice and caring and not calculating and scheming as is generally believed by people outside it. So, what I mean to say is that sincerity always pays. I have not tried to deceive anyone, so no one has tried to deceive me. The problems arise when you try to be smarter than the others, when in your ignorance you take it for granted that the people you are dealing with are less intelligent than you. I have not tried to do so and therefore I am amply rewarded with their love and affection. You do a good turn to others and others will do a good turn to you. That is my motto in life. If I am where I am today it is only because of my sincere trust in people, of my acceptance of what they really worth. I always try to give in return what I have received from others. That is why, I believe, I have been accepted and loved for so long. What more could I have asked for? With all humility I would say that I have received from people more than I deserve perhaps", Raj Babbar says.

Career-wise Raj Babbar, who has worked in more than one hundred and thirty-five films so far and now has several films on hand, cannot be said to have reached the saturation point of his success. Raj Babbar says: "If by success one means the material success, then I have reached it a long time back, perhaps soon after my first hit film. But the creative success is a relative term. I have worked in a number of creatively fulfilling films have been acclaimed for any performances in them, but I cannot say that I have touched the creative success I aspire for. Creatively what I feel happy about is that I have not been made, as the film-makers are want to do, a stereotyped actor so that people cannot pinpoint the roles and say that Raj Babbar is good only in this kind of roles and not in that kind. If I have played the role of a seducer in Insaaf Ka Tarazu', I have also played the role of a crusader of a just cause in `Aaj Ki Awaj' and I have been accepted and acclaimed by the audience in both the films.

But have I worked in my last creatively successful film? This is a question no true artiste can give a right answer to. To me every new filnı of mine is an experiment in acting, a process of discovering the depth of man's emotions or in short, understanding the man himself. Human mind is a complex apparatus. So many things work in it simultaneously that one cannot ascribe one's motivation for what he has done at a given time. And what is acting after all? Is it not a job of peeling off the layers of the mind of a character an actor is given to portray? If an actor does not know, or even try to know, why a character does what he does, he will not be able to give a convincing portrayal of the character he is playing. So, to me, acting is the learning process of understanding the man. That is why I have accepted such divergent roles as a thief and a righteous man.

I have done my bit of running around the trees. But I do not say that henceforth I will stop doing so in films. For my survival in the industry I may have to do so. But given a chance I would rather go beyond doing what I have done on the screen so far. Given a chance I will portray on the screen various characters—one different from the other. And I am happy to say that I have been given such a chance. In my some films, I have played characters which are as different as a conventional hero from an anti-hero, a farmer from a rioter, to cite an example. In films like 'Kanwarlal', 'Andha Yudh', 'Tauheen', 'Waaris', 'Heensa' and to some extent in 'Aasmaan Se Ooncha', audiences have seen me not only in a different garb and get-up but altogether in a different light. I accepted these films because I wanted to grow as an actor and not to get bogged down doing the done thing over and over again."

If Raj Babbar is trying to comprehend the human mind through the characters, he has been given to portray on the screen, he is also on a different level trying to understand the society around him. But, he says, "I am not messiah for the society's ills. As a citizen of the country, I have the right to articulate my views and I just express them whenever I see that the government—the ultimate authority over the society—is not doing what it should do. As a responsible citizen, how can I afford to remain silent or prefer to be blind when the society reels under one problem or the other because of inactivity, or rather the incapability of the government? How can I not oppose the government's erring film policy and its refusal to understand the economics of filmmaking, and again when it exports us to make good films?"

Findings of the Survey Work

One hundred political supporters of Raj Babbar were surveyed in Delhi in January 1996. The main findings are as below:

1. Out of one hundred political supporters; twelve were educated upto Matric, fifteen were upto intermediate, eighteen were upto B.A., ten were upto B.Sc., eleven were upto B.Com, sixteen were upto

Table 4.1
Raj Babbar's Films, Leading Heroines and Directors upto present period

Sl. No.	*Year*	*Name of Film*	*Leading Heroine*	*Director*
1	2	3	4	5
1.	1980	Insaf Ka Taraju	Zeenat Aman	B.R. Chopra
2.	1980	Aap To Aese Na The	Ranjita	Ambarish Sangal
3.	1980	Najrana Pyar Ka	Sarika	S.M. Sagar
4.	1980	Saajan Mere Mein Saajan Ki	Kajal Kiran	Hiren Nag
5.	1980	Sau Din Sas Ke	Reena Roy	Vijay Sadana
6.	1981	Arman	Ranjita	Anand Sagar
7.	1981	Hum Paanch	Dipti Nawal	Bapu
8.	1981	Kalyug	Rekha	Shyam Benegal
9.	1981	Punam	Punam Dhillon	Harmesh Malhotra
10.	1981	Prem Geet	Anita Raj	Sudesh Issar
11.	1981	Raaj	Sulakshna Pandit	Harmesh Malhotra
12.	1981	Tajurba	Smita Patil	Nikhil Saini
13.	1981	Umrao Jaan	Rekha	Muzaffar Ali
14.	1981	Ye Rishta Na Toote	Bindiya Goswami	K. Vijayan
15.	1982	Aapas Ki Baat	Punam Dhillon	Ashok Ahuja
16.	1982	Bhigi Palaken	Smita Patil	Shishir Mishra
17.	1982	Daulat	Sarika	Mohan Shagal
18.	1982	Dulha Bikata Hai	Anita Raj	Anwar Pasha
19.	1982	Jivan Dhara	Rekha	T. Ramarao

(*Contd.*)

1	2	3	4	5
20.	1982	Laxmi	Reena Roy	B.S. Thapa
21.	1982	Nikah	Salma Aga	B.R. Chopra
22.	1983	Achchha-Bura	Anita Raj	Rishikesh Mukharji
23.	1983	Agar Tum Na Hote	Rekha	Lekh Tandon
24.	1983	Arpan	Parvin Bobby	J. Om Prakash
25.	1983	Kalka	Sarika	Loksen Lalwani
26.	1983	Mein Awara Hoon	Rati Agnihotri	Asim Samant
27.	1983	Majdoor	Rati Agnihotri	Ravi Chopra
28.	1983	Mehandi	Ranjita	Asit Sen
29.	1983	Naukar Biwi Ka	(Guest Heroine)	Raj Kumar Kohli
30.	1983	Panchavan Manjil	Zarina	Jagdish Sadana
31.	1983	Rishta Kagaj Ka	Rati Agnihotri	Ajay Goyal
32.	1984	Aaj Ki Awaj	Smita Patil	Ravi Chopra
33.	1984	Anand Aur Anand	Smita Patil	Dev Anand
34.	1984	Intaha	Reena Roy	Shibu Mitra
35.	1984	Jeene Nahin Doonga	Roshani	Raj Kumar Kohli
36.	1984	Kanoon Meri Mutthi Mein	Smita Patil/Ranjita	K. Prasad
37.	1984	Maati Mange Khoon	Rekha	Raj Khosla
38.	1984	Pet, Pyar Aur Pap	Smita Patil	Durai
39.	1984	Shapath	Smita Patil	Ravikant Nagaiach
40.	1985	Aetabar	Dimple Kapadia	Mukul Anand
41.	1985	Durga	Hema Malini	Shibu Mitra
42.	1985	Ek Chitthi Pyar Ki	Reena Roy	Vijay Sadana

(Contd.)

1	2	3	4	5
43.	1985	Hakiqat	Swpna	T. Ramarao
44.	1985	Hum Do Hamare Do	Smita Patil/Shoma Anand	B.R. Ishara
45.	1985	Jawab	Smita Patil	Ravi Tandon
46.	1985	Lava	Dimple Kapadia	Ravindra Pipat
47.	1985	Maha Shaktiman	Minakshi Sheshadri	V.S. Swami
48.	1985	Mera Ghar Mere Bachche	Smita Patil	Chander Bohra
49.	1985	Salma	Salma Aga	Ramanand Sagar
50.	1985	Ulta-Sidha	Rati Agnihotri	Subodh Mukherji
51.	1985	Yaar Kasam	Zeenat Aman	K. Prasad
52.	1986	Angare	Smita Patil	Rajesh Seth
53.	1986	Baat Ban Jaye	Zeenat Aman	Bharat Rangachari
54.	1986	Dahalij	Meenakshi Sheshadri	Ravi Chopra
55.	1986	Door Desh	Parvin Bobby	Bobby Ambarish Sangal
56.	1986	Jhuthi	Rekha	Rishikesh Mukherji
57.	1986	Kirayedar	Padmini Kolhapure	Basu Chaterji
58.	1986	Suhagan	Padmini Kolhapure	K. Raghavendra Rao
59.	1986	Tisara Kinara	Smita Patil	Krishna Kant
60.	1986	Triveni	Rati Agnihotri	Rajan Thakur
61.	1987	Aawaam	Punam Dhillon	B.R. Chopra
62.	1987	Insaniyat Ke Dushman	Anita Raj	Raj Kumar Kohli
63.	1987	Jan Hatheli Pe	(Guest Heroine)	R. Jhalani
64.	1987	Mukaddar Ka Faisala	Smita Patil	Ketan Mehta
65.	1987	Mirch-Masala	Smita Patil	Ketan Mehta

(Contd.)

1	2	3	4	5
66.	1987	Sansaar	Archana Joglekar	T. Ramarao
67.	1988	Hum Farishte Nahin	Punam Dhillon	Jatin Kumar
68.	1988	Kabja	Dimple Kapadia	Mahesh Bhatt
69.	1988	Vaaris	Smita Patil	Ravindra Pipat
70.	1988	Andha Yuddh	Pallavi Joshi	Dayal Nihalani
71.	1988	Aurat Teri Yahi Kahani	Minakshi Sheshadri	Mohan G. Prasad
72.	1988	Kanvar Lal	Sujata Mehta	S.S. Ravi Chandra
73.	1988	Mahavira	(Guest Heroine)	Naresh Sehgal
74.	1988	Mera Muqaddar	(Guest Heroine)	K. Pappu
75.	1988	Namumkin	Zeenat Aman	Rishikesh Mukherji
76.	1988	Rama-O- Rama	Kimi Katkar	Mirja Brothers
77.	1988	Sajish	Anita Raj	Raj Kumar Kohli
78.	1988	Vijay	(Guest Heroine)	Yash Chopra
79.	1988	Zakhmi Aurat	Dimple Kapadia	Avtar Bhogal
80.	1988	Hisab Khoon Ka	Punam Dhillon	Surendra Mohan
81.	1989	Hum Bhi Insan Hein	(Guest Heroine)	Mani Vannan
82.	1989	Mahadev	(Guest Heroine)	Raj Sippi
83.	1989	Mohabbat Ka Paigam	Meenakshi Sheshadri	Tammu
84.	1989	Paanch Fauladi	Salma Aga	Mohan Bhakhri
85.	1989	Surya	(Guest Heroine)	Ismail Shroff
86.	1990	Aaj	Anamika	Kuljeet Pal
87.	1990	Aaj Ke Shanshah	Kimi Katkar	Not Available
88.	1990	Agnikaal	Sonu Valiya	Abbas-Mastan

(Contd.)

1	2	3	4	5
89.	1990	Amiri-Garibi	Poonam Dhillon	Harmesh Malhotra
90.	1990	Shadyantra	Hema Malini	Rajan Johari
91.	1990	Shera-Shamshera	Farha	S.R. Pratap
92.	1990	Andher Gardi	Kimi Katkar	Ashok Tyagi
93.	1990	Ghayal	Mausmi Chaterji	Raj Kumar Santoshi
94.	1991	Gunahgaar Kaun	Sujata Mehta	Ashok Gayakvad
95.	1991	Kasam Kaali Ki	Anita Raj	Qamar Nakhi
96.	1991	Kanoon Ki Zanjir	Swpna	R.M. Raja
97.	1991	Swarg Jaisa Ghar	Anita Raj	Swaroop Kumar
98.	1992	Karmyoddha	Dimple Kapadia	Dayal Nihalani
99.	1992	Aaj Ka Gundaraj	(Guest Heroine)	Ravi Raja
100.	1992	Kal Ki Awaj	Neena Gupta	Ravi Chopra
101.	1992	Waqt Ka Badshah	(Guest Heroine)	Manmohan S. Kabir
102.	1992	Tauhin	Dimple Kapadia	Madan Joshi
103.	1993	Aankhe	(Guest Heroine)	David Dhawan
104.	1993	Aulad Ke Dushman	(Guest Heroine)	Raj Kumar Kohli
105.	1993	Badi Bahan	Meenakshi Sheshadri	Kalpataru
106.	1993	Dalaal	(Guest Heroine)	Partho Ghosh
107.	1993	Maya Memsab	Dipa Sahi	Ketan Mehta
108.	1993	Rudali	Dimple Kapadia	Kalpana Azmi
109.	1994	Janm Se Pahle	Farha	B.R. Ishara
110.	1994	Andaj	Farha	David Dhawan
111.	1994	Do Fantoosh	Farha	Sikander Bharti
112.	1994	Rakhvale	Farha	Sudershan Lal
113.	1995	Yaarana	Madhuri Dixit	David Dhawan
114.	1995	Barasaat	Madhuri Dixit	Raj Kumar Santoshi

Table 4.2

Detailed Study of Raj Babbar's One Hundred Political Supporters in Delhi in January 1996

S. No.	Name of the Person	Sex	Age (in years)	Urban/ Rural	Religion	Whether SC/ST	Family's income P.M. (in Rs.)	Education	Occupation	No. of His watched Political Films	View about His Political Future
1	2	3	4	5	6	7	8	9	10	11	12
1.	Ummed Singh	Male	31	Rural	Hindu	Nil	3100.00	B.A.	Business	11	May be elected to Lok Sabha
2.	Janaki Devi	Female	27	Urban	Hindu	SC	2400.00	Matric	Housewife	08	More popular in future politics
3.	S.K. Tripathi	Male	29	Urban	Hindu	Nil	3200.00	M.A.	Service	12	Very Good
4.	Himmat Singh	Male	26	Rural	Sikh	Nil	4000.00	M.Com.	Business	15	Brighter as a politician
5.	Irfan Ali	Male	34	Urban	Muslim	Nil	3800.00	B.Sc.	Service	13	Good
6.	M. William	Male	27	Rural	Christian	Nil	3300.00	B.Com.	Student	15	More popular in future politics
7.	Usha Verma	Female	24	Rural	Hindu	Nil	3000.00	B.Sc.	Student	08	Good
8.	Nafees Ahmad	Male	23	Rural	Muslim	Nil	2500.00	B.A.	Student	11	Brighter as a politician
9.	Ram Prasad	Male	42	Urban	Hindu	SC	1800.00	Inter	Service	18	Very Good
10.	Vinay Sharma	Male	40	Rural	Hindu	Nil	3400.00	M.Com.	Service	13	May be elected to Lok Sabha
11.	Rosy Jacob	Female	37	Urban	Christian	Nil	4500.00	M.Sc.	Service	12	Good
12.	R.C. Jain	Male	29	Urban	Jain	Nil	3900.00	M.Com.	Business	16	More popular in future politics
13.	Vinod Ahuja	Male	24	Rural	Hindu	Nil	4400.00	B.Com.	Student	13	Very Good
14.	Jagat Narain	Male	33	Urban	Hindu	SC	3900.00	B.A.	Business	11	Brighter as a politician
15.	Banwari Lal	Male	30	Urban	Hindu	SC	3400.00	Inter	Service	08	May be elected to Lok Sabha

(Contd.)

1	2	3	4	5	6	7	8	9	10	11	12
16.	B.R. Yadav	Male	28	Rural	Hindu	Nil	2700.00	M.A.	Business	07	May be elected to Lok Sabha
17.	Kamlesh Kumari	Female	23	Urban	Buddhist	SC	1800.00	Inter	Housewife	09	Very Good
18.	Makhan Lal	Male	27	Rural	Buddhist	SC	1500.00	Matric	Service	10	May be elected to Lok Sabha
19.	Hem Chand	Male	28	Urban	Hindu	Nil	2400.00	B.Com.	Business	13	More popular in future politics
20.	Balban Singh	Male	29	Urban	Sikh	Nil	2700.00	Inter	Service	11	Brighter as a politician
21.	Hans Raj	Male	36	Rural	Hindu	SC	1900.00	Matric	Service	06	Good
22.	Mamta Devi	Female	33	Rural	Hindu	SC	1800.00	Inter	Housewife	09	Very Good
23.	Nirmal Kaur	Female	31	Rural	Sikh	SC	2200.00	Matric	Service	11	More popular in future politics
24.	Raunak Singh	Male	27	Urban	Sikh	Nil	4400.00	B.A.	Business	17	More popular in future politics
25.	Baldev Prasad	Male	39	Rural	Hindu	SC	3900.00	Inter	Service	12	Good
26.	Hukam Narain	Female	23	Rural	Hindu	SC	2700.00	B.Sc.	Student	13	May be elected to Lok Sabha
27.	Venna Singh	Female	26	Urban	Hindu	Nil	3400.00	B.Com.	Housewife	16	Very Good
28.	Lavinder Singh	Male	24	Urban	Sikh	Nil	4300.00	M.A.	Student	09	Brighter as a politician
29.	Saroj Kumari	Female	27	Rural	Hindu	SC	4000.00	M.A.	Service	11	May be elected to Lok Sabha
30.	Urmila Devi	Female	34	Urban	Hindu	Nil	3400.00	M.Sc.	Housewife	07	More popular in future politics
31.	Kamlesh Jain	Female	31	Urban	Jain	Nil	4500.00	M.A.	Service	09	Brighter as a politician
32.	Bharati Sharma	Female	23	Urban	Hindu	Nil	3700.00	B.Com.	Student	12	May be elected to Lok Sabha
33.	Kalka Prasad	Male	25	Rural	Buddhist	SC	2400.00	B.A.	Student	08	Very Good
34.	Akshay Jain	Male	36	Urban	Jain	Nil	4600.00	M.Com.	Business	13	May be elected to Lok Sabha
35.	Akash Jain	Male	22	Urban	Jain	Nil	3900.00	M.Com.	Business	06	Good
36.	Anupam Taneja	Male	36	Rural	Hindu	Nil	4100.00	B.A.	Service	07	Brighter as a politician

(Contd.)

1	2	3	4	5	6	7	8	9	10	11	12
37.	Ved Prakash	Male	39	Rural	Hindu	SC	3100.00	Inter	Service	09	More popular in future politics
38.	Tariq Khan	Male	27	Urban	Muslim	Nil	2600.00	Matric	Business	05	Brighter as a politician
39.	Bahadur Singh	Male	28	Rural	Hindu	SC	1800.00	Matric	Service	07	Very Good
40.	M. Jacob	Male	26	Urban	Christian	Nil	3500.00	M.A.	Service	14	More popular in future politics
41.	Om Prakash	Male	29	Urban	Hindu	Nil	2800.00	B.Com.	Business	12	Very Good
42.	Hema Vats	Female	24	Rural	Hindu	Nil	2900.00	B.Sc.	Student	08	May be elected to Lok Sabha
43.	Waheeda Khan	Female	27	Urban	Muslim	Nil	3300.00	Inter	Housewife	05	Good
44.	Arun Kumar Jain	Male	45	Urban	Jain	Nil	3700.00	M.Com.	Business	08	Brighter as a politician
45.	Madhu Jacob	Female	33	Urban	Christian	ST	3400.00	M.Sc.	Service	09	Very Good
46.	Sunita Kumari	Female	31	Rural	Hindu	SC	3600.00	B.A.	Housewife	12	May be elected to Lok Sabha
47.	Mahendra Singh	Male	26	Rural	Hindu	Nil	3400.00	M.Com.	Service	11	Very Good
48.	Vinod Kumar	Male	27	Urban	Hindu	SC	2400.00	Matric	Service	05	Very Good
49.	Bhagwan Das	Male	23	Rural	Buddhist	SC	1900.00	B.A.	Student	16	May be elected to Lok Sabha
50.	Angoori Devi	Female	34	Rural	Hindu	SC	1400.00	Matric	Housewife	05	Good
51.	Asha Rani Jain	Female	33	Urban	Jain	Nil	3700.00	B.A.	Service	11	More popular in future politics
52.	Gurdayal Singh	Male	37	Urban	Sikh	Nil	4000.00	Inter	Business	15	Brighter as a politician
53.	H.N. Singh	Male	35	Rural	Hindu	Nil	4500.00	M.Com.	Business	10	Very Good
54.	Mangal Singh	Male	27	Rural	Hindu	Nil	3700.00	B.Com.	Service	07	Brighter as a politician
55.	Mujaffar Hussain	Male	45	Urban	Muslim	Nil	4500.00	Matric	Service	13	May be elected to Lok Sabha
56.	Bhaskar Tripathi	Male	24	Urban	Hindu	Nil	4600.00	B.Com.	Student	14	Brighter as a politician
57.	Harful Singh	Male	23	Rural	Sikh	SC	2700.00	Inter	Service	08	Very Good

(Contd.)

1	2	3	4	5	6	7	8	9	10	11	12
58.	Man Prakash	Male	21	Rural	Buddhist	SC	2400.00	B.Sc.	Student	12	May be elected to Lok Sabha
59.	Prem Chand	Male	23	Urban	Hindu	Nil	1800.00	B.A.	Student	11	Good
60.	O.P. Haksar	Male	49	Urban	Hindu	Nil	4700.00	M.A.	Business	05	Brighter as a politician
61.	Mamta Kukreja	Female	23	Rural	Hindu	Nil	3400.00	M.Com.	Service	08	More popular in future politics
62.	Raj Narain Singh	Male	26	Rural	Hindu	Nil	2900.00	Matric	Business	06	Very Good
63.	Omvati	Female	29	Rural	Hindu	SC	1400.00	Matric	Housewife	09	May be elected to Lok Sabha
64.	Christy Wilson	Female	29	Urban	Christian	Nil	2900.00	M.Sc.	Service	09	Brighter as a politician
65.	Krishna Sharma	Female	24	Rural	Hindu	Nil	2700.00	B.Sc.	Student	07	Very Good
66.	Sanjay Tandon	Male	25	Urban	Hindu	Nil	2600.00	B.Com.	Student	09	May be elected to Lok Sabha
67.	Madhu Sexena	Female	27	Urban	Hindu	Nil	3400.00	M.A.	Housewife	11	Very Good
68.	Amla Basu	Female	29	Urban	Hindu	Nil	4500.00	M.Sc.	Housewife	14	More popular in future politics
69.	Aruna Jain	Female	34	Rural	Jain	Nil	4400.00	B.Sc.	Housewife	07	Brighter as a politician
70.	Oscar Jacob	Male	39	Urban	Christian	Nil	4200.00	B.A.	Service	09	May be elected to Lok Sabha
71.	Bhagwan Singh	Male	36	Rural	Hindu	SC	1600.00	Inter	Business	12	Very Good
72.	Hema Singh	Female	31	Urban	Hindu	Nil	4500.00	B.Com.	Service	09	May be elected to Lok Sabha
73.	Sohan Lal	Male	29	Rural	Buddhist	SC	4100.00	M.A.	Business	13	Good
74.	Sunder Kaur	Female	33	Rural	Sikh	Nil	2400.00	M.A.	Housewife	09	More popular in future politics
75.	Gulam Mohammed	Female	46	Urban	Muslim	Nil	1800.00	Matric	Service	05	Brighter as a politician
76.	Shailendra Singh	Male	24	Urban	Hindu	Nil	2200.00	B.Sc.	Student	08	May be elected to Lok Sabha
77.	Upendra Singh	Male	25	Urban	Hindu	SC	2400.00	B.A.	Student	06	More popular in future politics
78.	Sharda Tripathi	Female	26	Urban	Hindu	Nil	3700.00	M.A.	Housewife	13	May be elected to Lok Sabha

(Contd.)

1	2	3	4	5	6	7	8	9	10	11	12
79.	Shridhar Verma	Male	49	Rural	Hindu	Nil	3400.00	B.A.	Business	16	More popular in future politics
80.	Manisha Verma	Female	33	Urban	Hindu	Nil	4800.00	M.A.	Housewife	08	May be elected to Lok Sabha
81.	Virendra Singh	Male	24	Urban	Hindu	SC	2200.00	B.A.	Business	07	Very Good
82.	Arti Taneja	Female	27	Rural	Hindu	Nil	2300.00	M.A.	Housewife	13	More popular in future politics
83.	Mary Wilson	Female	26	Urban	Christian	ST	2100.00	M.Sc.	Student	16	Brighter as a politician
84.	Sunder K. Taneja	Male	36	Urban	Hindu	SC	4100.00	M.A.	Business	18	Good
85.	M. Ga[illegible]sh	Male	24	Urban	Hindu	Nil	4600.00	M.Com.	Service	12	May be elected to Lok Sabha
86.	Chitra Mudgal	Female	27	Rural	Hindu	Nil	2500.00	B.Sc.	Housewife	07	Brighter as a politician
87.	Sushma Chopra	Female	26	Urban	Hindu	Nil	3200.00	B.Com.	Student	11	May be elected to Lok Sabha
88.	Harbans Kaur	Female	25	Urban	Sikh	Nil	2700.00	B.A.	Housewife	05	May be elected to Lok Sabha
89.	Kishan Chand	Male	23	Rural	Hindu	SC	2400.00	Inter	Student	07	Very Good
90.	Rosy John	Female	25	Urban	Christian	ST	3300.00	B.Sc.	Student	16	May be elected to Lok Sabha
91.	Sonia Sethi	Female	29	Urban	Hindu	Nil	4100.00	M.A.	Housewife	13	More popular in future politics
92.	Satish Chand	Male	33	Rural	Hindu	Nil	3100.00	B.A.	Business	10	Brighter as a politician
93.	Harbans Singh	Male	45	Urban	Sikh	Nil	2700.00	Inter	Business	13	May be elected to Lok Sabha
94.	Lavleen Shukla	Female	31	Urban	Hindu	Nil	3400.00	B.A.	Housewife	06	Good
95.	Zile Singh	Male	29	Rural	Hindu	Nil	1900.00	Inter	Service	08	May be elected to Lok Sabha
96.	Laxman Sinha	Male	29	Urban	Hindu	Nil	4600.00	M.Sc.	Service	09	Very Good
97.	Ram Murti	Male	33	Urban	Hindu	Nil	4300.00	M.Com.	Business	16	May be elected to Lok Sabha
98.	Trilok Singh	Male	49	Rural	Sikh	SC	2400.00	Inter	Business	06	Brighter as a politician
99.	Vivek Shukla	Male	35	Urban	Hindu	Nil	2700.00	B.A.	Service	09	May be elected to Lok Sabha
100.	B.P. Tewari	Male	27	Urban	Hindu	Nil	3600.00	M.A.	Service	11	More popular in future politics

M.A., seven were upto M.Sc and eleven were upto M.Com.

2. Out of these one hundred persons; fifty seven persons were urban and forty three were rural.
3. Out of one hundred political supporters; sixty two political supporters were Hindus, six were Muslims, eleven were Sikhs, eight were Christians, seven were Jains and six were Buddhists.
4. Out of these one hundred persons; thirty two were SC/ST and sixty eight were non -SC/ST.
5. Out of one hundred political supporters; sixty four were males and thirty six were females.
6. Out of these one hundred persons; thirty four belonged to service, twenty four belonged to business, twenty two were students and twenty were housewives.
7. Out of one hundred political supporters, thirteen supporters belonged to monthly family's income group upto Rs. 2000.00, thirty one belonged to Rs. 2001.00 to Rs 3000.00, thirty four belonged to Rs. 3001.00 to 4000.00 and twenty two belonged to over Rs. 4000.00.
8. Out of these one hundred persons; seven persons watched Raj Babbar's films upto five, forty four persons watched his films upto six to ten, thirty nine persons watched his films upto eleven to fifteen and ten persons watched his films upto sixteen to twenty.
9. Out of one hundred political supporters; twenty five supporters were of age-group upto twenty five years, thirty six were upto twenty six to thirty years, twenty were upto thirty one to thirty five years, eleven were upto thirty six to forty years age group and eight were over forty years age.

10. Out of these one hundred persons; twenty nine persons said that as their views he may be elected to Lok Sabha, twenty one persons said that his political futu.e is very good, twelve persons viewed his good political future, twenty expressed about his brighter political future as a politician and eighteen persons viewed more popular in future politics.

It is found that all surveyed persons were serious about his political activities. It is also showed that Raj Babbar was popular in every section of Delhi's population.

Chapter 5

Surveyed Political Study of Rajesh Khanna

The key contestants for this prize seat were Congress' Rajesh Khanna, BJP nominee Shatrughan Sinha and Janata Dal sponsored Jai Bhagwan Jatav. Two were top matinee idols and one hailed from the humble origin of a weaver and a shoemaker family. On the eve of launching their poll campaign, the three opposing contestants talked about political issues, their respective parties, the people and themselves.

Rajesh Khanna said, "I shall begin my campaign from the Lord Jagannath temple in Hauj Khas and people around."

Contested the election from here virtually for the third time, the cinestar who had been living in Delhi mostly since the May polls last year (1991) appeared more of a politician than a glamorous filmstar. Dressed in a saffron lungi and white chicken kurta sitting in his DDA apartment in Vasant Kunj, New Delhi, Mr. Khanna said he was confident that the local party bosses were supporting him. In an oblique reference to the controversy of his candidature for the by-election earlier, he said, "Yes, it's been like a test by fire everytime. But then coming through successfully has made me feel stronger. The Congress is one family and as in any family squabbles here too can take place. But, then everything becomes all right and the family members are more closely knit than before. I have great regard for Bhagatji (the Delhi Pradesh Congress Committee President). He is my senior and I trust he will always lead the way for the success of the party which will also be my success."

"As in the previous election time apart from national issues I feel it is every member's responsibility to improve the conditions of the people nearer home. There is also the question of high prices and law and order. I shall talk to the people at length about them", he said. "I strongly believe that the income-tax limit should be raised to Rs. 50,000. The salaried and the middle income groups have to bear the brunt of high prices and rising cost of living; surely, they should be given this consideration. I had advocated this in my election campaign earlier and shall do so even now", said the bespectacled star-turned-politician. Asked what he felt about groupism in the local party unit, he said, "I think of it as a cohesive unit. I have no group and no lobby. The congress party is my group and Mr. Narsimha Rao the leader. I look on this election as a fight not between two stars of the film world, but one between the Congress and its policies and the BJP with its beliefs. I am confident that I shall win. Not because the filmstar Rajesh Khanna. I am confident because my party, the congress, has unmatched credibility and with the political stability it provides come the attendant benefits of progress and development." Talking about his electioneering experience, he said, "Earlier, I was new to it all. The problems of the people came to me through various channels. Often in a coloured and filtered manner. Now, it is different. I have been here, among the people and know their problems and troubles. For me, the campaign is an extension of my close acquaintance with the people. Slogans and speeches no longer have relevance. What matters is the people and what best can be done for them. They are my people. I belong to them."

With bouncy enthusiasm and self-confidence declared the BJP nominee Shatrughan Sinha: "Our victory is certain. The infighting in the congress party, the mud-slinging in public and the last minute announcement of the congress candidate have been an added gain for the BJP. It is the congress which has made me a heavy weight in the by-election today. To borrow Mr. Narasimha Rao's expression, we should be grateful to our invisible friends." Informally, attired in a blue shirt and pyjamas lounging in his sitting room with his wife, Mr. Sinha said the New Delhi Constituency was familiar terrain now. "I know party workers, the people and the area well." There were several issues, national and local which were significant. "The highest degree of corruption which is continuing unchecked and abetted in the highest quarters like the Bofors cover-up attempt or the share brokers scandal, to name a few. The fact is that suffering of the common people and salaried groups in terms of economy has reached a peak. These are issues which everyone understands and which will make them realise that the congress has never delivered the goods as promised", he said.

Referring to the congress leaders, he said: " the hypocracy among them is astonishing. The top leaders talk for economy drives and cut in expenditure but I ask them what about their own expenses. The number of foreign jaunts the ministers have and the number of staff and perks like cars and others is anyone's guess. The high sounding intentions and preaching is meant for others and confined to words. In practice, it is otherwise." Mr. Sinha said he did not meet former Prime Minister and Samajwadi Janata Party leader. "I do not even need his blessings. I have the blessings of BJP leaders like Mr. Atal Behari Vajpayee, Dr. Murli Manohar Joshi, Mr. L.K.

Advani and Mrs. Vijayraje Scindia. This is enough. I had been invited to meet Mr. Chandra Shekhar but I feel somebody just planned it with some other motive. My wife and I did noı meet him." Mr. Sinha also accused the congress of not giving Delhi statehood. "Even the proposed legislative may not ultimately come through. When BJP wins the New Delhi seat and is ready to gain control here, the Congress may well dilly-dally about the legislative assembly. They would not want that Delhi be the fifth BJP ruled state in the country. But with the committed voters, we have and the misperformance of the Congress party coupled with the BJP track record our success is certain", he said confidently.

The 43-year-old businessman Jai Bhagwan Jatav who contested election for the first time said it was the time the people of the constituency voted for a worker rather than a leader. "Invariably in the past those that have contested elections from here have been top leaders of political parties. They get elected and busy with national matters. But a worker in Parliament could voice the problems of the common people and make their grievances felt." Mr. Jai Bhagwan felt that both the BJP and Congress had let down the people. "The congress promise of containing the price-line and corruption. The BJP won the last election on the plank of building the temple in Ayodhya. But, in effect, not of the two parties have done what they said. The people are not so naive as not to realise this nor so gullible as to believe them. The constituency comprises large numbers of backward communities and government employees. It is their support that we will assuredly get."

The Janata Dal catch slogans were, "Bhajpa Congress dono yaar, desh bechne ko tayar." (Both Congress and BJP are ready to sell the country) and "Faisla aap karye, abhineta ya janneta" (decide between an actor and a public leader). Economic policies of the government, corruption, doubling of DTC fares, recession, lack of adequate developmental work and poor public distribution system were some of the issues of his election plank. Mr. Jai Bhagwan said w. ile he was addressing meetings and visiting areas he will formally launch his election campaign from Bhogal on May 19, 1992. The main meetings were addressed by Janata Dal leaders including former Prime Minister V.P. Singh, party president S.R. Bommai, Mr. Ram Vilas Paswan, Mr. Sharad Yadav and Mufti Mohammad Sayed, among others.

Rajesh Khanna as Congress (I) Candidate

An hour before Rajesh Khanna's name was formally announced by the party high command on May 13, 1992; the warring congress factions in Delhi finally decided to leave it to the party high command to decide the candidate for the New Delhi parliamentary seat after two different meetings of faction leaders appealed to the Prime Minister to take a final decision in the matter. An evening meeting chaired by the president of the Delhi Pradesh Congress Committee, Mr. H.K.L. Bhagat, unanimously decided to request the Congress president Mr. P.V. Narasimha Rao, to select the nominee for the New Delhi constituency and vowed that the "DPCC will fully and with dedication support any candidate chosen by the Congress president." The meeting came as a dampner after two days of hectic political activity when supporters of Mr. Bhagat presented memoranda to the Prime Minister urging him to reconsider the candidature of cinestar, Rajesh Khanna, and instead nominate a local heavyweight like Mr. Bhagat to take on the Bhartiya Janata Party. The meeting was attended by the former chief metropolitan councillor, Mr. J.P. Goel and other leaders of the pradesh election committee who owe their allegiance to Mr. Bhagat. The brief meeting left it to the party high command to decide on who shall contest the elections.

At another meeting held earlier in the same day, leaders belonging to the Jagdish Tytler faction of the party met the Prime Minister and appealed to him that the candidate selected by him would have the backing of all the Congress workers. The meeting which was attended by Mr. Kishan Swarup, Mr. K.S. Gujral, Mr. Jagdish Anand, Mr. Jayaprakash Agrawal, Mr. Harcharan Singh Josh, Mr. Inder Singh Solanki and Mr. Jagdish Tokas called for a broad-based campaign committee and expressed concern at the 'working of some leading Congress leaders to damage the chances of the Congress candidate in the ensuing bye election'. The leaders also urged Mr. Rao to address a meeting of party workers in Delhi.

According to one party leader, the fact that Mr. Rao gave an audience to the Tytler group to air their point of view made it clear that Mr. Bhagat's attempt to outmanouevre Mr. Rajesh Khanna had failed. Mr. Khanna had already filed his nomination during the 1991 parliamentary bye-elections which was postponed after the death of an independent candidate. His main rival in this round of election was BJP's Shatrughan Sinha.

By-Election's Manifesto

The All India Congress Committee supported the Congress nominee for the New Delhi Parliamentary constituency byelection Rajesh Khanna's stand that efforts will be made to raise the income tax exemption limit to Rs. 60,000 on June 6, 1992. This was announced by minister, water resources V.C. Shukla who was also the AICC observer for this byelection at a well-attended press meet in New Delhi on June 6, 1992. He said the Congress was committed to provide maximum relief to the people but the entire thing would have to be thought of in a balanced and responsible manner. The Bharatiya Janata Party leaders stating that they would withdraw their candidate Shatrughan Sinha from the electoral fray if the government announce that the income-tax limit would be raised to Rs. 60,000, he said shows that the BJP was only contesting the polls for income-tax payers. The major portion of the New Delhi Lok Sabha constituency comprises non-tax payers as they belonged to the least affluent lot. Obviously, the BJP was not concerned about this economically weaker sections for they were willing to opt out of the fray if the measures were announced for the income-tax payees, he added.

Talking about the BJP rules states, Mr. Shukla said the BJP had gained power in Rajasthan, Himachal Pradesh, Madhya Pradesh and Uttar Pradesh. After sometime of their rule when elections were held in Madhya Pradesh they got only 12 of the 40 seats in the elections, in Rajasthan the majority of the seats were won by the Congress and in Himachal Pradesh the BJP did not get a single seat in the municipal elections. Even in the cantonement board elections in various parts Mr. Shukla said the BJP got a drubbling from the congress. There was not even one exception where the BJP got a majority, he added. The BJP member parliaments, member legislative assemblies and others had also themselves criticised the BJP leadership on different occasions, Mr. Shukla said. The party, he said, was confident that Mr. Khanna would win and that too with considerable margin. The cinestar turned politician had topped in whatever field he worked and would do well in the party as well, he added.

Earlier, in the day (June 6, 1992) Rajesh Khanna accompanied by his actress wife Dimple Kapadia led a rally from Rajghat covering the entire New Delhi constituency.

Rajesh Khanna Disappointed

Rajesh Khanna, Congress MP from the New Delhi constituency, said on February 28, 1993, he was disappointed that Finance Minister Manmohan Singh ignored Government employees by not increasing the income tax exemption limit to Rs. 60,000. Mr. Khanna assured Government servants that he would continue his fight for increasing the income-tax exemption limit. Delhi BJP vice-president Charti Lal Goel demanded that Rajesh Khanna, Congress MP from New Delhi, quit for failing to keep his electoral promise of getting the income-tax exemption limit raised to Rs. 60,000. Mr. Goel pointed out that this had been made an election issue by Khanna and the Congress in the New Delhi by-elections.

Sikh Bodies Supported Rajesh Khanna

In the New Delhi Lok Sabha by elections 1992, some Sikh organisations expressed solidarity with the Congress candidate Mr. Rajesh Khanna at a meeting in New Delhi on May 28, 1992 evening. In this meet, hosted by the party's election agent, Mr. R.K. Dhawan was held in the lawns of his government bungalow in Lodi Estate, New Delhi. The Sikhs called for support to Mr. Khanna in the name of stability and "a befitting reply to the fundamental, communal and casteist forces threatening the unity and integrity of the country." Among those present were Mr. Balwant Singh, member, Delhi Sikh Gurdwara Committee, Mr. Harcharan Singh, president, Indian National Sikh Manch, Mr. H.S. Kohli, president, National Sikh Organisation, and Mr. Joginder Pal Singh, president, Guru Nanak Singh Mission, Mr. Rajender Singh president, All India Punjabi Editors' Conference, also expressed solidarity with Mr. Rajesh Khanna.

Later, Mr. Dhawan told journalists a few Sikh leaders here and there had got together at the BJP meet. Mr. Harcharan Singh Josh, senior Congress politician, said several leading Sikh religious and cultural organisations had joined hands with them. Mr. Dhawan reiterated how important stability was, as no

Table 5.1
Rajesh Khanna's Films, Leading Heroines and Directors upto present period

Sl. No.	*Year*	*Name of Film*	*Leading Heroine*	*Director*
1	2	3	4	5
1.	1966	Aakhiri Khat	Anupama	Chetan Anand
2.	1967	Raaj	Babita	Ravindra Dave
3.	1967	Baharon Ke Sapne	Asha Parekh	Nasir Husain
4.	1969	Bandhan	Mumtaz	Narendra Bedi
5.	1969	Do Raste	Mumtaz	Raj Khosla
6.	1969	Doli	Babita	A. Subbarao
7.	1969	Ittafak	Nanda	Yash Chopra
8.	1969	Khamoshi	Wahida Rehman	Asit Sen
9.	1970	Anand	Wahida Rehman	Rishikesh Mukherji
10.	1970	Sachcha Jhutha	Mumtaz	Manmohan Desai
11.	1970	Kati Patang	Asha Parekh	Shakti Samant
12.	1970	Safar	Sharmila Tagore	Asit Sen
13.	1970	The Train	Nanda	Ravi Nagaiach
14.	1971	Amar Prem	Sharmila Tagore	Shakti Sippi
15.	1971	Andaj	Hema Malini	Ramesh Sippi
16.	1971	Badnam Farishte	Sharmila Tagore	Kamar Narwi
17.	1971	Chhoti Bahu	Sharmila Tagore	K.B. Tilak
18.	1971	Dushman	Mumtaz	Dulal Guha

(Contd.)

1	2	3	4	5
19.	1971	Haathi Mere Saathi	Tanuja	C. Devar
20.	1971	Maryada	Mala Sinha	Arvind Sen
21.	1972	Anurag	Mausmi Chaterji	Shakti Samant
22.	1972	Apna Desh	Mumtaz	Jambo
23.	1972	Bavarchi	Jaya Bhaduri	Rishikesh Mukherji
24.	1972	Dil Daulat Aur Duniya	Sadhana	P.N. Arora
25.	1972	Joru Ka Gulam	Nanda	A. Bhim Singh
26.	1972	Maalik	Sharmila Tagore	A. Bhim Singh
27.	1972	Mere Jivan Saathi	Tanuja	Ravi Nagaiach
28.	1973	Shahajada	Rakhi	K. Shankar
29.	1973	Aavishkar	Sharmila Tagore	Basu Battacharya
30.	1973	Daag	Sharmila Tagore / Raakhi	Yash Chopra
31.	1973	Namak Haram	Rekha	Rishikesh Mukherji
32.	1973	Raja Rani	Sharmila Tagore	Sachin Bhaumik
33.	1974	Aaiana	Mumtaz	K. Balachandar
34.	1974	Aapki Kasam	Mumtaz	J. Om Prakash
35.	1974	Ajnabi	Zeenat Aman	Shakti Samant
36.	1974	Five Rifles	(Guest Heroine)	I.S. Johar
37.	1974	Humshakal	Tanuja / Mausmi Chaterji	Jambo
38.	1974	Prem Nagar	Hema Malini	K.S. Prakashrao
39.	1974	Roti	Mumtaz	Manmohan Desai

(Contd.)

1	2	3	4	5
40.	1975	Prem Kahani	Mumtaz	Raj Khosla
41.	1976	Bandalbaj	Sulakshna Pandit	Shammi Kapoor
42.	1976	Mahachor	Nitu Singh	Narendra Bedi
43.	1976	Mahbooba	Hema Malini	Shakti Samant
44.	1976	Tyag	Sharmila Tagore	Dindayal Sharma
45.	1977	Aashiq Hoon Baharon Ka	Zeenat Aman	J. Om Prakash
46.	1977	Anurodh	Dimple Kapadia	Shakti Samant
47.	1977	Chalta Purja	Parvin Bobby	Bhappi Soni
48.	1977	Chhaila Babu	Zeenat Aman	Joy Mukherji
49.	1977	Karm	Vidhya Sinha/Shabana Azmi	B.R. Chopra
50.	1977	Palakon Ki Chhanv Mein	Hema Malini	Meraj
51.	1978	Bhola Bhala	Rekha/Mausmi Chaterji	Satpal
52.	1978	Prem Bandhan	Rekha	Ramanand Sagar
53.	1978	Amardeep	Shabana Azmi	K. Vijayan
54.	1978	Chakravyuh	Nitu Singh	Basu Chaterji
55.	1979	Janta Havaldar	Hema Malini	Mehmood
56.	1980	Aanchal	Raakhi/Rekha	Anil Ganguli
57.	1980	Bandish	Hema Malini	K. Bapaya
58.	1980	Phir Vahi Raat	Kim	Dainy
59.	1980	Red Rose	Poonam Dhillon	Bharati Raja
60.	1980	Shaitan Mujrim	Jyoti	Najar Khan

(Contd.)

1	2	3	4	5
61.	1980	Thodi Si Bevfai	Shabana Azmi	Ismail Shroff
62.	1981	Dard	Hema Malini	Ambarish Sangal
63.	1981	Dhanwan	Reena Roy	Surendra Mohan
64.	1981	Fifti-Fifti	Tina Munim	Shomu Mukherji
65.	1981	Kudarat	Hema Malini	Chetan Anand
66.	1982	Ashanti	Zeenat Aman	Umesh Mehra
67.	1982	Dil-E-Nadan	Smita Patil/Jaya Prada	Shridhar
68.	1982	Disco-Dancer	(Guest Heroine)	B. Subhash
69.	1982	Rajput	Hema Malini	Vijay Anand
70.	1983	Agar Tum Na Hote	Rekha	Lekh Tandon
71.	1983	Avtar	Shabana Azmi	Mohan Kumar
72.	1983	Janwar	Zeenat Aman	Ali Raja
73.	1983	Nishan	Rekha	Surendra Mohan
74.	1983	Sautan	Tina Munim/Padmini Kolhapure	Sawan Kumar
75.	1984	Aaj Ka M.L.A. Ram Avtar	Shabana Azmi	Dasari Narain Rao
76.	1984	Asha Jyoti	Rekha/Reena Roy	Dasari Narain Rao
77.	1984	Awaj	Jaya Prada	Shakti Samant
78.	1984	Dharam Aur Kanoon	Jaya Prada	Joshi
79.	1984	Maksad	Jaya Prada	K. Bapaiya
80.	1984	Naya Kadam	Shri Devi/Jaya Prada	K. Raghvendra Rao
81.	1984	Papi Pet Ka Sawal	Rati Agnihotri/Tina Munim	Sohan Lal Kanwar

(Contd.)

1	2	3	4	5
82.	1985	Aakhir Kyon	Smita Patil	J. Om Prakash
83.	1985	Alag-Alag	Tina Munim	Shakti Samant
84.	1985	Aawara Baap	Minakshi Sheshadri	Sohan Lal Kanwar
85.	1985	Babu	Hema Malini	A.V. Trilok Chand
86.	1985	Bewafai	Tina Munim	R. Tyagrajan
87.	1985	Hum Donon	Hema Malini	B.S. Glad
88.	1985	Insaf Mein Karoonga	Tina Munim/Padmini Kolhapure	Shibu Mitra
89.	1985	Master Ji	Shri Devi	K. Raghavendra Rao
90.	1985	Oonche Log	Salma Aga	Brij
91.	1985	Jamana	Ranjita/Poonam Dhillon	Ramesh Talwar
92.	1986	Adhikar	Tina Munim	Vijay Anand
93.	1986	Amrat	Smita Patil	Mohan Kumar
94.	1986	Anokha Rishta	Smita Patil/Sabia	I.V. Shashi
95.	1986	Nasihat	Shabana Ajmi	Arvind Sen
96.	1986	Shatru	Shabana Ajmi	Pramod Chakravarti
97.	1987.	Awam	Smita Patil	B.R. Chopra
98.	1987	Gora	Sulakshana Pandit	Desh Gautam
99.	1987	Najarana	Smita Patil	Ravi Tandon
100.	1987	Sitapur Ki Geeta	Hema Malini	Shibu Mitra
101.	1988	Vijay	Hema Malini	Yash Chopra
102.	1988	Woh Phir Aayegi	Farha/Munmun Sen	B.R. Iashara
103.	1989	Ghar Ka Chirag	Dipika	Sikander Bharati
104.	1990	Swarg	Madhavi	David Dhawan
105.	1991	Rupaye Das Karod	Dipika	Sikander Bharati
106.	1995	Khudaai	Madhavi	Jani Bakhshi

Table 5.2

Detailed Study of Rajesh Khanna's One Hundred Surveyed Political Supporters in Delhi in September 1997

S.No.	Name of the Person	Sex	Age (in years)	Urban/ Rural	Religion	Whether SC/ST	Family's income P.M. (in Rs.)	Edu- cation	Occup- ation	No. of His watched Political Films	View about His Political Future
1	2	3	4	5	6	7	8	9	10	11	12
1.	V.P. Sharma	Male	32	Urban	Hindu	Nil	3000.00	B.A.	Service	08	Good
2.	Rekha Agarwal	Female	26	Urban	Hindu	Nil	2500.00	M.A.	Housewife	04	May be Minister
3.	Sant Ram Verma	Male	45	Rural	Hindu	Nil	1800.00	Matric	Business	11	Very Good
4.	Hukum Singh	Male	32	Rural	Sikh	SC	2100.00	B.A.	Service	07	May be Re-elected
5.	Ram Prakash	Male	22	Urban	Hindu	SC	1400.00	Inter	Service	13	Brighter as a politician
6.	Kartar Singh	Male	27	Urban	Sikh	Nil	3600.00	M.Sc.	Business	08	May be Re-elected
7.	Nafees Hussain	Male	55	Rural	Muslim	Nil	1700.00	Matric	Service	11	Very Good
8.	Sumit Mehta	Male	21	Urban	Hindu	Nil	4000.00	B.Sc.	Student	15	More popular in future
9.	Asha Devi	Female	27	Rural	Hindu	SC	2700.00	Matric	Housewife	09	May be Re-elected
10.	Davis Samuel	Male	31	Urban	Christian	Nil	2200.00	M.Com.	Service	07	Very Good
11.	Asifa Khan	Female	24	Urban	Muslim	Nil	2600.00	B.A.	Student	11	May be Minister
12.	Arvind Kumar	Male	29	Rural	Hindu	Nil	1800.00	Matric	Business	09	More popular in future
13.	Mamta Jain	Female	27	Urban	Jain	Nil	3400.00	M.Sc.	Service	13	Should be President of India
14.	Akash Sinha	Male	33	Urban	Hindu	Nil	2400.00	M.B.A.	Service	06	More popular in future
15.	Amarjit Singh	Male	45	Urban	Sikh	Nil	4000.00	M.Com.	Business	13	May be Minister
16.	Avtar Singh	Male	27	Urban	Sikh	Nil	3500.00	C.A.	Business	06	Brighter as a politician
17.	Meenakshi Gandhi	Female	29	Rural	Hindu	Nil	2700.00	M.Sc.	Service	09	More popular in future

(Contd.)

1	2	3	4	5	6	7	8	9	10	11	12
18.	Rama Kant	Male	34	Rural	Duddhist	SC	1800.00	Inter	Service	08	May be Re-elected
19.	Haridev	Male	22	Rural	Buddhist	SC	1400.00	Matric	Service	11	Very Good
20.	Asha Devi	Female	19	Urban		Nil	2100.00	Matric	Housewife	12	Good
21.	Sita Devi	Female	24	Urban	Hindu	SC	1600.00	Inter	Housewife	13	Brighter as a politician
22.	Nioml Hussain	Male	31	Urban	Muslim	Nil	2200.00	B.A.	Service	11	More popular in future
23.	Alok Gupta	Male	27	Rural	Hindu	Nil	2400.00	M.A.	Business	17	Brighter as a politician
24.	Arti Tawari	Female	34	Urban	Hindu	Nil	3300.00	B.A.	Service	09	May be Re-elected
25.	Urmila Nagar	Female	27	Urban	Hindu	Nil	4000.00	M.Sc.	Service	13	Very Good
26.	Rekha Jain	Female	29	Urban	Jain	Nil	4200.00	M.A.	Housewife	11	May be Re-elected
27.	Satish Kakkad	Male	31	Urban	Hindu	Nil	2900.00	M.Com.	Service	13	Brighter as a politician
28.	Pritam Singh	Male	32	Rural	Sikh	Nil	3700.00	B.Com.	Business	14	May be Re-elected
29.	Bihari Lal	Male	33	Rural	Hindu	SC	2800.00	Inter	Service	13	Brighter as a politician
30.	Baban Singh	Male	31	Urban	Sikh	SC	2400.00	Matric	Service	12	May be Re-elected
31.	Jyoti Narula	Female	32	Rural	Hindu	Nil	2100.00	Inter	Housewife	11	Good
32.	Avinash Sharma	Male	32	Urban	Hindu	Nil	3100.00	M.Sc.	Service	08	Brighter as a politician
33.	M.Mathuew	Male	34	Urban	Christian	Nil	1800.00	B.A.	Service	12	Very Good
34.	Mary Johnson	Female	37	Urban	Christian	Nil	2300.00	M.A.	Housewife	07	Brighter as a politician
35.	Kamal Kaur	Female	28	Rural	Sikh	Nil	1700.00	B.A.	Housewife	11	May be Re-elected
36.	Karan Singh	Male	27	Rural	Hindu	SC	2400.00	Inter	Business	11	May be Minister
37.	Anju	Female	18	Urban	Hindu	Nil	2600.00	B.A.	Service	09	Should be president of India
38.	Davis Thomas	Male	27	Rural	Christian	Nil	2700.00	M.Sc.	Service	05	More popular in future
39.	Akshay Jain	Male	29	Urban	Jain	Nil	4000.00	M.A.	Business	08	May be Re-elected
40.	Amar Singh	Male	31	Urban	Hindu	Nil	2400.00	M.A.	Service	08	Brighter as a politician

(Contd.)

1	2	3	4	5	6	7	8	9	10	11	12
41.	Harbans Singh	Male	34	Urban	Sikh	Nil	2700.00	M.A.	Business	09	Very Good
42.	Mohan Lal Sharma	Male	36	Rural	Hindu	Nil	3300.00	Inter	Business	12	May be Re-elected
43.	Bansi Lal Verma	Male	34	Rural	Hindu	Nil	2400.00	Matric	Business	09	More popular in future
44.	Ram Ratan	Male	31	Rural	Hindu	SC	2100.00	Inter	Service	11	Very Good
45.	Pyara Singh	Male	24	Urban	Sikh	Nil	2300.00	Matric	Business	07	May be Re-elected
46.	Jasprit Singh	Male	23	Urban	Sikh	Nil	2400.00	B.A.	Service	09	More popular in future
47.	Amar Nath	Male	26	Rural	Hindu	Nil	2700.00	M.A.	Service	11	Very Good
48.	Bachan Singh	Male	25	Rural	Hindu	SC	1900.00	Matric	Service	07	May be Re-elected
49.	Mahendra Singh	Male	27	Urban	Hindu	Nil	2700.00	M.Com.	Service	09	May be Re-elected
50.	Indra Narain	Male	26	Urban	Hindu	Nil	2900.00	M.A.	Service	08	Very Good
51.	Rajendra Prasad	Male	24	Rural	Hindu	Nil	3600.00	M.Com.	Service	07	More popular in future
52.	S.P. Ahuja	Male	27	Urban	Hindu	Nil	2400.00	B.A.	Business	08	Brighter as a politician
53.	Upendra Singh	Male	26	Rural	Hindu	SC	2100.00	Inter	Service	13	May be Re-elected
54.	Kartar Singh	Male	19	Urban	Sikh	Nil	2300.00	B.A.	Service	08	Brighter as a politician
55.	M. Zafar	Male	39	Urban	Muslim	Nil	2700.00	M.Sc.	Service	09	More popular in future
56.	Raisa Khan	Female	34	Urban	Muslim	Nil	2400.00	M.A.	Service	11	May be Re-elected
57.	Ranjit Singh	Male	28	Urban	Sikh	Nil	3400.00	B.A.	Business	08	More popular in future
58.	Anjubala	Female	27	Rural	Hindu	Nil	2100.00	Matric	Housewife	11	Very Good
59.	Anand Swaroop Mathur	Male	29	Urban	Hindu	Nil	2300.00	Inter	Business	08	May be Re-elected
60.	Atma Ram	Male	34	Rural	Hindu	SC	2400.00	Matric	Service	11	May be Minister
61.	Anupama Jain	Female	22	Urban	Jain	Nil	2500.00	Inter	Housewife	07	Brighter as a politician
62.	Maya Agnihotri	Female	38	Urban	Hindu	Nil	3300.00	B.A.	Service	09	Brighter as a politician

(Contd.)

1	2	3	4	5	6	7	8	9	10	11	12
63.	S.C. Chaturvedi	Male	34	Urban	Hindu	Nil	2100.00	M.A.	Business	11	May be Re-elected
64.	Balak Ram	Male	25	Rural	Buddhist	SC	2300.00	B.A.	Servicfe	09	Very Good
65.	Kaushalya Devi	Female	26	Urban	Hindu	Nil	3200.00	M.A.	Service	08	May be Re-elected
66.	Vimla Rani	Female	27	Rural	Hindu	Nil	2400.00	Inter	Housewife	09	More popular in future
67.	J.P. Sharma	Male	29	Urban	Hindu	Nil	2700.00	B.A.	Business	08	May be Re-elected
68.	R.P. Arora	Male	31	Urban	Hindu	Nil	2900.00	M.A.	Service	09	More popular in future
69.	Dayal Mishra	Male	41	Rural	Hindu	Nil	2400.00	B.A.	Service	08	May be Re-elected
70.	Savita Pandey	Female	34	Urban	Hindu	Nil	3100.00	M.A.	Housewife	11	May be Minister
71.	Rama Devi	Female	27	Rural	Hindu	SC	2500.00	B.A.	Service	10	Brighter as a politician
72.	Vijay Sadana	Male	29	URban	Hindu	Nil	2600.00	M.A.	Business	01	Brighter as a politician
73.	P.B. Dasgupta	Male	29	Urban	Hindu	Nil	3400.00	B.A.	Service	10	More popular in future
74.	Malati Joshi	Female	27	Urban	Hindu	Nil	3300.00	M.A.	Housewife	09	Very Good
75.	Mahavir Singh	Male	29	Rural	Hindu	SC	2100.00	Matric	Service	11	Should be President of India
76.	Jagdish Kalra	Male	24	Urban	Hindu	Nil	2400.00	B.Com.	Student	13	May be Re-elected
77.	Vanita Handa	Female	22	Urban	Hindu	Nil	2700.00	B.Sc.	Student	11	Good
78.	Pawan Shukla	Male	21	Rural	Hindu	Nil	3200.00	B.A.	Student	09	May be Minister
79.	Parmatma Sharma	Male	19	Rural	Hindu	SC	3100.00	Inter	Student	07	More Popular in future
80.	Vandana Singh	Female	25	Urban	Hindu	Nil	2500.00	B.A.	Student	10	May be Re-elected
81.	Aashish Jain	Male	24	Urban	Jain	Nil	3100.00	B.A.	Business	09	More popular in future
82.	Jaslin Kaur	Female	23	Urban	Sikh	Nil	1900.00	Matric	Student	11	May be Re-elected
83.	Rahul Verma	Male	28	Rural	Hindu	Nil	2400.00	B.A.	Service	10	Should be President of India
84.	Aditi Modi	Male	32	Urban	Hindu	Nil	4000.00	M.A.	Business	06	May be Minister
85.	Vimal Kumar	Male	22	Rural	Hindu	SC	2100.00	Inter	Service	08	Very Good

(Contd.)

1	2	3	4	5	6	7	8	9	10	11	12
86.	Sagar Kataria	Male	25	Urban	Hindu	Nil	2400.00	B.A.	Service	13	More popular in future
87.	Ankur Pradhan	Male	35	Rural	SC		2100.00	Inter	Service	11	Brighter as a politician
88.	Priyanka Sadhakar	Female	34	Urban	Hinshu	Nil	3200.00	B.A.	Housewife	12	Brighter as a politician
89.	Abhishek Gandhi	Male	26	Urban	Hindu	Nil	2800.00	B.Sc.	Student	08	May be Re-elected
90.	Jagdev Singh	Male	27	Rural	Sikh	Nil	2500.00	M.A.	Service	11	May be Minister
91.	Gaurav Tanya	Male	29	Urban	Hindu	Nil	2400.00	M.Com.	Business	09	More popular in future
92.	Mangla Devi	Female	32	Rural	Hindu	SC	1800.00	Matric	Housewife	11	Brighter as a politician
93.	Sajjan Kumar	Male	29	Urban	Hindu	Nil	2400.00	M.Com.	Service	09	Very Good
94.	N.K. Mathur	Male	25	Rural	Hindu	Nil	2500.00	B.Com.	Student	06	Brighter as a politician
95.	Alankar Shukla	Male	24	Urban	Hindu	Nil	1900.00	B.A.	Student	08	More popular in future
96.	Adim Garg	Male	23	Rural	Hindu	Nil	2100.00	M.A.		09	May be Minister
97.	Satya Narain	Male	28	Urban	Hindu	Nil	2400.00	M.A.	Service	10	More popular in future
98.	S.S. Tripathi	Male	24	Urban	Hindu	Nil	3100.00	M.Sc.	Service	08	Brighter as a politician
99.	Jagriti Singh	Female	23	Urban	Hindu	SC	2200.00	B.A.	Student	09	May be Minister
100.	Pooja Dwivedi	Female	34	Urban	Hindu	Nil	3400.00	M.A.	Housewife	07	More popular in future.

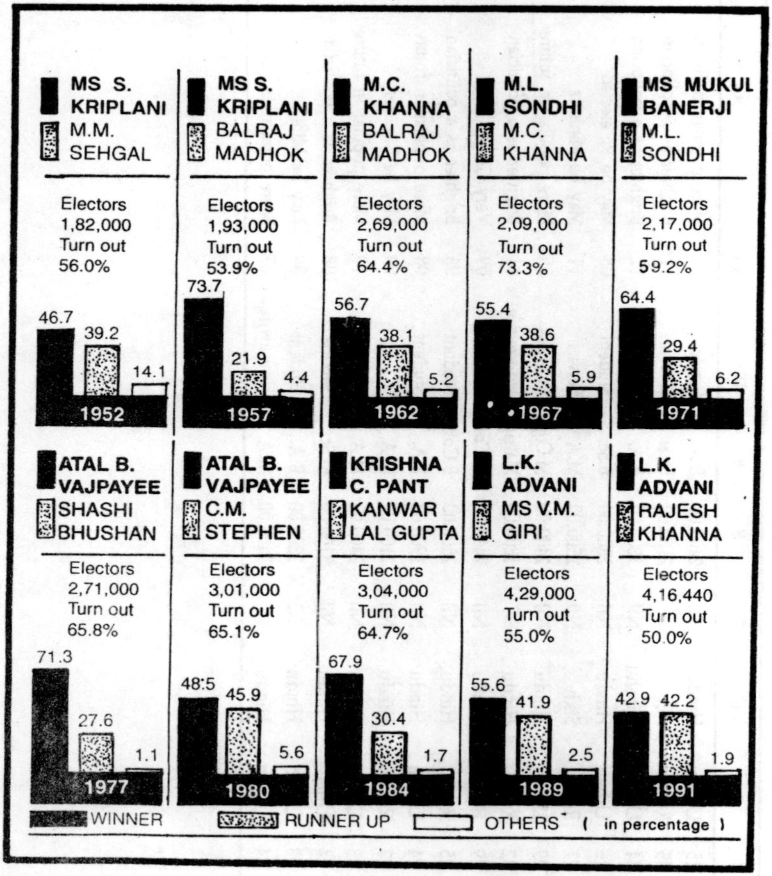

Diagram 5.1

1952-1991 Electoral Performance in New Delhi Lok Sabha Constituency.

development could take place without it. Mr. Khanna also addressed the meet.

Findings of the Survey Work

One hundred political supporters of Rajesh Khanna were surveyed in Delhi in September 1997. The main findings are as follows:

1. Out of one hundred political supporters; fifteen were educated upto matric, fifteen also were upto intermediate, twenty six were upto B.A., three were upto B.Sc., three also were upto B.Com, twenty one were upto M.A., eight were upto M.Sc, seven were upto M.Com, only one was M.B.A. and also only one was C.A.
2. Out of these one hundred persons; sixty two persons were Urban and thirty eight persons were Rural.
3. Out of one hundred political supporters; seventy were males and thirty were females.
4. Out of these one hundred persons; twenty nine persons were of age group upto twenty five years, thirty six were upto twenty six to thirty years age-group, twenty seven were upto thirty one to thirty five years, four were upto thirty six to forty years age-group and four also were over forty years age.
5. Out of one hundred political supporters; sixty nine political supporters were Hindus, five were Muslims, Fourteen were Sikhs, four were Christians, five were Jains and three were Buddhists.
6. Out of these one hundred persons; twenty one were SC/ST and seventy nine were non-SC/ST.
7. Out of these one hundred political supporters; fifty belonged to service, twenty two belonged to Business, twelve were students and sixteen were housewives.

8. Out of these one hundred persons; thirteen persons belonged to monthly family's income group upto Rs. 2000.00, sixty one belonged to Rs. 2001.00 to Rs. 3000.00, twenty five belonged to Rs. 3001.00 to 4000.00 and only one person belonged to over Rs. 4000.00.

9. Out of these one hundred persons two persons watched Rajesh Khanna's films upto five, fifty eight persons watched his films upto six to ten, thirty nine persons watched his films upto eleven to fifteen, and only one person watched his films upto sixteen to twenty.

10. Out of these one hundred persons; four persons viewed his good political future, fifteen persons said that his political future is very good, twenty five persons said that as their views he may be re-elected to Lok Sabha, eleven persons said he may be minister in future, twenty persons said his political future as a politician is brighter, twenty one persons hoped his more popularity in future and four persons viewed he should be President of India.

It is found that Rajesh Khanna is very popular in every community in Delhi. Surveyed political supporters of Rajesh Khanna have also keen interest in his political films.

Chapter 6

Surveyed Political Study of Shatrughna Sinha : M.P.

(Rajya Sabha Member)

Braving the scorching sun to bathe in sweat. Bharatiya Janata Party nominee Shatrughan Sinha undertook a whirlwind tour of the New Delhi constituency to meet with his supporters, particularly in the J-J clusters. The cine-star also visited the slum areas in the rural pockets of the constituency. Beginning his day-long election campaign with early morning prayers at Lal Sai Mandir in Lajpat Nagar, Mr. Sinha went around Vinobha Puri, Gandhi Jhuggi Camp, Kasturba Niketan, Krishna Market, Nehru Nagar and Rajiv camp in a procession that finally terminated in a large public meeting at Hari Nagar Ashram. Later, the BJP nominee addressed another largely attended meeting at Andrews Ganj. Mounting a frontal attack on the non-performance of the Congress Government at the centre, the cine-star-turned politician cautioned the voters against voting for the Congress. "If you do that even by mistake, the party will take it as an acceptance of its present-day anti-people actions", he warned while listing the failures of the Government on all fronts.

Mr. Sinha stated that it was not a question of making or breaking a Government but of expressing opposition to those measures that pushed the populace into a world of darkness. "The unprecedented rise in the prices of essential commodities, continued atrocities against the women and deteriorating law and order situation were there for all to see", he stated while calling upon the electorate to provide the necessary check to the Government in its pursuit of deceit and delusion. He referred to the recent scandals involving the former Foreign Minister in the now infamous `Bofors cover-up' and also the multi-crore stock scam. "The people at the top positions are involved in `loot' and voters must express their anger", he said. Labelling the New Delhi by-election as historic given the importance of signals the results were expected to send all over the country, he hinted that the congress party had already begun to search for alibis in consequence of the expected defeat at the hustings.

Mr. Sinha who was showered with flower-petals and cheered by his supporters during the poll campaign expressed satisfaction that with the wide spread support of the people, he will not only defeat his opponents but win the elections with a record margin. Meanwhile, National secretary of the BJP Madan Lal Khurana met with the senior officers of the Delhi Police in the morning to ensure adequate security measures during the poll. He alleged that 'musclemen' were being brought by the Congress party from the neighbouring states particularly Haryana to foment trouble during the poll. Calling upon the Lt. Governor of Delhi to take appropriate steps to maintenance law and order in view of the presence of 'Congress-toughs', Mr. Khurana who was also the campaign manager of the party nominee accused the ruling party of having already lost its nerve in the face of 'sure defeat' at the husting. 'The allegations of the so-called rigging' and bogus-polling hurled by the congress party at its opponents appeared as if it were a dress-rehearsal for working out a defence in the face of defeat, he charged while fcreseeing a landslide victory for the BJP nominee.

Meanwhile, Mrs. Poonam Sinha undertook 'Padyatra' in large areas of the constituency. She visited many houses at Golf Links, Khan Market, Kaka Nagar and Bharati Nagar. Accompanied by a large number of women workers of the party, Mrs. Sinha also met with a large number of women leaders belonging to many organisations. She was assured support for her husband in the election. Party president Dr. Murli Manohar Joshi addressed three public meetings to garner support for Mr. Sinha. He also met with the members of the Uttranchal Pradesh Sangharsh Samiti who announced support to the party nominee. Large number of BJP workers from Bihar under the leadership of Dr. Shailendra Nath Srivastava, former M.P. and vice-president of the State unit, continued with their door-to-door campaign particularly in areas inhabited by Biharis to seek support for Mr. Shatrughan Sinha whom they labelled as the 'son of Bihar'.

Shatrughan Sinha visited Dargah and Hanuman Temple

In a show devoid of election gimmickry, and indeed everything that had to do with electioneering, Mr. Shatrughan Sinha, Bhartiya Janata Party (BJP) candidate for a New Delhi seat undertook a "padyatra" in the Nizamuddin Basti area on May 22, 1992. Beginning by offering prayers at the Dargah of Amir Khusro and Hazrat Nizamuddin Aulia he covered the area quickly onfoot, going through the narrow serpentine lanes on foot, waving at people, accepting garlands and rounding off with a short speech.

Mr. Sinha was at the Dargah for close to an hour. It was not exactly a sombre affair with a large crowd following him wherever he went. The BJP candidate, occasionally waved at those who came to see him. But there was no slogan-shouting within the Dargah, quite in contrast with Mr. Sinha's visit to the Hanuman Temple on Baba Kharak Singh Marg. In fact throughout Mr. Sinha's visit to the area there was hardly any slogan-shouting. Besides, only a couple of banners could be seen. BJP party workers, who had an aggressive campaign-style, kept a low profile. Besides one did not even hear shouts of "Jai Shri Ram, Har Har Mahadev." Mr. Sinha later said his visit to the area had nothing to do with his election effort. He had come there only to offer prayers at the Dargah. In a short speech from atop an open jeep at the end of his trip to Nizamuddin Basti, Mr. Sinha thanked the people for giving him a warm welcome and promised to visit the area soon. Throughout his short speech, the BJP candidate kept pointing out that his visit to the basti and the dargah had nothing to with his election campaign.

Mr. Sinha received an enthusiastic welcome during his visit. Most of those who followed him through were children. The other area which Mr. Sinha visited included Lajpat Nagar where the BJP had fared well in recent years.

Shatrughan Sinha's wife Mrs. Poonam Sinha made campaign a gay affair in 1992

Mrs. Poonam Sinha, wife of Mr. Shatrughan Sinha, the Bhartiya Janata Party (BJP) candidate for the New Delhi by-election, was always ready with a smile, ready to eat and drink with the voters during the numerous 'padyatras' through slums. In her round of Princess Park on June 4, 1992, she was accompanied by women workers and three teenage girls who put up a good show shouting slogans on the mike while she walked around the various shanties and hutment colonies. Two supporters with 'dholaks' suddenly appeared and drummed away enthusiastically. Children swarmed all around trying to collect party stickers and badges. A youth surrounded by nearly 50 children egged them on to clap and shout slogans. "She seems very sincere", said a woman resident watching her go. "The big bindi suits her", said another. "Her enthusiasm is infectious", said a third as she laughed at what Mrs. Sinha was saying on the mike from her Gypsy: "I've come to seek your blessings. Give me ten minutes of your precious time. You must vote for......(here she showed the audience a photograph of Mr. Sinha) him. You know I can't take his name.....!"

From 7.30 a.m. to midnight, Mrs. Sinha hardly had time for rest. Chalo, Chalo (come on), she urged her group as they enjoyed a cup of tea. "There was no time to idle". Initially, she had campaigned with her husband, standing by his side, smiling, waving and folding hands to the crowds which came pouring out to see the canvassing. But after, she went separately, especially to the areas where the rival party, the congress had always polled more votes than BJP. Unlike her husband, who seldom got down from his Gypsy during his padyatras, Mrs. Sinha preferred going on foot as much as possible so that she can woo voters `door to door'. In the evenings she joined her husband to campaign with him. In Princess Park a woman welcomed her in the traditional manner with an `aarti'. Mrs. Sinha was asked to break a coconut. With a sure, energetic suring of her arm, Mrs. Sinha banged the coconut on the ground. Some of the juice split on her simple black and white `salwar-kameez' and even on her face. She wiped the drops away with the back of her hand and smiled broadly. "The time has come to bring about a change", she told her audience of mainly women and children. "Vote for Sinha Saheb and I promise you he will not disappoint you. You have seen how he acts in films. He will raise his voice in Parliament for your causes with more fervour".

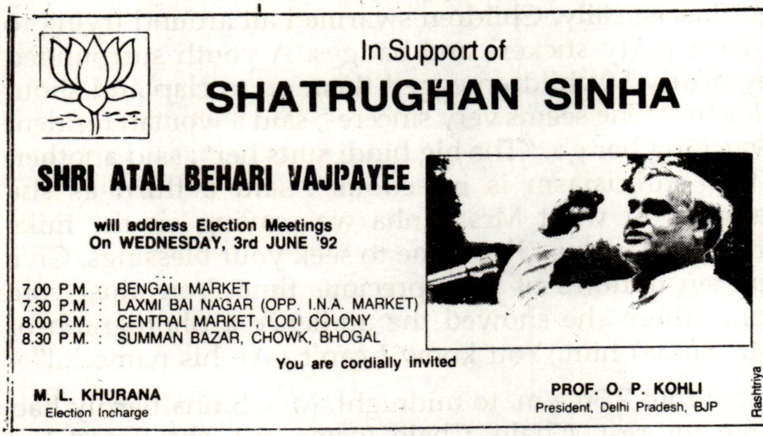

An Advertisement in Support of Shatrughna Sinha during bye-election of Lok Sabha from New Delhi in 1992

Did her arrival really effect a change in the voters' heart? "I think we can do with some change", said one woman resident. "You know how the poor are. They get sold on whoever promises them a better deal. Now she says her husband will get this or that done. May be, we can give him a try", said another. "This is a Congress strong-hold. You mark my words, 85 percent of the votes from this area will go to the Congress. Her (Mrs. Sinha's) coming will make no difference", said an old man. "This is her (Mrs. Sinha's) third trip here", said another woman. "When Rajesh Khanna (Congress) came he did not even bother to get down from his jeep.

These people are working hard over canvassing. I think it will pay dividends. People here are ready to die for Mrs. Tajdar Babar (city women Congress Chief)", said a middle-aged man.

Police Disclosed Plot to Kill Shatrughan Sinha in 1994

A Bombay city based gang of contract killers was paid Rs. ten lakhs by Dawood aide Chotta Shakil, to assassinate the film star, Mr. Shatrughan Sinha, in April 1994. The plot was, however, aborted at the last minute. This startling disclosure was made by the Joint Police Commissioner (crime) of Bombay, Mr. M.N. Singh, in a press conference at the police headquarters on October 14, 1994. In a major breakthrough, six members of this gang including its kingpin Mohammed Hasan alias Sheru were arrested under TADA by a team of city's Crime Branch in Bangalore on October 5, 1994. Two members of the gang waited outside Mr. Sinha's bungalow in an auto-rickshaw in April 1994. As the star left his house, the killers whipped out their weapons. Seeing the guns, the rickshaw driver fled and gang hastily abandoned their plans of killing the star.

The gangsters also confessed to being given a contract by the Dubai-based Chotta Shakil to kill the late corporator Mr. Ramdas Nayak in the same month. The plan was again abandoned at the last minute owing to the security around the slain corporator, Mr. M.N. Singh said. "We have almost solved the Nayak Case. Only the arrests remain to be made", said the Joint Commissioner hinting at the hand of the Dubai based Shakil in Ramdas Nayak's assassination. Five firearms including a carbine, two pistols, two revolvers and 201 rounds of ammunition of different calibres and cash and jewellery worth Rs. 3.5 lakhs were recovered from the gang. The other gang members arrested including Abdul Ghafoor Faqi, Shamim Ahmed Suleiman Shaikh alias Nikki and Syed Mohsin Khan. Another associate Salim Sonde, was arrested in Pune on October 6, 1994.

Table 6.1

Detailed Study of Shatrughna Sinha's One Hundred Surveyed Political Supporters in Delhi in March 1997

S. No.	*Name of the Person*	*Sex*	*Age (in years)*	*Urban/ Rural*	*Religion*	*Whether SC/ST*	*Family's income P.M. (in Rs.)*	*Edu-cation*	*Occup-ation*	*No. of His watched Political Films*	*View about His Political Future*
1	*2*	*3*	*4*	*5*	*6*	*7*	*8*	*9*	*10*	*11*	*12*
1.	Rakesh Malhotra	Male	25	Urban	Hindu	Nil	3500.00	B.A.	Student	12	May be C.M. of Bihar.
2.	Uma Malhotra	Female	32	Urban	Hindu	Nil	3100.00	M.A	Service	15	May be elected to Lok Sabha
3.	Aruna Jain	Female	30	Rural	Jain	Nil	2600.00	B.Sc.	Housewife	10	Success as B.J.P. Leader
4.	Ram Lal	Male	28	Rurai	Hindu	SC	1800.00	B.A	Service	18	More popular in future politics
5.	Anthony Thomas	Male	27	Urban	Christian	Nil	2400.00	B.Com.	Business	17	May be C.M. of Bihar
6.	Sadiu Hussain	Male	36	Rural	Muslim	Nil	2700.00	M.A.	Service	19	Success as B.J.P. Leader
7.	Sansa Chand Dubey	Male	27	Urban	Hindu	Nil	4500.00	M.Com	Business	12	May be C.M. of Bihar
8.	Tara Chand Dubey	Male	34	Urban	Hindu	Nil	4100.00	M.Sc.	Service	18	Success as B.J.P. Leader
9.	Bhure Lal	Male	29	Rural	Hindu	SC	3700.00	B.Com.	Service	15	May be C.M. of Bihar
10.	Shyam Lal Yadav	Male	37	Rural	Hindu	Nil	3400.00	Matric	Business	20	More popular in future politics
11.	Akash Gupta	Male	34	Urban	Hidnu	Nil	3000.00	Inter	Service	15	Should be President of India
12.	Gagan Gupta	Male	30	Urban	Hindu	Nil	2800.00	B.A.	Business	10	May be C.M. of Bihar
13.	Anuradha Ganeshan	Female	28	Urban	Hindu	Nil	3600.00	M.A.	Housewife	15	Should be President of India

(Contd.)

1	2	3	4	5	6	7	8	9	10	11	12
14.	Varun Kaul	Male	29	Urban	Hindu	Nil	3900.00	M.A.	Service	15	May be C.M. of Bihar
15.	Liyaqat Ansari	Male	33	Rural	Muslim	Nil	2400.00	Matric	Business	08	Success as B.J.P. Leader
16.	Tarun Majurndar	Male	39	Urban	Hindu	Nil	2700.00	B.Com.	Service	10	Should be President of India
17.	Raj Kumar Sharma	Male	42	Rural	Hindu	Nil	2900.00	B.Sc.	Business	18	More popular in future politics
18.	B.P. Singh	Male	37	Rural	Hindu	SC	2400.00	Inter	Service	20	May be elected to Lok Sabha
19.	Saida Khatoon	Female	33	Urban	Muslim	Nil	2700.00	Matric	Business	18	Should be President of India
20.	Chandra Kant Tripathi	Male	36	Urban	Hindu	Nil	3600.00	M.Com.	Service	22	Success as B.J.P. Leader
21.	Charulata Bamerji	Female	33	Rural	Hindu	Nil	3000.00	M.Sc	Housewife	24	May be C.M. of Bihar
22.	Atual Kumar Jain	Male	24	Urban	Jain	Nil	3200.00	B.A.	Service	18	Should be President of India
23.	Ajay Agarwal	Mlae	27	Urban	Hindu	Nil	4100.00	M.A.	Business	15	May be C.M. of Bihar
24.	Banarasi Das	Male	24	Rural	Buddhist	SC	1900.00	B.Sc.	Student	13	May be elected to Lok Sabha
25.	Chetan Gurnani	Male	36	Urban	Hindu	Nil	2500.00	M.A.	Serivce	17	More pupular in future politics
26.	Alok Chauhan	Male	33	Rural	Hindu	SC	2200.00	B.A	Service	19	Success as B.J.P. Leader
27.	Rajnikant	Male	27	Urban	Hindu	Nil	2700.00	M.A.	Business	12	May be C.M. of Bihar
28.	Alfred Wilson	Male	25	Urban	Christian	ST	3100.00	B.Com.	Student	15	More popular in future politics
29.	Tariq Hussaine	Male	24	Urban	Muslim	Nil	3400.00	B.Sc.	Student	10	May be elected to Lok Sabha
30.	Vandana Jain	Female	27	Urban	Jain	Nil	4000.00	M.Sc.	Student	12	Success as B.J.P. Leader
31.	Vasudev Naiyer	Male	29	Rural	Hindu	Nil	4500.00	M.A	Service	15	May be C.M of Bihar
32.	Ramesh Chandra Verma	Male	34	Rural	Hindu	Nil	4100.00	M.Com.	Business	25	More popular in future politics
33.	Ram Dulare	Male	31	Urban	Hindu	SC	3400.00	Matric	Business	12	May be elected to Lok Sabha

(Contd.)

1	2	3	4	5	6	7	8	9	10	11	12
34.	Har Narian	Male	36	Urban	Hindu	Nil	3200.00	Inter	Service	10	May be C.M. of Bihar
35.	Madan Kaur	Female	33	Rural	Sikh	SC	1800.00	Inter	Housewife	15	Success as B.J.P. Leader
36.	Basant Kaur	Female	41	Urban	Sikh	Nil	2600.00	B.A.	Service	18	May be C.M. of Bihar
37.	Beant Kaur	Female	29	Urban	Sikh	Nil	3400.00	Matric	Housewife	16	Should be President of India
38.	Neelam Ahuja	Female	33	Urban	Hindu	Nil	4300.00	B.A.	Housewife	08	Success as B.J.P. Leader
39.	R.L. Srivastan	Male	31	Rural	Hindu	Nil	3600.00	M.A	Business	12	More popular in future politics
40.	Kaushalya Deve	Female	23	Rural	Hindu	SC	3100.00	Matric	Housewife	16	May be C.M. of Bihar
41.	Kanak Lata	Female	19	Urban	Buddhist	SC	2300.00	Inter	Student	18	Should be President of India
42.	Sunit Kumar	Male	23	Rural	Buddhist	SC	2600.00	B.Com.	Student	20	May be elected to Lok Sabha
43.	Sajjan Singh Kothari	Male	27	Urban	Hindu	Nil	3600.00	M.Com.	Service	24	Should be President of India
44.	Saquib Hussain	Male	29	Rural	Muslim	Nil	3100.00	M.Sc	Business	25	May be elected to Lok Sabha
45.	J.L.Gupta	Male	31	Urban	Hindu	Nil	2700.00	B.Com	Business	24	Should be President of India
46.	Barqat Ali	Male	28	Urban	Muslim	Nil	3400.00	M.A.	Service	12	May be elected to Lok Sabha
47.	Gaffar Khan	Male	31	Rural	Muslim	Nil	3300.00	Inter	Business	18	May be C.M. of Bihar
48.	M.L. Williams	Male	36	Urban	Christan	ST	2600.00	B.Com.	Service	2.3	More Popular in future politics
49.	Zulfiqar	Male	33	Urban	Muslim	Nil	2900.00	B.Sc	Business	11	May be C.M of Bihar
50.	Mohammad Said	Male	31	Rural	Sikh	SC	3500.00	Matric	Business	15	Should be President of India
51.	Nihal Singh	Male	42	Rural	Sikh	SC	3100.00	Matric	Business	15	Should be President of India
52.	Naranjan Prasad	Male	32	Urban	Hindu	Nil	2700.00	Inter	Service	10	May be elected to Lok Sabha
53.	Banwari Lal	Male	24	Urban	Hindu	Nil	2400.00	B.A.	Business	18	May be C.M. of Bihar
54.	Harcharan Singh	Male	29	Urban	Sikh	Nil	4200.00	M.Com.	Service	14	More popular in future politics

(Contd.)

1	2	3	4	5	6	7	8	9	10	11	12
55.	B.S. Ahrya	Male	33	Rural	Hindu	Nil	3400.00	M.Sc.	Business	18	Should be President of India
56.	Surya Kant	Male	36	Rural	Hindu	SC	2400.00	Inter	Service	10	May be C.M. of Bihar
57.	Farzin Ali	Male	31	Urban	Muslim	Nil	2100.00	Matric	Business	15	May be elected Lok Sabha
58.	Fakhrudin Ali	Male	24	Urban	Muslim	Nil	2400.00	B.A	Student	12	Success as B.J.P Leader
59.	Janaki Devi	Female	26	Urban	Hindu	SC	2200.00	B.Sc	Student	18	Should be President of India
60.	Khusi Ram Verma	Male	29	Urban	Hindu	Nil	2700.00	M.A.	Service	12	Success as B.J.P. Leader
61.	Jayanti Prasad	Male	25	Rural	Hindu	SC	2300.00	Inter	Service	16	Should be President of India
62.	J.P. Bundela	Male	39	Rural	Hindu	Nil	2600.00	B.A.	Business	08	Should be President of India.
63.	J.N. Dikshit	Male	25	Rural	Hindu	Nil	3400.00	M.Com.	Student	10	May be C.M. of Bihar
64.	Avtar Singh Gill	Male	27	Urban	Sikh	Nil	3100.00	M.Sc.	Service	08	May be elected to Lok Sabha
65.	Anwar Kaur	Female	32	Urban	Sikh	Nil	3400.00	B.Com.	Service	16	May be C.M. of Bihar
66.	Armendra Singh	Male	30	Rural	Sikh	SC	2500.00	B.A.	Business	14	Should be President of India
67.	Upendra Singh Uppal	Male	33	Urban	Sikh	Nil	2700.00	M.A	Service	16	More Popular in future politics
68.	Nem Chand Jain	Male	36	Urban	Jain	Nil	2900.00	M.Sc.	Business	20	May be C.M. of Bihar
69.	Suraj Mal Lodha	Male	27	Rural	Jain	Nil	3600.00	B.A.	Business	22	More popular in future politics
70.	Ram Lal	Male	29	Urban	Buddhist	SC	2600.00	Inter	Service	24	May be C.M of Bihar
71.	H.K. Singh	Male	39	Urban	Hindu	Nil	2900.00	B.Sc.	Service	25	Should be President of India
72.	Laxmi Devi	Female	27	Rural	Hindu	ST	2400.00	Matric	Housewife	18	May be elected to Lok Sabha
73.	Laxami Narain	Male	29	Urban	Hindu	Nil	2600.00	B.A.	Business	12	May be C.M. of Bihar
74.	Balbir Singh	Male	33	Urban	Sikh	Nil	2900.00	M.A.	Service	10	May be elected to Lok Sabha
75.	Rashmi Singh	Female	31	Rural	Hindu	Nil	2700.00	B.A.	Housewife	14	Success as B.J.P. Leader

(Contd.)

1	2	3	4	5	6	7	8	9	10	11	12
76.	Rudra Pratap	Male	36	Rural	Hindu	Nil	3400.00	M.A.	Service	15	May be C.M. of Bihar
77.	Vani Desh Pandey	Female	29	Urban	Hindu	Nil	3900.00	M.Sc.	Service	18	May be elected to Lok Sabha
78.	Lavlin Mishra	Female	24	Urban	Hindu	Nil	4200.00	M.Sc.	Student	16	Should be President of India
79.	Shiv Prasad	Male	29	Rural	Hindu	S.C.	2600.00	B.A.	Service	15	May be C.M. of Bihar
80.	Alok Ranjan	Male	33	Urban	Hindu	Nil	2800.00	M.A	Business	10	May be elected to Lok Sabha
81.	Gyan Devi	Female	28	Urban	Hindu	Nil	2400.00	Matric	Housewife	08	More popular in future politics
82.	Dharm Narain	Male	27	Rural	Hindu	SC	2200.00	Inter	Service	12	May be elected to Lok Sabha
83.	Bahram Singh	Male	34	Urban	Sikh	Nil	3700.00	M.A.	Business	14	May be C.M. of Bihar
84.	Banke Behari Lal	Male	36	Urban	Hindu	Nil	2800.00	B.A.	Business	16	Success as B.J.P. Leader
85.	Avinash Singh	Male	36	Rural	Hindu	Nil	3400.00	B.A.	Business	08	Should be President of India
86.	Salman Hussian	Male	25	Urban	Muslim	Nil	3100.00	B.Com.	Student	16	Success as B.J.P. Leader
87.	Sonali Gupta	Female	22	Urban	Hindu	Nil	4500.00	B.A.	Student	14	May be C.M. of Bihar
88.	C.K. Singh	Male	26	Rural	Hindu	S.C	4000.00	M.A.	Service	12	May be elected to Lok Sabha
89.	Kiran Taneja	Female	21	Urban	Hindu	Nil	2700.00	Inter	Student	10	More popular in future politics
90.	Pramod Hundu	Male	25	Urban	Hindu	Nil	3900.00	M.A.	Student	16	May be C.M of Bihar
91.	Deep [illegible]ur	Female	23	Rural	Sikh	S.C	2400.00	B.A.	Student	14	Should be President of India
92.	Mohan Kumar Jha	Male	26	Rural	Hindu	Nil	3400.00	M.A.	Service	10	May be C.M. of Bihar
93.	Khushal Singh	Male	29	Urban	Hindu	S.C	2500.00	M.A	Service	10	May be C.M. of Bihar
94.	Gulam Rasool	Male	24	Urban	Muslim	Nil	2300.00	B.A.	Student	16	Success as B.J.P. Leader
95.	Rishi Pal Jain	Male	27	Urban	Jain	Nil	3700.00	M.A.	Business	12	May be C.M. of Bihar
96.	Hemant Kumar	Male	29	Rural		Nil	3400.00	B.A.	Service	10	Success as B.J.P. Leader
97.	Kanchan Bala	Female	27	Urban	Hindu	Nil	3600.00	B.Com.	Housewife	14	May be elected to Lok Sabha
98.	Jai Singh	Male	33	Rural	Hindu	S.C.	3100.00	B.A.	Service	08	May be C.M. of Bihar
99.	Ved Ram	Male	31	Urban	Hindu	Nil	2500.00	B.Com.	Business	15	Should be President of India
100.	Sajjan Singh	Male	29	Urban	Hindu	Nil	2700.00	B.A	Service	10	More popular in future politics

Findings of Survey Work

One hundred political supporters of Shatrughna Sinha were surveyed in Delhi in March 1997. The main findings are as below:

1. Out of one hundred political supporters; ten were educated upto Metric; thirteen were upto Intermediate; twenty-three were upto B.A.; seven were upto B.Sc.; eleven were upto B.Com.; twenty-one were upto M.A.; nine were upto M.Sc. and six were upto M.Com.
2. Out of these one hundred persons, sixty one persons were urban and thirty-nine persons were rural.
3. Out of one hundred political supporters; seventy seven were males and twenty-three were females.
4. Out of these one hundred persons, nineteen persons were of age-group upto twenty-five years, thirty six were upto twenty-six to thirty years age-group, twenty-seven were upto thirty-one to thirty-five years, fifteen were upto thirty six to forty years age-group and only three were over forty years age.
5. Out of one hundred political supporters; sixty-two political supporters were Hindus, thirteen were Muslims, twelve were Sikhs, six were Jains and four were Buddhists.
6. Out of these one hundred persons; twenty-five were SC/ST and seventy five were non-SC/ST.
7. Out of these one hundred political supporters; forty one belonged to service, thirty one belonged to business, seventeen were students and eleven were housewives.
8. Out of these one hundred persons; three persons belonged monthly family's income group, upto Rs. 2000.00, forty nine belonged to Rs. 2001.00 to Rs.

3000.00, thirty nine belonged to Rs. 3001.00 to Rs. 4000.00 and nine persons belonged to over Rs. 4000.00.

9. Out of these one hundred persons; twenty three persons watched Shatrughna Sinha's films upto ten, thirty six persons watched his films upto eleven to fifteen, thirty one persons watched his films upto sixteen to twenty and ten persons watched his films more than twenty.

10. Out of these one hundred persons; thirty one persons said he may be Chief Minister of Bihar, nineteen said he may be elected to Lok Sabha, in views of sixteen persons in future he will be successful as B.J.P. leader, fifteen persons hoped his more popularity in future and nineteen persons viewed he should be President of India.

It is found that Shatrughna Sinha is also a leader of Delhi Unit of Bhartiya Janata Party. In common people, he is very popular in Delhi.

Chapter 7

I. Amitabh Bachchan and Politics
II. Late Smita Patil : Interest in Social Activities and Politics Through Her Films

I. AMITABH BACHCHAN AND POLITICS

No Question of Returning to Politics, said Amitabh Bachchan

Film star Amitabh Bachchan has no plans to make a political comeback. Asked about the possibility of his returning to politics, he replied, "No, never, *"Hamein rajniti karni hi nahin aati, hum rajniti kya karenge"* (I do not know the intricacies of politics, how can I indulge in politics). Mr. Bachchan and his wife, Jaya, spoke to 'The Times of India' News Service on November 29, 1994 in Lucknow, before leaving for Safai village in Etawah district to receive the state government's Yash Bharti award, from Uttar Pradesh then Chief Minister Mulayam Singh Yadav. Asked whether he saw a political motive in Mr. Mulayam Singh's decision to honour him with the Yash Bharti award, he replied: "Where does politics come in? He is honouring me and I am accepting that honour. It is quite simple." Joining in the conversation, Mrs. Bachchan felt it was creditable on the part of the chief minister to think of honouring artists from the state. Both of them agreed that receiving a non-filmi award was a different experience.

The celebrity couple's visit had lent a special aura to the chief minister's residence. The star-struck employees were introduced to the visitors and the culinary skills of each were highlighted—one of them was introduced as the one who had prepared the previous night's dinner, another had made the 'kacharis', the third had cooked the 'rabri' and so on. The star looked amused but moved. Mrs. Bachchan, who used to visit the city when her father was posted here, said she found it quite different since her last visit in 1984. The actress who heads the Children's Film Society of India, felt children were the best part of life. "Children give meaning to life, they make you perceive things with a difference", she said. Fresh from her directorial ventures (serials 'Dekh Bhai Dekh' and 'Saat Phere') on Doordarshan, Mrs. Bachchan is busy making other programmes for the small box. What does Mr. Bachchan do these days? "I just relax at home doing nothing. Since I am unemployed I read all the newspapers", said the superstar.

Amitabh Bachchan's Views about his Father Dr. Harivanshrai Bachchan

"My initial memories are of a father who was a strict disciplinarian. Even the slightest indiscipline was not tolerated even to the extent of removing a pencil which I did once quite unconsciously and I had to pay for it very clearly. I was punished—punished because, one, I, did it without telling and, two, because I did not put it back at the same place. Or if it was soiling the verandah during a mud fight with friends we would actually be made to go down on our knees. He was an absolute stickler for time and there was punishment if we failed to keep timings—punishment which meant standing in a corner or taking away our playing time which was very painful. He had a very short temper and if something went wrong all hell broke loose. As we grew he mellowed—mellowed to a point where he stopped reacting altogether. There has been a sea-change in his temperament. We were all mortally scared of him; many a time we would have to hide behind our mother.

My father is a vegetarian. But he did not mind meat being cooked in the house. He never drank so there was never this alcoholism in the house. For a very long time he had given up eating sweets even though I know than one of his weaknesses in life is Indian sweets. So there has been a lot of sacrifice which one has seen and much was done for our well-being. So one cannot help admiring these. He has always had a great will-power which in later years of my life gave me inspiration and the strength to fight back when ever I have been down and out. Will-power which was exercised with a determined purpose in mind rather than will-power for the sake of will-power. If he would set a deadline, say for completion of a book, then everything thereafter would happen and be done to meet that deadline. There was no entertainment, no distractions—it was just that particular job which had to be done. From him we learnt that the quality for a fight-back must be superior; if we fought something we have not fought frivolously. If there is anger in what we have done or said, I feel it is something within our genes because of what my father believed; because of what he wrote. There has been a lot of anger in his poetry; there has been a lot of revolt also—revolt in one's thinking and I remember one of his lines: "Hai abhi raat par diya jalana kab mana hai...." Yes, the night is dark but who stops you from lighting a lamp. So there are very subtle references but behind these, there is a very questioning kind of revolt......

I have drawn inspiration from what my father wrote particularly when one has been faced with a dilemma. The most obvious has been the recent political fight-back. I know it must have been a very strenuous time for my parents and I know they were deeply disturbed. Even though my father says he did not know much about it, I know that he used to read every bit of the negative which appeared about us in the newspapers. Then I remember one fine day he took out two of his poems and gave them to me. The content was that if someone tried to dishonour you, you must stand up straight and fight back: 'Agar dushman, khinch kar talwar, karta var, Usse nitya pratyashit yahi hai, chahhiye iske liy taiyyar rahna...'.

Throughout these six years of absolute hell that my brother and I went through, these lines would come back to me. I would read and re-read them. These and many more.... lines written in a different context, for different situations which became relevant to me personally.... lines which I would pull out whenever I was down and out including the one which I thought fit in best: 'Main chupana janta to jag mujhe sadhu samajhta, shatru mera ban gaya chhalrahit vyavahar mera....'. These are lines which gave me strength because these is what I genuinely felt at that time. If I knew how to hide, the world would have called me a saint but my own capacity is my 'chhalrahit vyavahar' because I do not have the capacity to play dirty. So all along there has been this great silent force that has been working and which has been an inspiration, a force, a guidance. In his poetry I have often sensed a revolt.... against the system, against a recognised attitude.... always provoking mankind and not necessarily adhering to what is the norm.... not simply looking at something which is set aside from the norm but also learning to appreciate it and at the same time justifying the norm that he has shifted to.... there is philosophy behind the whole thing.... the philosophy of acceptance of the way life is. May be literary recognition that was his came to him late in life but the fact is that he is quite reticent about it and I think it is a healthy attitude. And I have always drawn from that, though as a son I feel that more should have been done, more could have been done and I feel that, yes, he deserved much more.

Research on Amitabh Bachchan

While newspapers and people of various political hues went Amitabh Bachchan bashing for his alleged involvement in Bofors, his fans, without his knowing, rallied around him to salvage his plummeting image. Susmita Dasgupta, who is completing her Ph.D. on the super hero from Jawaharlal Nehru University, New Delhi, says for her M.Phil., she got most of her information from fans. They put their heads together to understand the strong feelings of 'hate', almost as strong as their love, that he could evoke. The fans felt that people look at him through their eyes so it was their responsibility to defend him.

Rajesh Saini in Jaipur switched from B.Sc. physics to law to be able to defend Amitabh better on the Bofors issue. Eddie of Delhi University was just 20 when he watched 'Agnipath' and decided to become like Amitabh. He is keen to become a publisher and begin his career by publishing Susmita's manuscripts. Pankaj Ganatra, 23, is in business in Calcutta but when Amitabh was under attack he began dressing like him and inviting Amitabh fans for premiers of his films. The fans, Susmita says, have internalised their hero. They walk, talk and even live like him. But surprisingly they do not plaster the walls of their homes with his pictures. Susmita claims she can identify an Amitabh fan in a roomful of people. The fans took in their stride Amitabh's peccadiloes, his affairs of the heart. There was no resentment against Rekha for her involvement with their hero. For them, she was like them, above all an Amitabh fan. Rekha just did not have the stature to be his wife, they maintain.

Amitabh, Susmita found, represented the concept of a man who was a threat to be the 'statusquoists'. The Akhil Bhartiya Vidhyarthi Parishad, she says attacked him when he was shooting 'Mein Azad Hoon'. The BJP's anger was with the entire cinema world. It was more of a man-to-man conflict than party conflict.

Susmita's M.Phil. concludes that "Amitabh represented the productive man. In Amitabh, the film world found the formula of eternal self generation." Cinema music found this same capacity for rejuvenation through Kishore Kumar and Lata Mangeshkar, and cricket in Pakistan through Imran Khan. Imran and Amitabh, belong to the same 'biradari' and invariably Amitabh fans are Imran fans. When Imran played cricket to raise funds for a cancer hospital, the Amitabh fan club in Jadavpur raised money. All the royalty from the books that she hopes to publish from her M.Phil. and Ph.D. work will also be donated to the hospital. Susmita's M.Phil. dissertation is dedicated to Vijay Chauhan, the hero 'Agnipath', portrayed by Amitabh. Susmita has seen each of Amitabh's films atleast six times. But 'Agnipath', which she rates a brilliant albeit complicated film, she has seen 20 times in different cinema halls in different cities. Susmita thinks 'Sholey' is central to the Amitabh Bachchan image. Amitabh himself thinks it is 'Deewar'. 'Anand', 'Don', 'Amar Akbar Anthony', 'Zanjeer' and 'Mukaddar ka Sikandar' have all helped portray a definite image of Amitabh, she says. But Susmita is quite clear that the actor and star image of Amitabh are quite different. In 'Saudagar' he is an actor not a star. Actors faithfully follow the storyline but the stars adopt the script with their vision and personalised interpretation of the characters they play.

TV-18 wants to televise her dissertation on the theme 'Why Muslims are Amitabh fans?' It was while watching 'Namak Halal' in Calcutta that Susmita noticed the reverence the Muslims had for Amitabh. All his films go through the Islamic route and are big hits there. After watching an Amitabh movie, a senior international civil servant based in Sudan is believed to have exclaimed 'He is like a prophet.' 'Dressing up for the super hero', was part of the Amitabh cult. In colleges she found fans shampooing their hair and sprucing up for Amitabh movies. Susmita bathes before she sits down to work on the dissertation. In Calcutta, Pankaj would fast for three days before organising an Amitabh Bachchan premier. Her enthusiasm to research and write on Amitabh, however, was not shared by the great hero initially. Though he gave her a two-hour interview, he seemed confused as to why she should want to do her M.Phil. on him. But when the project was completed and sent to him he was surprised and pleased. With his cooperation she has been able to meet several people from the film world for her Ph.D. work. If Amitabh has a macho image on the screen, at home he is 'feminine' and absent-minded, says Susmita. He will fuss over his guest at the dining table asking for 'achchar' and 'papad'. He will lose his spectacles and blame everyone around.

Amitabh Bachchan inaugurated a Studio in Noida, near Delhi

The film industry had finally treaded towards northern region of the country. The honour to play host had been bestowed on a developing modern township bordering Delhi, Noida. Its advent was formalised with the inauguration of a fully equipped studio Kabuki, by the matinee idol Amitabh Bachchan in Noida on April 13, 1991. The occasion also marked the 'muhurat' of the first ever full length feature film to be shot in this upcoming film city. Mr. Bachchan also gave the clap for the muhurat shot of the Bengali film titled 'Bondhu' which featured another leading film artiste Dany Denzongpa. Mr. Bachchan paid glouring tributes to former chief minister of U.P. Mr. Vir Bahadur Singh for planning a film city in Noida. He disclosed that during his short tenure as member of the Lok Sabha, Mr. Singh who was then chief minister of the state, frequently interacted with him and showed keen interest to do 'something' for the film industry. The idea finally took shape in the form of the Noida film city, he added.

Talking to reporters after the inaugural ceremony, the super star said he had once for all decided to bid adieu to politics. "I would not even campaign for the Congress-I during the ensuing parliamentary elections. It is a firm decisions," he added. Referring to the present state of the film industry, he admitted that the standard had drastically gone down. The great paucity of written words was one of the main reason for this downward slide, he felt. Comparing the film industry of three decades back to the present one, he poetically remarked, "Us Waqat bahut thehrav tha. Jeevan mein kavita thi jo abh nahin hai," (There was consistency and life had a charm). He disagreed that the present state of turmoil in the country has its causes in the film industry. Films showed more violence but no film propagated sectarian and secessionist tendencies. And which film influenced communal violence, he asked. "To my mind, the film industry gets the ideas from society and not *vice-versa*", he added.

Regarding his future plans, he said he would take time off after completing his present assignments. "I am already 50. After completing two, three films which I am present working in, I will decide what kind of roles I should perform. I cannot do roles, which I did ten years back," he added.

II. LATE SMITA PATIL : INTEREST IN SOCIAL ACTIVITIES AND POLITICS THROUGH HER FILMS

Smita Patil, one of the very few talented actresses that it had seen in recent times, passed away in the midnight of December 13, 1986. According to the doctor who had attended on her at the Jaslok Hospital in South Bombay, where she had been brought in a state of coma from her residence on Carter Road in North Bombay early Previous night, She died and of "Viral Encephalitis" and "disseminated intravascular coagulpathy", which had caused a fall in her blood platelets and fibrinogen loading to internal hae-morrhage. Smita had suffered a bout of flu on December 8, 1986. On December 12, 1986, she was found bleeding through her nose and mouth and was then rushed to Jaslok Hospital, Bombay. On the way to the hospital she fell into a coma from which she never regained consciousness in spite of the panel of doctors, headed by Dr. R.P. Soonawalla, gynaecologist and Dr. Wadia, the eminent neuron surgeon.

Smita Patil's Place on Indian Cinema

The all-India Hindi film was stormed by a galaxy of brilliant heroines-Rehana Sultan, Raakhee, Jaya Bhaduri, Rekha, Sridevi, Jayaprada and of course, the golden triangle-Zeenat Aman, Parveen Babi and Hema Malini, Rehana, after 'Chetna' and 'Dastak', became a slave to her own image and was lost in the wilderness of the Bombay Cinema, Raakhee made a mark in '27 down' (and later in 'Paroma' and Amma) but marriage had taken a toll of her career. So it was with the 'Guddi' girl Jaya Bhaduri. Along with Zarina Wahab and Rameshwari, she was a great hope. All three could not blossom in the poisonous environment of the masala film. Rekha reached great height of popularity with her performances in the masala cinema. But looking back, what does she have to be remembered after her ? Just two roles-'Umrao Jaan' and 'Utsav'. Both Sridevi and Jayaprada have yet to make a socially relevant and meaningful film, despite their immense hold on the moviegoers. As for the golden triangle, Parveen Bobby, like Geeta Bali, remained a girl in search of role of a role. Zeenat Aman demolished all the past images of the screen heroine and project a liberated woman, especially in 'Hare Rama Hare Krishna'. Did she beyond it? No, her image shackled her. Hema Malini, who tried consciously to shape her carrier, ended up with only three memorable roles. 'Meera' 'Razia Sultan' 'and Rano in' 'Ek Chadar Maili Si'.

As against them, take the case of Shabana Azmi and Smita Patil. Neither the history of the Indian film art nor of screen histrionics in India, in respect of female performers, can be written without reference to their works. From 1974, when Shabana made her straining debut in Shyam Benegal's 'Ankur', till 1986 when Tarang was released on the national book-up, any discussion of Indian Cinema from any angle-histrionic, aesthetic, sociological or artistic (except technique)—has to go back and forth between the works of just these two artistes. This is not an elitist judgment but a conclusion that would hold its validity against all odds. At least 20 films of Shabana Azmi and as many of Smita Patil will go down as social documents of our time for the simple reason that the masala cinema has no time for contemporary issues. Is 'Ram Teri Ganga Maili' a social document ? Hence, at a young age, these girls sat on international juries and are known, discussed and admired abroad. Shabana Azmi holds the world record with four national best actress awards—with an unprecedented three in a row. Smita Patil with two national best actress awards, and Sarada with three, the total tally of these three young women come to 9 out 19 given away upto 1986. If Smita Patil had lived longer, she, along with Shabana or Sarda, could have brough. to the country the same honour which Nargis did three decades ago.

The premature and tragic death of Smita Patil is blow to Indian Cinema. And to the so called 'art-waala', it is an irreparable loss, for Smita Patil not only left behind a 20-day old infant but also the also 22-year old still uncertain 'art' cinema. Shabana Azmi and Smita Patil were the two wheels of the cart of 'art' cinema which lies derailed now. These two extra ordinarily gifted women, supported by two unusually gifted actors—the versatile Nasseeruddin Shah and the Virile Om Puri—took the message of thinking cinema to the people, built for it a mass base and achieved a mass following. What an irony that the parallel-waalas started off with a rebellion against the star system and themselves created a new breed of stars, whose lumuniscence could not be dinned by the masala cinema. These four and Sarada (in Malayalam) gave to the people of India a new screen star, who was closer to the experiences of the multitudes outside the movie houses. In other words, they created a new star sensibility. Think of it, it all happened over the last one and a half decades. The earth is really shining very fast. Smita Patil is the fifth most celebrated Maharashtrian actress after Durgabai, Shanta Apte, Nalini Jaywant and the peerless Nutan. Discoveres by Dr. Jabbar Patel, groomed by Shyam Benegal, tested by Satyajit Ray and Mrinal Sen and harnessed by a dozen others, Smita Patil rose lied a meteor, as did Shabana Azmi. Her film 'Saamna', in Marathi the debut film of director Dr. Jabbar Patel, was released in the spring of 1975. (Her first released film 'Raja Shiv Chhatrapati' was directed by Chandravadan). It was, after Satyadev Dubey's 'Shantata Court Chaloo Aahe', the second Marathi film in a new mould. Unlike the latter, producer

Ramdas Phutane and director Jabbar Patel had lensed 'Saamna' entirely outdoors. It was a film about exploitation and was opposed by the sugar barons of Marathawada. A brief lull ensue1 in which Smita Patil appeared in side roles in two Shyam Benegal films, 'Charandas Chor', the first satirical film for children, and 'Nishant', in which she appeared with Sabana, for whom it was the second film. Together they made Several films. The gossip Press sought to sow discord between them, as they had done earlier between Mohammed Rafi and Kishore Kumar and later between Dr. Jabbar Patel and his theatre colleague Amol Palekar. When Smita was in a coma, one of the first persons to reach her place was Shabana Azmi. In Mahesh Bhatt's 'Arth', Smita, playing the model Kavita Sanyal, had walked out of the life of the hero, to save his marriage with Pooja, interpreted by Shabana. Being women and sensitive artistes, they had a much deeper consideration for each other than the gossip press could grasp, because it is steeped, in the cut-and-tried relationship of the masala cinema. Like the declaration Kishore Kumar issued: 'I am a fan of Rafi' Shabana and Smita came together in Shyam Benegal 'Mandi' (1983) to make it a histrionic duet of Indian cinema. Shabana is the lonelier without Smita, just parting of Rafi more than anyone else.

This mention of personal equations between these two great heroines is intended to allude to their care do in the film medium. While Shabana made 'Paar', she also made 'Amar Akbar Anthony'. Smita made 'Umbartha' with as much devotion to her role as she did in 'Shakti' or 'Namak Halal'. And there lies the point. The masala film is made for recycling the box office image of a male 'Sntaar' and heroine fills the bill only to the extent of providing light diversion as the object of male perversities in song-dance sequences. That is the masala waala's concept of sex. Rekha is made the unlikely mother of a grown up daughter in 'Insaaf Ki Awaaz' and is shown, despite being cast as a trained police officer, lynched by hooligans, while a lone Anil Kapoor supposed to be an advocate, smashes a whole gang of them single-handedly. This corruption of the concept of the heroine took a heavy toll of all those talented women who entered movies—from Rehana Sultan down to Sridevi or Richa Sharma (whole only job in 'Insaaf Ki Awaaz' is to bare her lower limbs). Zeenat Aman and Parveen Babi did not resist tne male exploitation and lost the gamble. Hema Malini did, as had Waheeda Rehman, and outlasted the other two. If she had too would have been forced to go the Richa Sharma way. But this restraint caused Hema a lot in the Cumulative trash of the masala cinema. She had to wait a quarter century to do roles, such as 'Meera', 'Razia Sultan' and 'Rano'. A quarter century is an awfully long time in the life of an artiste.

Hema Malini like Zeenat and Parveen, was sustained on the throne of stardom by the sinister logic of the masala cinema which chained them to the image of the golden bird in a cage, or better still, of the goose that lays the golden egg. Can anyone imagine the agony of Hema Malini and others like her in seeking to become an artiste, a cut above the glamour girl for the pleasures of the deviate hero ? With the talent they had, they too must have aspired to play the roles Shabana and Smita Played—roles that assured them growth as artistes and brought renown and recognition, a shade better than the applause she received playing, a tongawaali in 'Sholay'. Hema and others too must have desired to walk to the rostrum of Vigyan Bhawan to receive the Silver Lotus from the President of India. But their desiness were frustrated by the suffocation of the massala cinema whose heroes, except Sanjeev Kumar and Sunil Dutt, never saw beyond themselves. So long as Mehboob, Bimal Roy and Guru Dutt lived, a new comer Waheeda Rehman could hope to play the street-walker Gulabo (in 'Pyassa'-1957), a young Nutan could aspire to play 'Sujata' -1959: an educated Kamini Kaushal could play 'Biraj Bahu', a dancer-actress Vyjayanthimala could play Chandramukhi (in 'Devdas'-1955), a talented Nimmi could play Sonia (in 'Amar'-1954), a buoyant Nalini Jaywant could play Sushama (in 'Shikast'-1953), a sedate Nirupa Roy could play the dispossessed peasant woman (in 'Do Bigha Zamina'-1953), a Madhubala could become a national dream by playing the Malan (in 'Mahal'), and a Meena Kumari could attain immortality by playing Sheetal (in 'Deera'). The heroines in these films had a symbiotic relationship with the film and grew in artistic stature with the film. Alas, Hema and her other contemporaries could never achieve this harmony between their heat and their work.

If thousands of common people joined the funeral procession of Smita Patil (on a working day December 15, 1986), as they had done when Madhubala or Meena Kumari or Nargis had died, it was because of the memory of the women they had portrayed on the screen. It was not their bodies that the people cherished but their souls and the souls of the women who lived in their persons when they were impersonating a Dhanno, a Biraj, Chandramukhi a Sheetal... ... . This, there is the mystique of Smita Patil, Shabana Azmi and Sarada. Their films did not camouflage life but unmasked it. They built their reputation on such films and earned recognition.

As a result, they did not have to come to the commercial waala. The commercial waala went to them. Shabana fully and Smita to a certain extent worked in the masala cinema on their own terms. Hence, the masala-waalas could not subjugate or destroy them, as they had the other heroined. The identity and place of Shabana and Smita remained intact even when they made 'Ashanti' or 'Namak Halal'. Shabana and Smita even become the envy of the most glamorous and the most successful box office stars—male or female. In other words, they could assert themselves. In other words, they could assert themselves. That two young girls accomplished this all within the span of a decade reveals the hower of that creative spark which resides in every human heart but was benumbed in the other heroines when they bowed to the logic of the masala film. It is this pulsation of the soul that distinguishes the human from the non-human. Be it the transition of Indian society, or the complex socio-economic issues of our time, the many facets of Indian womanhood on the art of acting and interpretation of life through acting, or even the journey of our movies, no one can write an account of our film culture without mentioning.

— The Rabaari Woman Bindu of 'Manthan'-1976;

— Of the tarmented actress Usha of 'Bhumika' the self-sacrificing tribal girl Chindi of 'Jait Re Jait'-1977;

— The dispossessed villager's wife Khairun longing in separation from her husband in 'Gaman'-1978;

— The existentialist slum woman Amma who sees life in the raw in 'Chakra' the Harijan woman Ujana fooling a king in 'Bhavani Bhavai', the disabled catholic girl Joan Pinto in 'Albert Pinto Ko... ... ..., the prosperous actress enacting a rural woman in a village of want in 'Apaler Sandhane' and the hapless tribal lass Nagi raped and murdered in 'Aakrosh'-1980;

— The social reformer Sueabha who fights against women's exploitation in a reformatory and is herself given up by her-in-laws in 'Jmbartha', and the helpless Harijan wife Dukhia torn by the death of her husband on the day of their daughter's marriage in 'Sadgati'-1981;

— The self... ... assured model Kavita Sanyal who rears a drone seeking to run away from his wife in 'Arth'... ... 1982;

— The witness of virgin-hunting in a Karnataka village in 'Giddh'-1984;

— The seduced and abandoned attendant at a temple in 'Chidambaram and the maid servant (of an industrialist) who keeps the proletarian protest alive in 'Tarang'-1985.

These are but a few of her many roles that mirrored the human condition in our time. Except for Shabana and Smita did anyone else project such a range of human relationships through her films? On top of it, Smita was the only actress of Indian Cinema who worked in films in seven languages. This then is the place of Smita Patil—Indian Cinema's girl next door whom we shall not see again.

PART III

Chapter 8

Surveyed Political Study of Shivaji Ganesan

I. SHIVAJI GANESAN : AN EXTRA-ORDINARY PERSONALITY

On October 1, 1927, a boy named Villupuram Chinnaiah Pillai Ganeshamurthy alias Sivaji Ganesan was born into a humble family. His father was a modest railway worker and an Indian freedom fighter who was in and out of prison for his political beliefs and activities. As the poor lonely mother struggled hard to keep the wolf away from her thin cracked doors, the boy Ganesan dropped out of school and ran away from home to join a 'Boys company' and go on stage as an actor. While at school he had watched a 'therukoothu' (street theatre) performance of the play based on the life and turbulent times of a Tamil chieftain, a rebel. One of first in India to raise the sceptre of freedom and fight against the autocratic East India Company, named Veera Pandya Kattaboman. The character, his rebellious spirit, his love for his mother land and freedom deeply impressed this sensitive lad, and instilled in him a sense of patriotism, a hatred for the ruling British, who were ill-treating his father, and a love for theatre. This interest had taken deep roots in his heart, soul and skin and driven him to abandon his home and 'boys' company.

'Boys' companies were theatre troupes in Tamil Nadu consisting only of boys, in their pre-teens and teens. All roles in plays, male and female were enacted by boys, and this concept found great favour and proved highly successful.

II. ACTRESS PADMINI'S VIEWS ABOUT SIVAJI GANESAN

Padmini told a film journalist Ayyappa Prasad in 1991—"My first film with Sivaji Ganesan was in 1951-52. The film was 'Panam' produced by Kavignar Kannadasan and directed by N.S. Krishnan. I remember the first scene in the film with him was a marriage scene and on the same day his real marriage was to take place. After the scene he left to attend his wedding. After that I worked in forty-fifty films with him. The last two films which I did with him were 'Thaik Oru Talat' and 'Lakshmi Vandachu'. The big hit film that we were paired in was 'Thillana' that was before I left in 1968. 'Managayar Thilakam', 'Devai Piravai', 'Thanga Padamai' were some of the many films with him that ran. Out of the forty-fifty films that I have acted with him, I think only about four to five films may not have run for reasons one cannot fathom. 'Katabooman', 'Vietnam Veedu' are again well known hits that we have acted together in. In 1990, one of our students of the dancing school wanted to conduct her arangetram in India and I called up Sivaji Ganesan from abroad and told him that he must be the chief guest. He immediately agreed and came for the function. I assumed that he would not sit through the whole function because of his health. He was ill at that time. He said that he would go only after the final curtain was drawn. It was so nice of him to sit through the function and make it a grand success. Whenever he comes abroad to stay with his friend, I send him home cooked food. Ours is a long standing association of forty years. To date we have never had any rifts or misunderstandings, though we started out as young stars.

As a co-artiste he was very helpful. He would give us all the encouragement and applaud us we did a good job. He would do that with any newcomer too and with other artistes. He would ask us whether he gave a good shot or not. It was a two way communication. I remember an incident while shooting for the film 'Ethir Parathu': In the film we are lovers and Sivaji goes to join the army and circumstances force me to marry his father. Sivaji comes back and we meet. He makes advances towards me. I had to rain blows on him and slap him. I was nervous. How could I hit him? He said, 'do not worry', just hit me with all your strength; I hit him and continued to hit even after the director said 'cut out'. His face was swollen and for days he could not shoot. In another film he had to hit me and he hit me so hard that one of my earrings went flying off somewhere. If there was any important function in his house, I would be invited. I did not attend his marriage but attended his first son Ramu's birthday. He has also attended many important functions at my house.

I remember one touching gesture of his. We were shooting in Hognekal-Kaveri for the film 'Iru Dhruvangal'. My husband had a cardiac trouble and he was in Tellichery. Nobody knew how to convey the news to me when the telegram arrived. He took the bold step and told me. He offered his dates and said that the shooting be stopped so that I could go to meet my husband. He arranged for a car to take me to Tellichery. I think there is no person to replace Sivaji. He has proved to the whole world that he is a great actor. In the film 'Navarathri' he enacted nine different roles. Nobody can match this feat. The dialogue in "Kattabooman', who can say it like him. For 'Tillana Mohanambal', the director was Shanmugha Sundaram and he had a gang of persons like Balan Annan, A.V.M. Rajan and others. He divided us into two groups and gave us separate rooms so as to create the mood of rivalry. That was why the film was a success.

During the shooting of 'Kattabooman', I had a duet with Gemini and nobody told me that at the end of the shot a snake has to come in because everybody knew .hat I am afraid of snakes. When the snake suddenly popped up I ran for my life and nobody would allow me to go out of the sets. Sivaji was there and he told me that I need not worry because the snake's mouth was stitched but I was not willing to believe him. It was nice working with him after a long gap in 'Thaik Oru Talat' directed by Balachandran Menon. Just like olden days we used to sit together and discuss the past. He and I remember the past very well. I rang him up from London and spoke to him when I heard about his ailment in Singapore."

III. SPECIAL JURY AWARD TO SIVAJI GANESAN FOR THE YEAR 1992

A special Jury Award has been conferred on Sivaji Ganesan for his performance in 'Thevar Magan' (Tamil) for the year 1992, it was announced in New Delhi on April 5, 1993. Bhagavad Geeta, G.V. Iyer's second Sanskrit film, has won the Swarna Kamal, renamed as the Satyajit Ray Award. The national award for the second best feature film has gone to 'Padma Nadir Majhi' directed by Goutam Ghose. The jury announced the national award on April 5, 1993 lauded G.V. Iyer for successfully translating the immortal philosophy of the Bhagavad Geeta into a powerful cinematic idiom. G.V. Iyer's first Sanskrit film on Adi Shankaracharya had also won national acclaim. Balu Mahendra chaired the jury. The Indira Gandhi Award for the best among the first films of directors has gone to Pamela Rook's 'Miss Beatty's Children', while 'Sargam' (Malayalam), directed by Hariharan has been adjudged the best popular film. The Nargis Dutt Award for the best feature film on national integration was conferred on Mani Rathnam's 'Roja' (Tamil), while best film on family welfare is 'Shwet Paatharer Thala (Bengali) directed by Prabhat Roy.

Visu's 'Neenga Nalla Irukkanam (Tamil, where Tamil Nadu Chief Minister J. Jayalalitha plays a major role) was named the best film on prohibition, women and child welfare, anti-dowry, drug abuse. Best film on environment was adjudged 'Cheluvi' (Hindi), directed by Girish Karnad; Best Children's film: 'Mujhse Dosti Karoge' (Hindi), Directed by: Gopi Desai; Best Direction: Gautam Ghose; Best actor: Mithun Chakravarty (Tahder Katha); Best actress: Dimple Kapadia (Rudali); Best supporting actor: Sunny Deol (Damini); Best supporting actress: Revathi Menon (Thevar Magan); Best child artiste: Master Amit Phalke (Mujhse Dosti Karoge). The awards for best male and female playback singer went to Dr. Raj Kumar (Jeevana Chaitia, Kannada) and S. Janaki (Thevar Magan); Best Cinematography: Venu (Miss Beatty's Children); Best Screenplay: M.T. Vasudevan Nair (Sadayam); Best audiography: Pandurangan (Thevar Magan); Best Editing: M.S. Mani (Sargam); Art Direction: Sameer Chanda (Rudali); Costume designer: Mala Dey (Rudali); Music direction: A.R. Rahman (Roja); Lyrics: Vairamuthu (Roja). Special effects award went to K. Sashilal Nair (Angaar); Choreography: Laxmibai Kolhapurker (Ek Hota Vidhushak). The best non-feature film Award was bagged by 'In Search of Indian Theatre' directed by Abhijit Chattopadhyay; Best non-feature film of a director: 'Knock Out', Tamil, directed by B. Lenin; Best Anthropological film: 'Wangal—A Garo Festival' (English, by Bappa Ray); Best biographical film: 'Pandit Bhimsen Joshi (Hindi, Guljar); Best Arts/Cultural film: The Recluse (Hindi, by Arvind Sinha) and Suchitra Mitra (Bengali, Raja Sen); Best scientific film: Chunauti (Dinkar Chaudhuri, Marathi).

Shivaji Ganesan is also honoured by Dada Saheb Phalke Award.

Table 8.1
Detailed Study of Shivaji Ganesan's One Hundred Political Supporters in Delhi in July 1997

S. No.	*Name of the Person*	*Sex*	*Age (in years)*	*Urban/ Rural*	*Religion*	*Whether SC/ST*	*Family's income P.M. (in Rs.)*	*Edu- cation*	*Occup- ation*	*No. of His watched Political Films*	*View about His Political Future*
1	2	3	4	5	6	7	8	9	10	11	12
1.	Laxmi Rajan	Female	25	Urban	Hindu	Nil	3000.00	M.A.	Housewife	15	May be C.M. of Tamil Nadu
2.	Vankat Damodaran	Male	40	Urban	Hindu	Nil	4000.00	B.A.	Service	20	May be Renominated to Rajya Sabha
3.	P. Ramchandran	Male	39	Rural	Hindu	SC	3600.00	M.A.	Service	10	Should be President of India
4.	Latha Chandran	Female	36	Urban	Hindu	Nil	3400.00	Inter	Housewife	25	May be C.M. of Tamil Nadu
5.	V. Krishanan	Male	31	Urban	Hindu	Nil	3100.00	B.A.	Business	25	More popular in future
6.	M. Mathew	Male	26	Urban	Christian	Nil	2400.00	Matric	Service	05	May be Re-nominated to Rajya Sabha
7.	Janki Raman	Female	27	Urban	Hindu	Nil	5000.00	B.A.	Housewife	10	More popular in future
8.	R. Dasan	Male	31	Rural	Hindu	SC	2400.00	M.A.	Service	15	May be C.M. of Tamil Nadu
9.	M. Ibraham	Male	40	Urban	Muslim	Nil	1800.00	Matric	Service	08	May be Re-nominated to Rajya Sabha
10.	Usha Sheshan	Female	32	Urban	Hindu	Nil	3300.00	M.A.	Service	12	Should be President of India
11.	Latha Dasan	Female	27	Rural	Hindu	SC	2100.00	B.A.	Housewife	17	May be C.M. of Tamil Nadu
12.	Mary Thomas	Female	24	Urban	Christian	Nil	2400.00	Matric	Service	15	More popular in future
13.	R. Krishnan	Male	42	Urban	Hindu	Nil	4200.00	M.Sc.	Business	10	Should be President of India
14.	Meenakshi Vaman	Female	29	Rural	Hindu	Nil	2700.00	Inter	Housewife	20	More popular in future
15.	Kartar Singh	Male	27	Urban	Sikh	SC	1900.00	Matric	Service	09	May be C.M. of Tamil Nadu
16.	Akshay Jain	Male	29	Rural	Jain	Nil	2200.00	B.Sc.	Business	12	More popular in future

(Contd.)

1	2	3	4	5	6	7	8	9	10	11	12
17.	Sumit Mehta	Male	33	Urban	Hindu	Nil	2700.00	M.Com	Business	18	Should be President of India
18.	Vanda... Das	Female	25	Urban	Hindu	Nil	3400.00	M.Sc.	Service	22	May be Re-nominated to Rajya Sabha
19.	Virendra Kumar	Male	36	Rural	Hindu	SC	2200.00	Inter	Service	18	More popular in future
20.	Kamlesh Kaur	Female	31	Rural	Sikh	Nil	2500.00	B.A.	Housewife	15	May be C.M. of Tamil Nadu
21.	Leonord David	Male	26	Urban	Christian	Nil	2800.00	M.A.	Service	10	May be C.M. of Tamil Nadu
22.	Jagat Singh	Male	22	Rural	Hindu	SC	2100.00	B.A.	Student	15	More popular in future
23.	Harjit Singh	Male	29	Urban	Sikh	Nil	2700.00	M.A.	Business	10	Should be President of India
24.	Manoj Kumar	Male	27	Rural	Hindu	SC	2600.00	Matric	Service	15	More popular in future
25.	Nafis Ahmad	Male	29	Urban	Muslim	Nil	3400.00	Inter	Business	18	Should be President of India
26.	Rajia Ahmad	Female	22	Urban	Muslim	Nil	3000.00	B.Sc.	Student	10	May be C.M. of Tamil Nadu
27.	Janaki Devi	Female	29	Rural	Buddhist	SC	2200.00	Matric	Housewife	04	More popular in future
28.	Amit Kumar	Male	21	Rural	Hindu	SC	2300.00	Inter	Student	08	May be C.M. of Tamil Nadu
29.	Hans Raj	Male	29	Rural	Hindu	Nil	3100.00	Matric	Business	16	May be C.M. of Tamil Nadu
30.	Jagdish Prasad	Male	36	Rural	Hindu	SC	2200.00	B.Sc.	Service	08	More popular in future
31.	Suchint Kumar	Male	27	Urban	Hindu	Nil	2700.00	B.Com.	Service	20	Should be President of India
32.	Achla Narula	Female	29	Urban	Hindu	Nil	3400.00	M.Com.	Business	22	May be C.M. of Tamil Nadu
33.	Jyotsna Raghuvansi	Female	33	Rural	Hindu	Nil	3100.00	B.Sc.	Housewife	18	More popular in future
34.	Jatin Khanna	Male	36	Urban	Hindu	Nil	4000.00	M.Sc.	Service	15	May be C.M. of Tamil Nadu
35.	Shri B^L gwan	Male	40	Rural	Hindu	SC	2400.00	Matric	Service	05	May be Re-nominated to Rajya Subha
36.	Nafisa Khan	Female	34	Rural	Muslim	Nil	2600.00	Matric	Housewife	10	May be C.M. of Tamil Nadu
37.	Rehana Ansari	Female	31	Urban	Muslim	Nil	3300.00	Inter	Service	15	More popular in future

(Contd.)

1	2	3	4	5	6	7	8	9	10	11	12
38.	Dipak Kumar	Male	27	Rural	Buddhist	SC	2500.00	Matric	Business	15	Should be President of India
39.	Parul Gupta	Female	29	Urban	Hindu	Nil	4000.00	M.A.	Business	12	May be C.M. of Tamil Nadu
40.	Swarn Singh	Male	31	Urban	Sikh	Nil	3500.00	M.Com.	Service	10	More popular in future
41.	Jasprit Kaur	Female	30	Rural	Sikh	Nil	4000.00	B.Com.	Housewife	05	May be C.M. of Tamil Nadu
42.	Marlin Davis	Female	24	Urban	Christian	Nil	3700.00	B.Sc.	Student	12	May be C.M. of Tamil Nadu
43.	Victor Davis	Male	22	Urban	Christian	Nil	3700.00	B.A.	Student	08	More popular in future
44.	Abida Hasan	Female	30	Rural	Muslim	Nil	2500.00	Inter	Housewife	20	May be C.M. of Tamil Nadu
45.	Prem Das	Male	28	Rural	Hindu	SC	2100.00	Matric	Service	08	More popular in future
46.	Virendra Uppal	Male	31	Urban	Hindu	Nil	2700.00	B.Com.	Service	08	May be Re-nominated to Rajya Sabha
47.	Bhaskar Rao	Male	25	Urban	Hindu	Nil	3600.00	B.Sc.	Student	12	May be C.M. of Tamil Nadu
48.	A. Charles	Male	42	Urban	Christian	Nil	3100.00	M.Com.	Service	15	More popular in future
49.	R. Manoharan	Male	25	Urban	Hindu	SC	2600.00	B.Sc.	Student	22	May be C.M. of Tamil Nadu
50.	Subba Rao	Male	29	Urban	Hindu	Nil	3500.00	M.Com.	Service	18	Should be President of India
51.	Rameshwar Singh	Male	34	Rural	Hindu	SC	2200.00	B.Com.	Business	15	May be C.M. of Tamil Nadu
52.	Rampyari Devi	Female	25	Rural	Hindu	Nil	2700.00	B.A.	Business	10	May be C.M. of Tamil Nadu
53.	Satpal Singh	Male	27	Urban	Hindu	Nil	3600.00	M.A.	Service	08	More popular in future
54.	Ganeshi Das	Male	27	Urban	Hindu	SC	3200.00	Matric	Business	15	May be C.M. of Tamil Nadu
55.	Onkar Singh	Male	36	Rural	Hindu	Nil	1600.00	Inter	Service	10	More popular in future
56.	Ramjan Khan	Male	31	Rural	Muslim	Nil	2400.00	B.A.	Business	15	May be C.M. of Tamil Nadu
57.	Madan Lal	Male	22	Rural	Hindu	SC	1800.00	B.Com.	Student	18	Should be President of India
58.	A.K. Khanduri	Male	27	Urban	Hindu	Nil	3500.00	M.Sc.	Student	21	May be C.M. of Tamil Nadu
59.	Devika Rani	Female	29	Urban	Hindu	Nil	3000.00	M.A.	Housewife	12	More popular in future

(Contd.)

1	2	3	4	5	6	7	8	9	10	11	12
60.	Lalit Narain Gupta	Male	35	Urban	Hindu	Nil	3200.00	B.Sc.	Business	05	May be Re-nominated to Rajya Sabha
61.	Banwari Lal	Male	45	Rural	Hindu	SC	1600.00	Matric	Service	08	May be C.M. of Tamil Nadu
62.	Uday Singh	Male	25	Urban	Hindu	Nil	3600.00	B.A.	Student	15	More popular in future
63.	J.N. Verma	Male	29	Urban	Hindu	Nil	2700.00	Matric	Business	10	May be C.M. of Tamil Nadu
64.	Kanchan Bala	Female	32	Rural	Hindu	SC	1800.00	Inter	Housewife	09	More popular in future
65.	Harmesh Gandhi	Male	43	Urban	Hindu	Nil	4500.00	M.Com.	Business	13	Should be President of India
66.	Shanti Devi	Female	40	Rural	Hindu	SC	1700.00	Inter	Housewife	11	May be C.M. of Tamil Nadu
67.	Satya Prakash Sethi	Male	37	Urban	Jain	Nil	4300.00	M.A.	Business	16	More popular in future
68.	Manak Chand Sogani	Male	34	Urban	Jain	Nil	4500.00	B.A.	Business	14	May be Re-nominated to Rajya Sabha
69.	Dhanlaxmi Jain	Female	25	Urban	Jain	Nil	4000.00	M.A.	Student	12	May be C.M. of Tamil Nadu
70.	Dharam Das	Male	26	Rural	Buddhist	SC	3400.00	B.A.	Student	16	More popular in future
71.	Uday Narain Singh	Male	36	Urban	Hindu	Nil	2900.00	M.Sc.	Business	08	May be C.M. of Tamil Nadu
72.	Jamna Prasad	Male	27	Rural	Hindu	SC	1800.00	Matric	Service	11	Should be President of India
73.	Ganga Singh	Male	24	Urban	Sikh	Nil	2700.00	B.A.	Student	09	May be C.M. of Tamil Nadu
74.	Anguri Devi	Female	36	Urban	Hindu	Nil	1900.00	Matric	Housewife	12	More popular in future
75.	Gomati Devi	Female	32	Urban	Hindu	Nil	2300.00	Inter	Business	06	May be C.M. of Tamil Nadu
76.	Bhairon Singh	Male	25	Rural	Hindu	ST	1900.00	B.Com.	Student	17	May be Re-nominated to Rajya Sabha
77.	Anil Maheshwari	Male	26	Rural	Hindu	Nil	4300.00	B.Sc.	Student	15	May be C.M. of Tamil Nadu
78.	Shaiani Nelson	Female	24	Urban	Christian	ST	2700.00	B.Com.	Student	16	More popular in future
79.	Karan Chand Sogani	Male	27	Urban	Jain	Nil	3600.00	M.Com.	Business	08	May be C.M. of Tamil Nadu

(Contd.)

1	2	3	4	5	6	7	8	9	10	11	12
80.	Hiranand Aswani	Male	29	Rural	Hindu	Nil	2700.00	B.A.	Service	10	More popular in future
81.	Dilavar Singh	Male	25	Urban	Sikh	Nil	3600.00	M.A.	Business	06	Should be President of India
82.	Ram Singh	Male	34	Urban	Hindu	Nil	3100.00	B.A.	Business	15	May be C.M. of Tamil Nadu
83.	J.N. Awasthi	Male	41	Urban	Hindu	Nil	2900.00	M.A.	Service	10	May be Re-nominated to Rajya Sabha
84.	Sanjay Verma	Male	23	Urban	Hindu	Nil	2600.00	B.A.	Service	15	May be C.M. of Tamil Nadu
85.	Arun Sharma	Male	37	Rural	Hindu	Nil	2400.00	M.A.	Business	10	More popular in future
86.	Rahul Bishnoi	Male	32	Rural	Hindu	Nil	2800.00	Inter	Service	08	Should be President of India
87.	Kishan Swaroop	Male	34	Rural	Hindu	SC	3400.00	M.Sc.	Business	18	More popular in future
88.	Vimal Munda	Male	24	Urban	Hindu	ST	2700.00	B.Sc.	Student	12	May be C.M. of Tamil Nadu
89.	Kamal Kishore	Male	27	Rural	Hindu	SC	1800.00	B.A.	Business	10	More popular in future
90.	Vishnu Kant	Male	29	Urban	Hindu	Nil	2300.00	M.A.	Service	05	May be Re-nominated to Rajya Sabha
91.	Gulam Mohammad Ansari	Male	45	Rural	Muslim	Nil	1900.00	B.A.	Business	18	May be C.M. of Tamil Nadu
92.	Janardan Gahlot	Male	27	Urban	Hindu	Nil	3100.00	M.A.	Student	08	More popular in future
93.	Rajesh Verma	Male	37	Rural	Hindu	Nil	2700.00	B.A.	Service	12	May be C.M. of Tamil Nadu
94.	Anand Swaroop Mathur	Male	34	Urban	Hindu	Nil	3500.00	M.Sc.	Business	18	Should be President of India
95.	Gurcharan Singh Ahuja	Male	33	Urban	Sikh	Nil	4500.00	B.Com.	Business	15	May be C.M. of Tamil Nadu
96.	Jarnail Singh Manchanda	Male	45	Urban	Sikh	Nil	4000.00	M.A.	Service	05	More popular in future
97.	Kamal Nayan Singh	Male	27	Rural	Hindu	SC	1800.00	Matric	Service	08	May be C.M. of Tamil Nadu
98.	Jay Bhagwan Jatav	Male	29	Rural	Hindu	SC	1900.00	Inter	Service	12	More popular in future
99.	Khajan Singh Gahlot	Male	35	Urban	Hindu	Nil	2700.00	B.A.	Business	15	Should be President of India
100.	Anusuyia Devi	Female	29	Rural	Hindu	Nil	2100.00	Inter	Housewife	20	Should be President of India

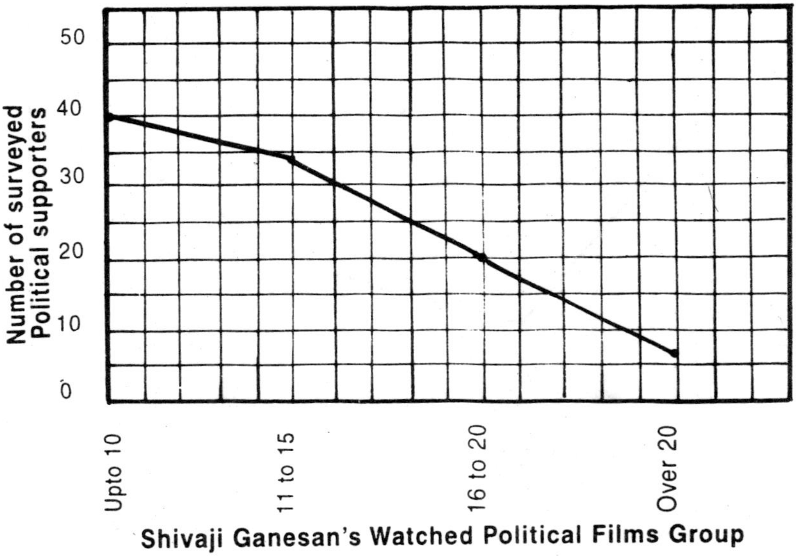

Diagram 8.1

His watched Political Films Group-wise Number of Shivaji Ganesan's One Hundred Surveyed Political Supporters in Delhi in July, 1997.

Out of one hundred surveyed political supporters of Shivaji Ganesan in Delhi, forty supporters are in upto 10 watched political films-group, thirty-four supporters are in 11 to 15 watched political films-group, twenty supporters are in 16 to 20 watched political films-group and only six supporters are in over 20 watched political films-group.

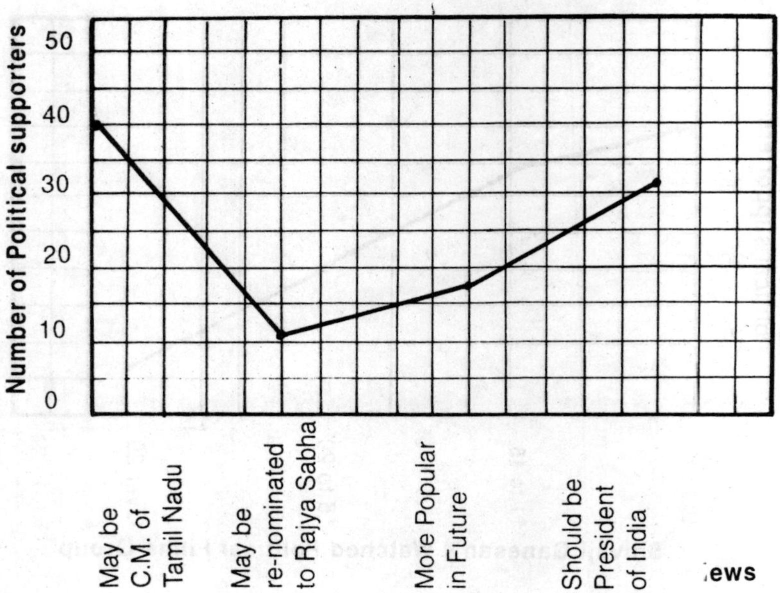

Diagram 8.2

Views-wise Number of Shivaji Ganesan's One Hundred Surveyed Political Supporters in Delhi in July, 1997. (Views about His Political Future)

Out of one hundred surveyed political supporters of Shivaji Ganesan in Delhi, according to forty supporters, he 'may be chief minister of Tamil Nadu'; according to eleven supporters, he 'may be re-nominated to Rajya Sabha' in future; according to seventeen supporters, he 'should be President of India' and according to thirty-two supporters, he may be more popular in future.'

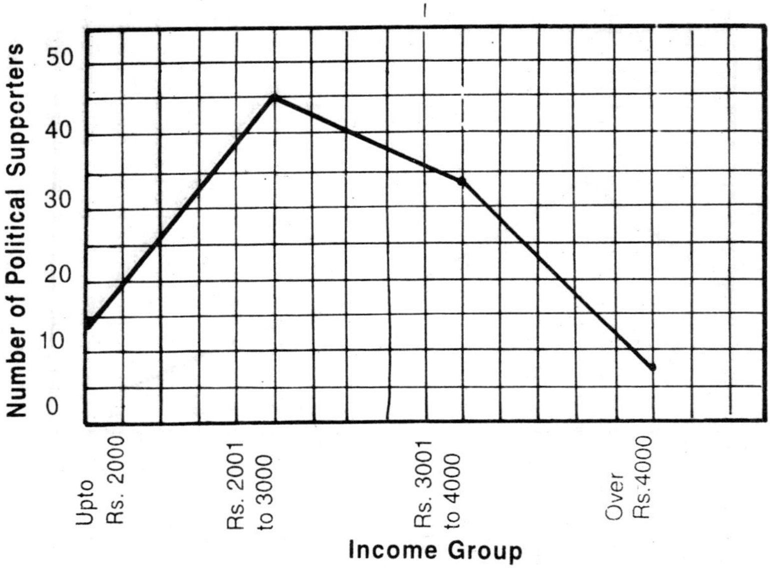

Diagram 8.3

Income Group-wise Number of Shivaji Ganesan's One Hundred Surveyed Political Supporters in Delhi in July, 1997.

Out of one hundred surveyed political supporters of Shivaji Ganesan in Delhi, fourteen supporters are in up to Rs. 2000 income groups, forty-five supporters are in from Rs. 2001 to Rs. 3000 income group, thirty-four supporters are in from Rs. 3001 to Rs. 4000 income-group and only seven supporters are in over Rs. 4000 income-group.

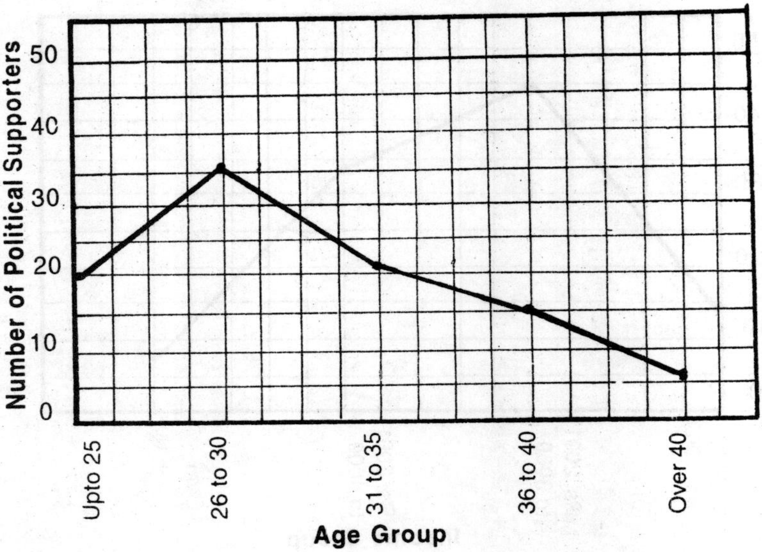

Diagram 8.4.

Age Group-wise Number of Shivaji Ganesan's One Hundred Surveyed Political Supporters in Delhi in July, 1997.

Out of one hundred surveyed political supporters of Shivaji Ganesan in Delhi, twenty supporters are in upto 25 age-group, thirty-six supporters are in 26 to 30 age group, twenty-two supporters are in 31 to 35 age group, fifteen supporters are in 36 to 40 age-group and only seven supporters are in over 40 age-group.

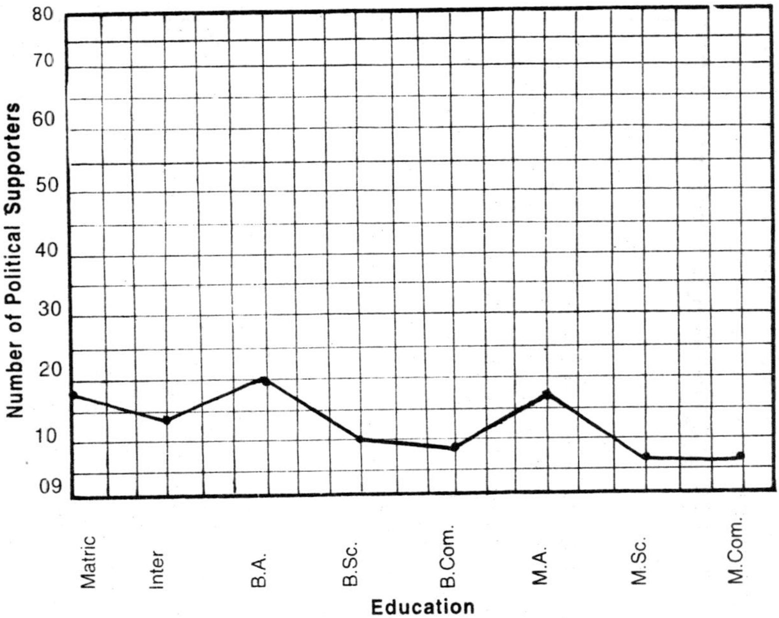

Diagram 8.5

Education-wise Number of Shivaji Ganesan's One Hundred Surveyed Political Supporters in Delhi in July, 1997.

Out of one hundred surveyed political supporters of Shivaji Ganesan in Delhi, seventeen supporters are only Matric passed, fourteen supporters are Inter examination passed, twenty supporters are B.A., ten supporters are B.Sc., eight supporters are B.Com., seventeen supporters are M.A., seven supporters are M.Sc. and also seven supporters are M.Com.

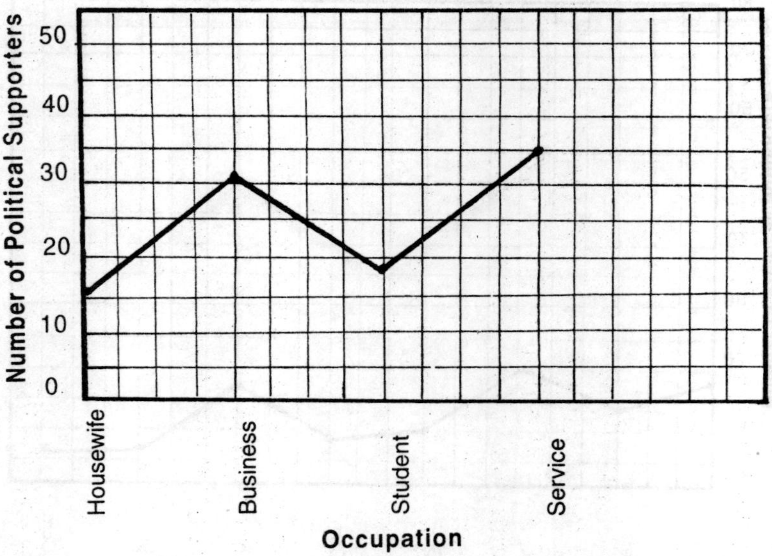

Diagram 8.6

Occupation-Wise Number of Shivaji Ganesan's One Hundred Surveyed Political Supporters in Delhi in July, 1997.

Out of one hundred surveyed political supporters of Shivaji Ganesan in Delhi, sixteen supporters are as housewives, thirty-one supporters are in business, eighteen supporters are as students and thirty-five supporters are in service.

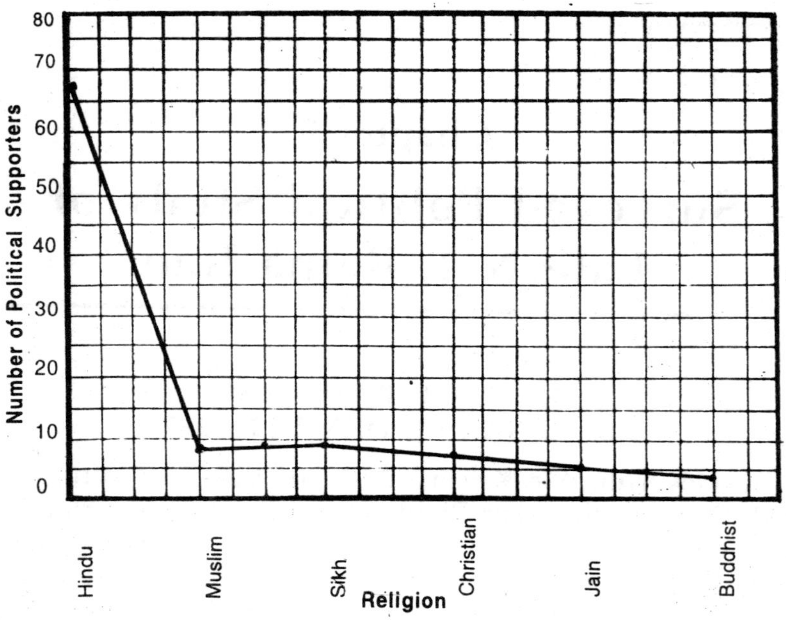

Diagram 8.7

Religion-wise Number of Shivaji Ganesan's One Hundred Surveyed Political Supporters in Delhi in July, 1997.

Out of one hundred surveyed political supporters of Shivaji Ganesan in Delhi, sixty-seven supporters are Hindus, eight supporters are Muslims, nine supporters are Sikhs, seven supporters are Christians, five supporters are Jains and only four supporters are Buddhists.

Chapter 9
Surveyed Political Study of Late N.T. Rama Rao

I. LATE N.T. RAMA RAO : AS SOCIAL REFORMER IN 1993

The Governor, Mr. Krishna Kant and the Chief Minister, Mr. K. Vijayabhaskar Reddy, left the venue of a public meeting organised to rally support for the anti-arrack movement in Andhra Pradesh as supporters of the congress and the Telugu Desam Party nearly came to blows at the Satya Sai Kalyana Mandapam in Hyderabad on January 2, 1993. There was utter chaos at the meeting convened by the United Forum for Prohibition, when the TDP leader, Mr: N.T. Rama Rao, strongly criticised the State Government for its 'dilatory tactics' in taking a decision on the question of introducing prohibition when there was overwhelming support in favour of ban on liquor. This was strongly protested by the state information minister, Mr. P. Penchalaiah. Taking this as a clue, the Congress workers rushed to the dais and raised slogans of 'NTR down, down,'. Not to be outdone, the TDP workers also moved forward and raised slogans against the Chief Minister and the Congress.

For nearly half on hour, it was total pell-mell as slogans rent the air. At one juncture, even the Governor and the Chief Minister stood up and repeatedly appealed for calm. When their pleas failed to restore order, the both left in a huff. The police remained silent spectators as the supporters of the two parties moved menacingly towards each other and some even got up on the dias and started raising slogans in support of their respective leaders. A group of workers led by the youth congress leader, Mr. P. Sudhakar Reddy, demanded an apology from N.T. Rama Rao. The TDP workers then threw a protective ring around NTR who remained rooted at the mike. Ministers too joined the fray and Mr. Vijayabhaskar Reddy was able to pacify a group of his party workers. But with Mr. Rama Rao's constant references to the State Government and its inability to impose prohibition irked the Congress supporters further and resulted in utter chaos. This was the signal for the Governor and the Chief Minister to leave the venue. Mr. Vijayabhaskar Reddy later termed the episode as unfortunate and put the blame squarely on Mr. N.T. Rama Rao, who, he felt, was trying to politicise the issue. "Once the Governor left the meeting, I, as the Chief Minister could not sit there", Mr. Reddy explained at a hurriedly called press conference at his residence in Jubilee Hills in Hyderabad. Mounting a scathing attack on the TDP leader, the Chief Minister said: "He (Mr. Rama Rao) does not want prohibition. Neither he is interested in the welfare of the poor. I need not repeat that he does not have an ideological commitment on the issue and his intention was only to get political mileage out of the movement." Terming as unfortunate the political speech of Mr. Rama Rao at the meeting, Mr. Reddy explained that the Governor appeared to have taken offence to the TDP leader asking whether the Government would permit prostitution, if the collection revenue was the sole criterion for not imposing prohibition.

Mr. Krishan Kant, who was listening attentively to the speakers, had asked one of the women sitting behind him to translate Mr. Rama Rao's speech. "As soon as he was told what the TDP leader was saying, he stood up abruptly and left and I had to follow him," a composed Mr. Vijayabhaskar Reddy explained. He said that Mr. Rama Rao continued with his speech using, choicest epithets to deride the ruling party. Even the requests of Mr. Ramoji Rao, who organised the meeting, not to make political speeches, went unheeded. Some women also pleaded with NTR not to spoil the movement by his speeches, but he continued his address. The Chief Minister said he had been assured by Mr. Ramoji Rao that it would be a non-political meeting and that leaders or all political parties would be participating. Though some political parties were utilizing the movement for prohibition for their own benefit, he had attended the meeting to explain the stand of Congress on the issue. Mr. Reddy said he sat through the speech amid slogan-shouting, "Though it was embarrassing, I sat because I wanted to explain the Government's stand. Reiterating that his party was committed to imposing prohibition, the Chief Minister said he had advocated a ban on liquor during his student days.

II. AN EXAMPLE OF LATE N.T. RAMA RAO'S POLITICS

To the dismay of Congressmen, Telugu Desam supremo N.T. Rama Rao had struck again. The TDP bagged two crucial Assembly seats Kovur and Kaibalur-in May, 1993 by-elections. The Congress leaders in the state were feeling pretty smug when the ruling party won two other by-elections from the politically volatile and faction-ridden Rayalaseema region in April, 1993. Chief Minister K. Vijayabhaskar Reddy was hopeful of bagging Kovur and Kaikalur too, which lie in the rich central coastal region. But TDP made a surprising breakthrough. The poll reverses revealed the tenuous hold by the Congress in Prime Minister P.V. Narasimha Rao's home state. It also pointed to the revived political fortunes of star-politician Rama Rao and his party. The TDP lost power in the 1989 Assembly elections, and political pundits had then expressed doubts even about its survival. But the party survived despite inner bickerings.

But the victory euphoria of NTR is shadowed by what appears to be a major scandal-in-the-making. A newspaper alleged that the 71-year-old matinee idol-turned-politician is at the deep end of a love affair. The woman in the leader's life is a lecturer and divorcee, Laxmi Siva Parwati, who set out to write a biography of the leader, and has grown into a close companion. There was stated to be initial opposition from his family members to the arrangement. But he is reported to have told them that he has been a loner since the death of his wife Basawa Tarakam eight years ago and there is no one to look after him. It is further speculated that the sons-in-law are vehemently opposed to the liaison as that would drastically affect the party's political standing. Asked about the rumours, NTR brushes them aside in his characteristic brusque style: "They say so many things about God. Does He come down to answer each one of them?" He does not wish to talk about his personal life.

The Kovur-Kaikalur defeat has however so disheartened the congressmen, that they have even begun to admit in private that the return of NTR is imminent. They even joke about how his younger son-in-law N. Chandrababu Naidu, who is the virtual party boss, will once again rule the roost if the TDP is back in power. Congressmen's fears may come true, and 1994 might well turn out to the year of Rama Rao's second coming. The by-election victories show that people still have faith in NTR and his party. Aware of his popularity, Rama Rao in his uninhibited way boasts: "The purity that I maintain in politics is well-known among the people. I am not a politician but a servant of the poor, he claims.

After decade in politics he has learnt many of the tricks of the trade, and is not as naive as he used to be when he first entered the fray back in 1982. But he is still in the habit of talking in hyperboles. Without NTR, there is no Telugu Desam," he asserts but does express faith that the party will not die. "Someone better than NTR may come as leaders are born out of circumstances.

A fissure seemed to have developed recently with the CPM insisting on contesting the Kovur by-election and barely managing to retain its deposit. How does he view it now? "The Telugu Desam approach is very clear. It is upto them and other parties to decide what they think of us." The answer is that of a politician: "I am not a politician like the congressmen, who cheat the people. For them, it is Congress-I. Only I.I.I. They think about themselves and not about the people. Holding forth against the congress comes easily to Rama Rao. He has thrived on calling congressmen names, using choicest Telugu phrases. It was his bold anti-congressism that brought him to power a decade ago. It was he who took the initiative and started holding 'conclaves' with other major opposition parties and was able to bring together leaders of the CPI, CPM, BJP, Janata Party and the National Conference on a single platform, heralding the birth of the National Front concept. Rama Rao later admitted that the National Front experiment was a 'mistake'. Asked about it now, he goes into a lengthy explanation about how political parties in general have not been able to live up to the expectations of the people who have reposed faith in them. He is not satisfied with the growth of political parties. "Everyone is still groping in the dark and the present trend will continue till politicians see the light."

How about the Telugu Desam? There is no second level of leadership worth the name. He is vague about it. "People have to utilise the opportunities given to them.

They have to grow with the party," he says. Rama Rao had created history by forming a party that came to power within nine months of its inception. And it was the anti-congress plank that did the trick, coupled with his silver screen popularity. The people have a lot of faith in him still, he feels. They have a lot of love and respect for him and his party. Why, then, did they defeat the Telugu Desam in the 1989 elections? "We have not been defeated. It is cheating by the congress, which rigged the elections." Rama Rao says, pointing out that the difference in the overall percentage of votes polled between the congress and TDP was only about three percent. The by-elections in Kovur and Kaikalur have proved that when the electorate is allowed to participate in a free and fair election, they would opt for the TDP rather than the congress. No doubt, sympathy played a major part in the Kouvr by-election where the son of the sitting member who died was elected.

Congressmen are not willing to let him gloat over his victory in the by-elections. Chief Minister Vijayabhaskar Reddy himself feels that winning a by-election would not enhance the prestige of the ruling party nor would losing it lower its image. The sympathy factor helped the TDP candidate win in the Kovur constituency. "Is it just enough to serve rice? Dal, curry and ghee have to go with it to make a wholesome meal," is how Rama Rao puts it when asked about the sympathy factor. But Dronamraju Satyanarayana, M.P., maintains that the good work done by the P.V. Narasimha Rao government at the centre and the Vijayabhaskar Reddy ministry in the state has not been given the publicity it should have among the masses.

Being essentially a film personality, NTR seems to have the knack of gauging the pulse of the people. He is sure of victory in the coming elections to the state assembly and declares it confidently. In a bid to complete shooting of a film 'Chandasasamudu' (Iron Man) before plunging into full-time politics in 1982, Rama Rao had suffered an injury when a bullock-cart ran over him. "I am alive because god has destined that I do something for the people," he had said. This statement had evoked much laughter. But it is he who seems to be having the last laugh now.

III. LATE N.T. RAMA RAO AS OPPOSITION LEADER

Ruckus marred a function organised to unveil the statue of singer Ghantasala Venkateswara Rao in Hyderabad on February 14, 1993, as congress workers protested noisily over the speech made by Telugu Desam supremo N.T. Rama Rao. The function was arranged by noted play-back singer S.P. Balasubramaniam in commemoration of Ghantasala at Lalita Kala Thoranam in the Public Garden. It was almost a repeat of the noisy scenes that were witnessed at the "United Forum against Arrack" meeting in January 1993 which Chief Minister K. Vijayabhaskar Reddy and Governor Krishan Kant left midway. The customary slogan 'Jai Telugu Desam' by the TDP supremo at the end of his 40-minute-long histronic speech sparked the row.

Irked at this some Congress-I workers led by one G. Narayana Reddy raised slogans of "Rajiv Gandhi Zindabad" which were countered by slogans of "NTR Zindabad" by actor Mohanbabu, who accompanied the Telugu Desam leader to the meeting. In the course of his speech Mr. Rama Rao recalled his long and fruitful association with Ghantasala and said that it was his good fortune to participate in the function and congratulated Balasubramaniam for doing what the entire film industry should have done. Asserting that true art had a purpose, he referred to the anti-liquor song 'kallu manandoyi and kallu teravandoyi' (give up toddy and open your eyes) in an old Telugu film and pointed out that it stressed the need for prohibition. At least now those in politics should open their eyes, he felt.

N.T. Rama Rao asked Supreme Court to make Ansari Panel Report Public

A petition was filed on February 23, 1993 by Telugu Desam Party leader N.T. Rama Rao in the Supreme Court seeking a direction to the Andhra Pradesh Government to make public the Ansari Commission report and punish the culprits who indulged in massive rioting in the state after assassination of the late Prime Minister, Mr. Rajiv Gandhi on May 21, 1991. According to Mr. Rama Rao the present Government of Chief Minister Vijay Bhaskara Reddy was suppressing the report so that congress MLAs like M. Mukesh, and P. Sudhir Kumar could go scot-free. The petition drawn by advocate B. Rajeswara Rao, settled by S. Ramchandra Rao and filed by Rani Chhabra, had made the Union Government, the Andhra Pradesh Government, Mr. Vijaya Bhaskara Reddy, the former Chief Minister N. Janardhana Reddy, MLAs Mukesh and Sudhir Kumar as respondents.

IV. JAYAPRADA VIEW ABOUT LATE N.T. RAMA RAO

Actress Jayaprada has been in politics for barely some days but she has already learnt the art of ducking uncomfortable questions. In an interview with V.R. Mani, correspondent of The Times of India, Madras, on December 22, 1994, Jayaprada, who joined the Telugu Desam Party in October 1994 and campaigned in 75 constituencies traversing 5,000 km, said she was yet to decide whether to take to politics full time or not. "It is too early to think of that because there is a lot of time yet," she said. Her answer to a query if she was at leastly partly responsible for the defeat of former chief minister N. Janardhana Reddy in Nellore district was a boisterous laugh.

"I am sweet sixteen and have a long way to go in films... Want to get the best actress national award and do art films... I have nine films on hand—six Hindi and three Bengali," she said. Lest that gives you the impression that she was not really serious about politics, she lets you know that right now she was giving equal importance to politics and her film career. But what would happen if her supremo, as she refers to N.T. Rama Rao, sent her to the Rajya Sabha as rumoured. "Of course, I will accept it," she said, without batting an eyelid. As an after-thought, she cautiously added: "...it (giving a berth) is left to the supremo and he will take the right decision.... I am a babe in politics, I will have to grow under his shadow." Jayaprada claimed politics had opened her eyes" for the first time to the reality outside. All this while she thought that life was as colourful as it mostly was in the dream world of films, she said.

"I never expected poverty will be so bad, so painful...", she said, adding that it had moved her very much. The younger generation is feeling insecure about its future and there is no security for women, she said, she wanted to make every woman a 'Rambolina', the female version of Rambo. As for herself, though, she wanted to live up to the image of 'Andhra aadapadichu' (daughter of Andhra) the people have created for her. The actress, who has paired with N.T. Rama Rao in 25 films, is certain that the chief minister would be able to deliver his poll promise of providing rice for Rs. 2 a kg. "The whole world knows that it is difficult but the greatness of N.T. Rama Rao is to 'make the impossible possible". "He is a leader with vision and wisdom,", she said. Did NTR (N.T. Rama Rao) want her in the party as a glamour girl, a substitute for Renuka Chaudhary, who was expelled from the party a few months ago? "The party need me and I had great regard for him (NTR)," she replied. She was, however, cautious when suggested that she could, in the long run, try to don the mantle of

NTR. "I am not dreaming for yet... I still grow under his shade... God should give him good health", she said. Jayaprada does not think that NTR's wife Laxmi Parvati would be doing the 'backseat driving', as is widely perceived. "He has been taking all decisions and no one can dominate him", she said. She also did not see any hitch in her relationship with Parvati. "She is a very nice lady, very friendly with me and I give her all respect," is what she had to say.

Findings of the Survey Work

Late N.T. Rama Rao had ambition to become Prime Minister of India. In this survey many persons hoped about his this ambition in September 1993 in Delhi.

Out of one hundred political supporters, thirty one supporters said in September 1993 that he may be Chief Minister of Andhra Pradesh again. Twenty five supporters believed he may be Prime Minister of India. Twenty political supporters hoped his more popularity in future politics. Twenty four said his future would be brighter as a politician.

Table 9.1

Detailed Study of Late N.T. Rama Rao's One Hundred Surveyed Political Supporters in Delhi in September 1993

S.No.	*Name of the Person*	*Sex*	*Age (in years)*	*Urban/ Rural*	*Religion*	*Whether SC/ST*	*Family's income P.M. (in Rs.)*	*Edu-cation*	*Occup-ation*	*No. of His watched Political Films*	*View about His Political Future*
1	*2*	*3*	*4*	*5*	*6*	*7*	*8*	*9*	*10*	*11*	*12*
1.	Ranga Reddy	Male	39	Rural	Hindu	Nil	3200.00	M.A.	Service	15	May be C.M. again
2.	Laxmi Rao	Female	32	Urban	Hindu	Nil	3600.00	B.A.	Housewife	13	May be Prime Minister of India
3.	Rajni Wilson	Female	19	Urban	Christian	ST	3900.00	Inter	Student	08	More popular in future politics
4.	M. Hashim	Male	27	Urban	Muslim	Nil	2400.00	Matric	Business	11	Brighter as a politician
5.	Ranga Rao	Male	24	Urban	Hindu	Nil	3400.00	B.Sc.	Student	16	More popular in future politics
6.	Nand Ram	Male	23	Rural	Hindu	SC	1800.00	B.A.	Student	03	May be Prime Minister of India
7.	Avtar Singh	Male	34	Urban	Sikh	Nil	3300.00	B.Com.	Business	02	May be C.M. again
8.	Kamal Nayan Jain	Male	27	Urban	Jain	Nil	4100.00	M.A.	Business	03	Brighter as a politician
9.	Uma Nayair	Female	33	Urban	Hindu	Nil	3400.00	M.Sc.	Housewife	02	May be Prime Minister of India
10.	Saraswati Rao	Female	24	Urban	Hindu	Nil	3500.00	M.A.	Housewife	16	May be C.M. again
11.	Khushal Singh	Male	26	Rural	Hindu	SC	1600.00	Matric	Service	07	More popular in future politics
12.	Raghu Bhatia	Male	27	Rural	Hindu	Nil	2300.00	Inter	Service	06	Brighter as a politician
13.	Ram Singh	Male	29	Rural	Buddhist	SC	1400.00	Matric	Service	04	May be C.M. again
14.	Jai Bhagwan	Male	32	Urban	Buddhist	SC	1300.00	Inter	Service	03	May be Prime Minister of India

(Contd.)

1	2	3	4	5	6	7	8	9	10	11	12
15.	Harbhajan Singh	Male	45	Urban	Sikh	Nil	3500.00	M.Com.	Service	02	May be C.M. again
16.	Om Prakash	Male	29	Rural	Hindu	SC	1400.00	Inter	Service	04	More popular in future politics
17.	Pragat Singh	Male	31	Urban	Sikh	SC	1800.00	B.Com.	Business	06	May be Prime Minister of India
18.	Asifa Hussain	Female	29	Rural	Muslim	Nil	2100.00	Inter	Housewife	04	May be C.M. again
19.	Tariq Hussain	Male	24	Urban	Muslim	Nil	2700.00	B.Com.	Student	18	May be Prime Minister of India
20.	Mujaffar Hussain	Male	34	Urban	Muslim	Nil	3300.00	M.Sc.	Service	13	Brighter as a politician
21.	M. Maical	Male	31	Rural	Christian	Nil	3100.00	M.Com.	Business	11	May be C.M. again
22.	Ram Babu	Male	30	Rural	Hindu	SC	1600.00	Matric	Service	07	May be Prime Minister of India
23.	Sunil Kumar Jain	Male	25	Urban	Jain	Nil	3800.00	B.Com.	Student	04	May be C.M. again
24.	Bhimsen	Male	45	Rural	Buddhist	SC	2700.00	B.A.	Service	07	May be Prime Minister of India
25.	Bhima Devi	Female	41	Rural	Buddhist	SC	2400.00	Matric	Housewife	05	Brighter as a politician
26.	Christy Sangma	Female	25	Urban	Christian	ST	3600.00	M.A.	Student	08	May be C.M. again
27.	Peter Ekka	Male	43	Urban	Christian	ST	4300.00	M.Sc.	Service	06	May be Prime Minister of India
28.	Laxman Singh	Male	42	Rural	Hindu	Nil	2700.00	M.Com.	Business	16	More popular in future politics
29.	Vikram Taneja	Male	37	Urban	Hindu	Nil	4600.00	M.Sc.	Service	12	May be C.M. again
30.	Ram Gopal Verma	Male	34	Rural	Hindu	Nil	3900.00	B.A.	Business	06	May be Prime Minister of India
31.	Inder Prakash	Male	27	Urban	Hindu	SC	1400.00	Matric	Service	04	More popular in future politics
32.	Ram Bhasin	Male	29	Urban	Hindu	Nil	2400.00	Inter	Business	08	May be C.M. again
33.	Ved Prakash Yadav	Male	33	Rural	Hindu	Nil	2700.00	B.A.	Service	05	May be Prime Minister of India
34.	Ramvir Singh	Male	29	Rural	Hindu	SC	2900.00	M.A.	Business	07	May be C.M. again
35.	Bobby Moore	Male	24	Urban	Christian	ST	2600.00	B.Com.	Student	08	May be Prime Minister of India

(Contd.)

1	2	3	4	5	6	7	8	9	10	11	12
36.	Akshaya Jain	Male	49	Urban	Jain	Nil	4800.00	M.Com.	Business	06	Brighter as a politician
37.	Ram Biduri	Male	34	Rural	Hindu	Nil	3700.00	M.A.	Business	08	May be C.M. again
38.	Usha Mahajan	Female	27	Urban	Hindu	Nil	3400.00	B.A.	Housewife	07	May be Prime Minister of India
39.	Shikha Jain	Female	23	Urban	Jain	Nil	4100.00	B.Sc.	Student	09	May be C.M. again
40.	Lokesh Sharma	Male	29	Urban	Hindu	Nil	3500.00	Matric	Business	11	More popular in future politics
41.	Tara Chand	Male	24	Rural	Hindu	SC	2400.00	Inter	Student	03	May be Prime Minister of India
42.	Ravi Shankar	Male	29	Urban	Hindu	Nil	2900.00	B.A.	Service	06	May be C.M. again
43.	Jamuna Prasad	Male	46	Rural	Hindu	SC	1500.00	Matric	Service	08	More popular in future politics
44.	Kamlesh Jain	Female	34	Rural	Jain	Nil	2300.00	Inter	Housewife	03	May be C.M. again
45.	Paramjit Kaur	Female	24	Urban	Sikh	Nil	3800.00	B.A.	Housewife	04	May be Prime Minister of India
46.	Ganga Devi	Female	26	Rural	Hindu	SC	2700.00	Matric	Housewife	07	May be C.M. again
47.	Deep Singh	Male	38	Urban	Sikh	Nil	3900.00	B.Sc.	Business	04	May be Prime Minister of India
48.	Vinay Sharma	Male	34	Urban	Hindu	Nil	2800.00	M.A.	Service	09	May be C.M. again
49.	Dharm Das	Male	27	Rural	Buddhist	SC	1600.00	Matric	Service	06	Brighter as a politician
50.	Manoj Kumar	Male	24	Urban	Hindu	Nil	1900.00	Inter	Business	13	May be C.M. again
51.	Hemant Jha	Male	28	Urban	Hindu	Nil	2300.00	B.Com.	Service	15	Brighter as a politician
52.	Mustafa Khan	Male	47	Urban	Muslim	Nil	2700.00	Inter	Service	03	May be Prime Minister of India
53.	Nilima Arora	female	26	Urban	Hindu	Nil	3600.00	M.Sc.	Student	07	More popular in future politics
54.	Mukes' Malhotra	Male	37	Rural	Hindu	Nil	3300.00	B.A.	Service	09	Brighter as a politician
55.	Bimlesh Kumar	Female	29	Rural	Hindu	SC	1700.00	Matric	Housewife	03	May be C.M. again

(Contd.)

1	2	3	4	5	6	7	8	9	10	11	12
56.	Deepa Sarin	Female	24	Urban	Hindu	Nil	2700.00	B.Sc.	Student	07	May be Prime Minister of India
57.	Salim Zakaria	Male	47	Urban	Muslim	Nil	4600.00	M.Com.	Business	09	Brighter as a politician
58.	Yakub Khan	Male	39	Rural	Muslim	Nil	3400.00	M.Sc.	Service	11	More popular in future politics
59.	Ummed Singh	Male	34	Rural	Hindu	SC	2400.00	Inter	Business	08	May be C.M. again
60.	Divya Ambedkar	Female	26	Urban	Buddhist	SC	2700.00	M.A.	Housewife	07	May be Prime Minister of India
61.	Ankur Jacob	Male	21	Urban	Christian	ST	2400.00	B.A.	Student	09	Brighter as a politician
62.	Sumit Khanna	Male	27	Urban	Hindu	Nil	2600.00	M.A.	Service	17	May be C.M. again
63.	Anupam Agarwal	Male	34	Rural	Hindu	Nil	2700.00	M.Com.	Business	08	May be Prime Minister of India
64.	Bal Krishna Pandey	Male	23	Urban	Hindu	Nil	4500.00	B.Sc.	Student	16	More popular in future politics
65.	Mamta Rani	Female	19	Rural	Hindu	SC	1900.00	Matric	Housewife	07	Brighter as a politician
66.	Sita Kumari	Female	26	Rural	Hindu	SC	2300.00	Inter	Service	11	More popular in future politics
67.	Jagdish Tiwari	Male	31	Urban	Hindu	Nil	2900.00	B.A.	Business	09	May be C.M. again
68.	Vanita Sharma	Female	27	Urban	Hindu	Nil	3600.00	M.A.	Housewife	17	Brighter as a politician
69.	Devinder Singh	Male	21	Urban	Sikh	Nil	4000.00	B.A.	Student	13	May be C.M. again
70.	Upendra Jain	Male	42	Rural	Jain	Nil	3800.00	Inter	Business	12	Brighter as a politician
71.	Veer Pal	Male	45	Rural	Buddhist	SC	2300.00	Matric	Service	17	More popular in future politics
72.	Vijay Singh	Male	37	Urban	Hindu	Nil	1800.00	Matric	Business	08	Brighter as a politician
73.	Amjad Hussain	Male	25	Urban	Muslim	Nil	2600.00	B.A.	Service	13	May be Prime Minister of India
74.	M. Zafar	Male	33	Rural	Muslim	Nil	3100.00	Inter	Business	12	May be C.M. again
75.	Kunwar Pal Singh	Male	31	Urban	Hindu	SC	2700.00	M.A.	Service	14	Brighter as a politician
76.	Kundan Lal	Male	27	Rural	Buddhist	SC	1600.00	Matric	Service	11	May be C.M. again
77.	Kumkum Devi	Female	26	Rural	Hindu	Nil	2200.00	Inter	Housewife	06	More popular in future politics

(Contd.)

1	2	3	4	5	6	7	8	9	10	11	12
78.	Neelam Batra	Female	23	Urban	Hindu	Nil	3400.00	B.Sc.	Student	14	May be Prime Minister of India
79.	S.S. Narula	Male	46	Rural	Sikh	Nil	3100.00	M.Sc.	Service	17	Brighter as a politician
80.	Rupa Jain	Female	24	Urban	Jain	Nil	4300.00	B.Com.	Student	08	May be C.M. again
81.	Budh Dev	Male	27	Rural	Buddhist	SC	2200.00	M.A.	Business	07	Brighter as a politician
82.	Vipin Chand	Male	24	Rural	Hindu	SC	1800.00	Inter	Student	13	More popular in future politics
83.	Mahendra Singh Saini	Male	46	Urban	Hindu	Nil	2600.00	M.Com.	Business	11	Brighter as a politician
84.	Rama Kant Dikshit	Male	39	Rural	Hindu	Nil	3900.00	B.A.	Service	09	More popular in future politics
85.	B.P. Verma	Male	27	Urban	Hindu	Nil	2700.00	B.A.	Business	09	Brighter as a politician
86.	Hukum Singh	Male	39	Rural	Sikh	SC	3100.00	Inter	Service	11	May be C.M. Again
87.	Hanuman Prasad	Male	28	Rural	Hindu	SC	1900.00	B.A.	Business	18	Brighter as a politician
88.	Anjula Rani	Female	24	Urban	Jain	Nil	4500.00	B.Sc.	Student	12	More popular in future politics
89.	F. Ahmad	Male	36	Rural	Muslim	Nil	3300.00	Inter	Service	07	May be Prime Minister of India
90.	Pinki Ahuja	Female	29	Urban	Hindu	Nil	2700.00	B.A.	Housewife	13	More popular in future politics
91.	Parmanand	Male	34	Urban	Hindu	ST	2500.00	M.A.	Service	16	May be C.M. again
92.	Virendra Kumar	Male	33	Rural	Hindu	Nil	2000.00	B.Com.	Service	08	More popular in future politics
93.	Bhairon Singh	Male	29	Urban	Hindu	Nil	3400.00	B.A.	Service	08	May be C.M. again
94.	Barkatullah	Male	34	Rural	Muslim	Nil	2500.00	Matric	Business	11	Brighter as a politician
95.	Karan Devi	Female	24	Rural	Hindu	SC	1400.00	Inter	Housewife	08	May be Prime Minister of India
96.	Sumit Kumar	Male	34	Urban	Hindu	Nil	3700.00	M.A.	Business	13	More popular in future politics
97.	Kamal Kaur	Female	23	Rural	Sikh	Nil	2500.00	B.Sc.	Student	09	May be C.M. again
98.	Ram Dayal	Male	43	Rural	Hindu	SC	1900.00	Matric	Service	07	Brighter as a politician
99.	Mitrasen	Male	39	Urban	Buddhist	SC	3600.00	M.A.	Service	15	May be Prime Minister of India
100.	Nayan Tara	Female	26	Rural	Hindu	Nil	4500.00	M.Com.	Student	14	Brighter as a politician

Chapter 10

I. J. Jayalalitha
II. V.N. Janaki Ramchandran
III. Late Utpal Dutt

I. J. JAYALALITHA

The Tamil film actress and Tamil Nadu Ex-chief Minister, Miss Jayalalitha was the most popular political leader in the state, according to a public opinion poll conducted by the department of statistics of Madras Christian College in 1991. The 21st annual survey also revealed that she enjoyed the strong support of 43 percent of the electorate. Only other instance when a political leader of the state enjoyed more than 40 percent support was in February 1983 when M.G. Ramchandran notched up the support of 46 percent of the electorate. One hundred and forty students of the statistics department of the Madra's Christian college visited nearly 500 villages and towns and ilicited information from over 2,000 respondents selected by random sampling techniques. Opposition leader the DMK president, Mr. M. Karunanidhi, enjoys 30 percent support. Partywise, Jayalalitha's AIADMK had the strong support of 43 percent, with 22 percent sympathising with it and 30 percent opposing it, while the DMK had the strong support of 30 percent of the people with 12 percent sympathising with it and as much as 53 percent being opposed to it. As for the Congress-I, it was a poor third, enjoying as it did the strong support of 17 percent, though 51 percent of the electorate sympathise with the party. Twenty two percent were opposed to the party. The other parties, the Janata Dal, BJP, PMK and the CPM and the CPI each enjoyed only around two percent of support. An interesting aspect of the survey is that both the AIDMK—Congress-I alliance has maintained its hold, the DMK—led front was to have gone up the popularity ratings at the cost of the PMK.

J. Jayalalitha : A Hope for Poor People

"I have confidence in you. As a woman, you will be well aware of the difficulties another woman faces. As a young girl, I find my future in dark. I need this world to live in.... Madam. I appeal to you, give me an opportunity to live in this world." This is a desperate plea made in a letter written by 21 years old S. Vasanthi, to the then Chief Minister, Miss J. Jayalalitha, in March 1992. Vasanthi, who had almost given up hopes of getting financial help from any quarter to enable her frail, emaciated frame to receive the life sustaining fluid blood, got a shot in the arm on July 20, 1992 with the then Tamil Nadu Chief Minister, Miss J. Jayalalitha, giving her Rs. one lakh from the AIADMK party funds. Following the publication of Vasanthi's heart rending story in the 'Indian Express' on July 20, 1992, the Express received a call from the then Chief Minister's Secretariat in the morning asking for Vasanthi's address. Within half an hour a car had been despatched to Vasanthi's residence with a message that the then Chief Minister wanted to see the young girl and her parents.

Vasanthi was a haemophiliac who has the 'bleeding disease', and she required blood transfusion once in a month or two months. Her problem began when she was three years old and started spurting blood from the mouth, and passing blood in the stools. The tragedy of her family was that three of her siblings, all of them brothers, have died of this disease. Predictably enough Vasanthi was an offspring from a consanguineous marriage, with Sivaram marrying his maternal uncle's daughter. In a voice choked with emotion Vasanthi told 'Indian Express,' "I was taken along with my parents to meet Madam Jayalalitha at her room in the secretariat. She made anxious inquiries about my problem, showed a lot of concern and spent almost 15 minutes with us. She gave me a fixed deposit certificate for Rs. one lakh deposited in the Tamil Nadu Transport Development Finance Corporation, and said it would fetch me a monthly interest of Rs. 1,234, and the amount could be used for my treatment. I do not know how to express my gratitude to the chief minister." Vasanthi's tragic tale has moved many others apart from the then Chief Minister. On July 20, 1992, the Express received many calls offering financial help to treat the young girl with a medical problem which required regular blood transfusion, apart from adequate medication round the year.

Now the Vasanthi has received some financial support, her parents and physician hope to get her thoroughly investigated so that specific treatment can be arranged for her. According to an official spokesman, Miss Jayalalitha decided to give her the money from party funds because under the existing rules there was provision for giving a maximum grant of only Rs. 20,000 from the Chief Minister's fund, and that too for an open heart surgery. Even this amount would not have sufficed for the girl's treatment. Explaining Vasanthi's condition, Gunasekharan said this was a disease transmitted usually by mothers to their children. Such patients have to be put on drugs to control the bleeding, and these have to be supplemented with Vitamin C and multivitamin tablets. The drugs to control the bleeding-coagulants—are easily available but they are expensive. To maintain an adequate dosage, a patient would need about Rs. 1000 to Rs. 2000 a month. The doctor said Vasanthi required further evaluation to assess her problem. "Quite a few tests are now available but the investigation will be very expensive. There is possibility of such investigation pin-pointing a particular factor, and this would help us to give her specific treatment."

J. Jayalalitha Meeting on Cauvery Issue with the Prime Minister in 1991

An all-party delegation form Tamil Nadu led by the then State Chief Minister, Miss J. Jayalalitha called on the then Prime Minister Mr. P.V. Narasimha Rao on December 3, 1991 in New Delhi, and submitted a memorandum urging the Union Government to immediately notify the interim orders of the Cauvery Water Disputes Tribunal. The mission of the delegation, in the wake of the Supreme Court opinion on the Presidential reference, was obviously to demonstrate to the Union Government that all people of Tamil Nadu, cutting across party lines were united on the question of sharing of the Cauvery waters. However, what was striking about the 30-minute meeting between the delegation and the Prime Minister was the conciliatory posture from the State leaders towards the Union Government. This was evident at the meeting from the full confidence expressed by Miss Jayalalitha "in the Prime Minister's ability to resolve the issue at a very early date."

Among those who formed part of the delegation were the then three Union Ministers from Tamil Nadu, Mr. P. Chidambaram, then Minister of state for Commerce, Mr. M. Arunachalam then Minister of State for Urban Development and Mr. P.R. Kumaramangalam then Minister of State for Law, Justice and Company Affairs and Parliamentary Affairs, the former Congress (I) Parliamentary Party Secretary, Mr. E. Anbarasu, the then Tamil Nadu Public Works Minister, Mr. Kannappan and leaders of all the political parties of Tamil Nadu as well as representatives from the Cauvery Delta Farmers Association. There was little to suggest on the response of the Prime Minister to the demand for immediate notification of the interim orders. "The Prime Minister gave the delegation a patient hearing and indicated that the government of India had accepted the Supreme Court's verdict given on the special Presidential reference and that the representations contained in the memorandum would be given due consideration", a press release issued on behalf of delegation said.

During the meeting Miss Jayalalitha explained the salient features of the memorandum and requested the then Prime Minister to gazette the interim award of the Tribunal without further delay. Leaders of various political parties as well as the representatives of the Cauvery Delta Farmers Association fully endorsed the views expressed by the then Chief Minister. The memorandum outlined in brief the circumstances under which the Cauvery Tribunal had pronounced the interim order, promulgation of Ordinance by the Karnataka Government to preempt implementation of the order, the presidential reference to the Supreme Court and the opinion rendered by the court. It said the Supreme Court had given the unanimous opinion that the interim order of the Tribunal constituted a report and a decision under Section 5 (2) of the Inter-State Water Disputes Act and had to be published in the official gazette of the Government of India as required under Section 6 of the Act to make it effective.

"In the above circumstances, we, the leaders of the various political parties, who have come as a delegation under the leadership of Chief Minister of Tamil Nadu, earnestly request the Prime Minister to take immediate action to publish the interim order of the Tribunal in the official gazette of the Governmei.t of India. We fervently hope and trust that our earnest request will be compiled with and justice rendered to the people of Tamil Nadu," the memorandum said. Prior to the submission of memorandum to the then Prime Minister, the then Chief Minister met members of the all-party delegation and discussed the view point to be presented before Mr. Rao. She read out the contents of the memorandum to be submitted to the then Prime Minister and took the consent of all the members on it.

Jayalalitha took Pot-Shots at Congress Disunity

Tamil Nadu's then Chief Minister J. Jayalalitha on February 9, 1993 took several potshots at the congress in the Assembly much to the discomfiture of opposition leader S.R. Balasubramanian. Demanding a clarification from the chair whether the Congress MLAs had walked out on February 8, 1993 as reported by newspapers, she observed that normally a party leader heads a walk-out, but on February 8, 1993, the CLP leader had remained seated while some others got up and left. "Even it is a two member party, only if both the members leave the house together, can it be called a walkout? We do not know whether they 'walked out' or went outside for refreshments. Our confusion in this matter has been confounded further with some newspapers reporting that the Congress staged a walk-out and others saying that the Vazhapadi group had walked out," she said and read out the relevant headlines from the Indian Express and The Hindus.

She asked speaker Sedaptti R. Muthiah to clarify two points—Whether there was a walk-out on February 8, 1993, and if so, whether the Congress had split. "We have always considered the congress as single party; we have not thought of them as the Vazhapadi group of Moopanar group." Mr. Muthiah then got up to say that in his capacity as a speaker he had no information of any split in the Congress, "As per Assembly records, this incident does not count as a walk-out'. The speaker also took the opportunity to caution newspapers on how they reported the proceedings of the house. "Only the names of the parties as in Assembly records should be used by newspapers," he said. "As far as matters relating to the House is concerned, there is no Vazhapadi or Moopanar group". The press should not set a wrong precedent by referring to "this group or that group", he warned.

The Assembly witnessed uproarious scenes after this, with congress members putting up a united front against the AIADMK and objecting to Chief Minister Jayalalitha's jibes. The congress MLAs rose in protest as one man when the CM made pointed remarks about the lack of discipline in the congress and contrasted it to the action taken by her party against dissident members. Sharp exchanges followed with the congressmen claiming that "Ours is a democratic party unlike yours" and the treasury benches attempting to shout down CLP leader S.R. Balasubramanian. Mr. Balasubramanian rose to clarify that February 8, 1993's incident was due to a "communication gap". Referring to CM's confusion on whether the Congress had split, he said the party remained strong and united. In this context, the CLP leader recalled DMK founder C.N. Annadurai's appeal to the then leader of the house, C. Subramaniam, not to blow up misunderstandings in the DMK, when the latter made some remarks about the 1961 split in the party.

This brought Government whip K.P. Pattabhiraman to his feet, objecting to the reference to Mr. Annadurai. The Congress members protested against this interrup–

tion and the speaker had to repeatedly appeal to the Congress members to take their seats. The CLP leader resumed his speech by pointing out dissidence was common to all parties. This led tc a chorus of protests from the AIADMK members, who claimed that there was no difference of opinion in their party. The CM intervened at this stage to say that there was no dissidence in the AIADMK. "When I speak, not one of my party men interrupts," she pointed out amidst thumping of desks by the Treasury benches. She had only wanted a clarification on whether some members had indeed walked out, she said, "If there are contradictions in your party, why blame us?" Mr. Balasubramanian however said it was not as if the AIADMK was without dissidence.

J. Jayalalitha's Fast for Cauvery Water

In a dramatic move that took by surprise party colleagues and political rivals alike, Tamil Nadu's, then Chief Minister J. Jayalalitha on July 19, 1993 went on an indefinite fast to press the Centre to implement the Cauvery tribunal's interim order awarding 205 tmc ft of water to the state. Jayalalitha carried her fast late into night on July 19, 1993 ignoring appeals by Prime Minister Narsimha Rao, Governor Channa Reddy and Karnataka Chief Minister Veerappa Moily to end the unusual agitation. "It's over two years since the interim award was announced. We have tried all humanly possible ways to get it implemented. This is the very last resort, the very last weapon in my armoury.... like the Brahmastra. When no other weapon works, the Brahmastra is used. This is my Brahmastra," Jayalalitha said soon after beginning her fast near MGR Samadhi on the Marina, Madras.

Her protest sparked off a chain reaction and reports of violence and fasting poured in from different parts of

Tamil Nadu, fuelled partly by rumours that the State Government had been dismissed. Partymen, including MLAs and MPs, undertook fasts and picketed Central offices at various places. Buses and train services were disrupted. At Madurai, AIADMK picketers went on the rampage at the railway junction, forcing hundreds of passengers to flee for safety. The mob indulged in large-scale violence, wreaking heavy damage on railway property. Earlier, they also ransacked a number of shops in the town. In New Delhi, the Water Resources Minister decided to rush the Central Water Commission chairman to Bangalore on July 19, 1993 discussions with officials of the two states.

Governor Reddy returned Madras cutting short his visit to Pondicherry and was closeted with Jayalalitha for one hour but failed to persuade her to call off her protest. He told her both Rao and Moily wanted her to end the fast. There was no direct request from the PMO to Jayalalitha. Reddy said Moily had expressed readiness to accommodate her request though not to the extent she desired. The CM, however, was firm she would end the fast only if the interim award is implemented. "I am grateful for his concern but there is no question of reconsideration," was her firm counter to Reddy's request. Dressed in a green and yellow sari and matching cape, Jayalalitha arrived at the MGR Samadhi at 9.15 a.m. on July 18, 1993. After paying respects to her mentor at the samadhi, she sat on a chair hurriedly acquired for her. "We've reached the end of our patience," she said. "We want full implementation of the interim order, with which we are not really satisfied; but this is the least we want and we won't settle for anything less," she also said.

Education in J. Jayalalitha's Tamil Nadu

In May 1993, Tamil Nadu took a pioneering step in the field of education: it announced that it would introduce a legislation to provide for compulsory enrollment and retention of children in primary schools. This far-reaching decision has brought back into focus the questions that hang over education-related issues like socio-economic conditions, the poor quality of teaching, and the indifference of the community—sometimes even parents. Then State Finance Minister V.R. Nedunchejhian had announced in the State Assembly that the Act 'would be selectively invoked to tackle the problem of drop-outs, and see that every child gets the benefit of basic education'. He said the ultimate aim is to progressively eliminate child labour in the State. Towards which end the Government is working in tandem with the UNICEF on a scheme. Nedunchejhian made it clear that such a programme would have to be realistic and endorsed by the people involved: 80 percent of the child labourers are girls.

Tamil Nadu has made rapid strides in the field of education. Universal enrollment and retention of children up to the age of 14, has been one of its priorities. In 1991, 63.7 percent of the state's population was literate. Tamil Nadu now ranks second to Kerala among the larger states of India on the literacy front. But there is still cause for concern. Does the schoolgoer actually acquire any knowledge? Former director of school education V.T. Titus says more than statistics on dropout rates, we would do well to find out how much the child really learns after a few years in school. "Even if the drop-out rate shows improvement, I would be worried about the child who stays in school for five years, but acquires very little knowledge."

The drop-out rates have shown a steady decline: 30 percent in 1981-82 to 23.15 percent in 1984-85, and to 18.27 percent in 1992-93 in the 6-11 age group. This is attributed to, among other factors, incentives like the noon-meal scheme (introduced by the MGR government), free uniforms, free text books and free bus travel. But about 20 percent still drop out before acquiring basic skills. And most often it is girls and SC/ST children who miss out.

J. Jayalalitha Opposed Terrorism in India

Then Tamil Nadu Chief Minister J. Jayalalitha, in her continued battle with the centre, on May 31, 1993 charged it with aiding and abetting the outlawed Liberation Tigers of Tamil Eelam (LTTE) to eliminate her. Talking to reporters at the Madras Airport after receiving the then new Governor Channa Reddy, Jayalalitha alleged that the centre was gunning for her by concocting false charges and casting aspersions on her integrity and intentions. "The person who must be the happiest at this turn of events is definitely Prabhakaran, the LTTE leader himself," she said. "If I am eliminated or driven out of office, I can say with certainty that hereafter no leader will come forward to oppose the LTTE, or any other terrorist or militant organisation, or terrorism in any form. That will be India's loss." She also went on record for the first time stating that she was not consulted over the appointment of Channa Reddy as the Governor of Tamil Nadu. Reacting sharply to a query on whether the centre had consulted her. She said that she was only informed by the centre about the resignation of Governor Bhisma Narain Singh and appointment of Reddy. "It is unfortunate that the centre does not follow conventions when it comes to opposition-ruled states," she said.

She, however, said she had the greatest respect and regard for Reddy. "He is no stranger to me. I have known him from the time he was the Andhra Pradesh Chief Minister." Referring to the LTTE, she claimed that she was "high on its hit list, if not number one on the list." She charged the central agencies—the CBI and the RAW—with forging letters and fabricating evidence to build up a false case against her. She said she had evidence in support of her charge, and would release the same to press at an appropriate time. "I am deeply anguished that false and baseless charges are made against the Tamil Nadu government by the Home Minister himself." "But I did not do so, I had the courage and determination to fight the LTTE. But it was unfortunate that after waging such a battle at personal risk, "this is the reward that I get," she said.

"It should not be forgotten that I was mainly responsible for getting the LTTE banned in India. From the time I took over as Chief Minister, till today, there has been no change in my attitude towards the LTTE, which is that it must be wiped out." When asked if she would resign in view of the supreme court upholding the high court order on the teachers' training institute, she said, "I do not see any reason to quit." Answering a specific query on whether Reddy would help patch up the differences with the centre, she said she did not know what was in his mind. She also said that the State Congress leaders were unnecessarily raising a hue and cry over not getting sufficient passes for the governor's reception. It was unfortunate that they had deliberately chosen to boycott the airport reception and gone to the press making false allegations, she added. "I did not want anything unpleasant during the reception and had directed the public department secretary to issue all the 50 passes for the swearing in ceremony and 500 passes for the airport reception to TNCC general secretary Dhandyuthapani as originally requested by him." Accordingly, the passes were sent through a special messenger on May 30, 1993, night. However, the TNCC representatives refused to receive the invitations, she said.

II. V.N. JANAKI RAMACHANDRAN

Mrs. Vaikom Nani Janaki Ramachandran (V.N. Janaki

Ramachandran), became the first woman Chief Minister of Tamil Nadu in 1988 after the death of her husband MGR (M.G. Ramachandran). Born at Vaikom in 1924, 35 kilometres from Kottayam in Kerala, as the daughter of Nani Amma of Vadakkekara Kandathil Parambil and Rajagopala Iyer, a musician and elder brother of late savant-lyricist Papanasam Sivan. After formal schooling the family moved to Nagapattinam and later to Kumbakonam. After five years her father shifted to Madras, and found work as an actor and lyricist in films with the help of late director K. Subramaniam, who was a patron of the Kumbakonam School where he was teaching. And it was also K. Subramaniam who encouraged V.N. Janaki to take to acting in films.

Janaki did not pursue her studies in Madras, but took to dancing and music. She then made an entry into films. Her first movie with MGR was 'Mohini' in the late 40s. While she was acting in films, she married Ganapathi Bhatt, who was an odd job man to late director Sunder Rao Nadkarni. Janaki had a son Surendran by this marriage. However, the marriage did not last. The relationship between her and M.G. Ramachandran (MGR) grew when she was cast with him in a few films. Soon they were married. She discontinued acting after her marriage to MGR. Though not actively involved in party politics, she was privy to almost everything that MGR did in politics and in the administration of the State. Again, though she never really wanted to play an important role in the post-MGR political scene, she was persuaded to enter politics by partymen who felt that this would help preserve her husband's party and legacy.

III. LATE UTPAL DUTT

It was in his very first film, 'Michael Madhusudan', that Utpal Dutt impressed viewers with his acting ability. A brilliant student of St. Xavier's College, he was a journalist working for 'The Statesman' when Modhu Bose selected him for the role. Initially there were doubts all around whether the newcomer would do justice to the role of the poet who, out of love for English, converted to Christianity but later returned to his mother tongue. Utpal Dutt not only allayed all such doubts but also left a lasting impression on the audience. The character must have found a resonance in the actor who lived the role, literally. For Utpal Dutt, in life, was a repetition of the phenomenon that was Madhusudan Dutta. Like the legend Utpal—due to an out and out anglicised upbring–ing—was closer to the English language and culture. And like Michael he too was transformed into a true Bengali devoted to and contributing massively to our poetry and drama.

What Utpal achieved in the language is amazing. He used it with enviable lase as we saw in 'Chhayanat' one of his earliest plays, and later in 'Angar' and 'Kallol'. And in 'Tiner Talwar' he showed a through grasp of the early 19th century Bengali dialect and colloquial usage. From 'Chhayanat' to 'Tiner Talawar' was, of course, a long road strewn with plays on subjects ranging from the Naxalbari Movement to the upheavals in the Eastern Europe and the French Revolution to the life of coal miners. It was long after the film, though, that Tapas Sen came to know of Utpal Dutt's love for theatre. He was then working with his own group, a small outfit which was later named 'Little Theatre Group'. It was essentially an English-oriented theatre group. And in 1949, when they (Tapan Sen and Utpal Dutt) first met in the coffee House through a common friend, Robi Sen Gupta, then talked and talked only theatre.

The first time they worked together was for a play at the ITF Pavilion off Park Street. 'Sangbadik' was Saroj Datta's translation of Constantin Simonov's 'The Russian Question'. During the production Tapas Sen realised, theatre was not just a pastime for Utpal, and soon after he left his job with the newspaper to be a full-time theatre worker. After a tour with Geoffrey Kendal's group, Shakespearana, Utpal settled down, heart and soul, into Bengali theatre. Along with friends like Robi Sen Gupta, Pratap Roy, Bunty Khan and Dilip Roy he staged Bengali plays including Tagore's 'Achalayatan' and 'Tapati'. But Geoffrey Kendal was a great influence on Utpal who acknowledged him as his theatrical guru. Utpal was a voracious reader who shifted loyalty totally to Bengali literature. With remarkable ease the handled its colloquialism in 'Titas Ekti Nadir Naam', on the lives of fishermen in North Bengal. Again, the locale for 'Ekla Chalo Re', on the terrorist uprising in British India, was East Bengal in the' 30s, and the language was true to the dialect of the region.

The growth of director Utpal Dutt was closely linked with the transformation of the man, both into a Bengali and a progressive, left-minded individual. The political ideology was indeed becoming stronger by the day, as we see from the plays that kept the Minerva Theatre—a commercial theatre managed and run by the Little Theatre Group-going for ten years. As a director he kept pace with his own social and political growth, and with happenings in his own country and abroad. But his very own contribution to Indian theatre remains in inculcating a social purpose in whatever he did. He did not hesitate in interpreting the world around him in a very direct manner. And this, even when it meant imprisonment by the then Congress Government or beating-up by the hired hooligans of political parties. In his courage to launch a frontal attack on the establishment Utpal will remain an inspiration for years to come. In his productions even Shakespeare came through as a socially aware playwright and not as one who treated art for art's sake. With Shakespeare of course he had a special relation. He alone could have done 'Julius Caesar' the he did in modern costume, down to wireless transmitters for soldiers! Small wonder that he was the only Shakespeare scholar from India invited to the quadricentennial celebration of the Bard in his birthplace, Startford-on-Avon.

After the phenomenal success of the Minerva plays like 'Angar' and 'Kallol', Utpal was approached by Jatra companies to write for them. He was an avid listener of Jatras as he was of classical music. Attracted by actors of the calibre of Panchu Sen and the two Phanibabus, he wrote some Jatras and directed them while continuing with Minerva. That was when he offered political confrontation in the Jatra format, in 'Jalianwalabagh', 'Rifle' and others. A total theatre person, Utpal was informed on set designs abroad as he was of the developments in stage lighting. He had a clear idea of what he wanted, and achieved it even with limited resources and obsolete conditions. Between the two of them the understanding seemed to be total. He reciprocated on whatever Tapas Sen thought, imagined or designed. In a distinct contrast to Tapas Sen's experience with Shambhu Mitra, Utpal, never intervened in what Sen did. He would wait till Sen was done, then tell him frankly if he wanted any change. Utpal Dutt had a total ensemble approach in treatment. It was never one or two persons doing their own job. He planned out his productions like a symphony orchestra where every single element has a definite role to play, yet fitted perfectly into the total design. No one was unimportant, all had something to contribute and Utpal was the one who infused this spirit in his entire team.

Utpal Dutt the friend was warm, humorous, jorial. But he could also be strict when it came to the group's discipline. Nothing would count then. During the rehearsals of 'Titas' Bijon Bhattacharya would come in totally unprepared with his part, without memorising his lines. This upset Utpal very much though Bijanda was a senior director and actor. One day he simply kicked the door, shouted 'Fetch me a taxi', and left, leaving everybody, including Bijanda, dumbfounded. Next day Bijanda came fully prepared with his part. Even as a writer of street plays he was an immense success and the propaganda plays like 'Kalo Haath' or 'Din Badaler Pala' drew larger crowds than any political leader could. Any single night they would perform at several places three or four miles apart. For, as in other mediums, he worked with complete devotion, and the immense strain that entailed took him away from us so prematurely.

PART IV

Chapter 11

Conclusion
I. Ronald Wilson Reagon
II. Great Charlie Chaplin

I. RONALD WILSON REAGON

Ronald Wilson Reagon was born in the tiny town of Tampico, Illinois, United States of America, on February 6, 1911. He was the second of the two sons (no daughters) of John Edward Reagon and his wife Nelle Wilson. Ronald's brother Neil had been born two years previously. Reagon senior, known to all as Jack, was a first-generation, black-haired Catholic Irishman who made his living as a shoe salesman, and whose experience as such ranged from being a clerk in a variety of stores to at times managing his own business. Jack Reagon took a serious interest in foot-wear and was considered to be good at his trade. The one apparent blemish in his character was a propensity for whisky, which left his youngest son with a lifelong dislike for alcohol. The occasional sight of Reagon's father "under the influence" appears to be the only major upsetting factor in a childhood which his contemporaries describe as being 'about as traumatic as apple pie.' The Reagons were a nice, ordinary, Midwest working-class family who adhered to the simple basics of American life and who were never involved in events either tragic or scandalous. Nelle Reagon was a Protestant of Scots-English stock, a lady sympathetic to her husband's weakness for drink but morally opposed to it, whose interests in literature and the arts provided a family counterbalance to his bluff and gregarious nature. Jack Reagon taught his sons to stand up for themselves in life, to fight fair whenever a fight was unavoidable, to respect the rights of the working man and to support the Democratic party.

The first nine years in the life of Ronald Reagon were spent in a number of residences in Illinois. His father took jobs wherever they were available and the Reagons did not own a home until many years later, when their son became a well-employed actor and bought the family a house in California. They lived for periods in Tampico, the south side of Chicago, Galesburg, Monmouth and again in Tampico before settling in Dixon, a town of ten thousand populations about ninety miles from Chicago. It is Dixon which Reagon fondly regards as his home-town and the setting of a life which he describes as being Tom Sawyer-like, without the outlandish adventures of Twain's imagination. Reagon inherited a hale and hearty personality from his father, along with a certain amount of anger over the foibles of the world. Reagon senior possessed a very sense of humour. He enjoyed telling jokes and was appreciated by his friends and customers as a good raconteur. He had the Irish 'gift of gab' and it would be difficult for his famous son to deny a similar characteristic. He was also a man with a great desire for success, who never found it, except vicariously, in his actor son. Jack Reagon did not live to see his son enter politics, but it doubtless would have pleased him greatly.

Young Ronald was undersized as a boy, but wiry and energetic. He was fond of the outdoor life and hunting, fishing, swimming in creeks, trekking through woods and climbing hills took up most of his out-of-school attention. He also had a marked love of sports, although this was somewhat curtailed by a case of short-sightedness which ruled out baseball but not football. Reagon became adopt at this game at an early age, which had considerable bearing on his later professional life. He recalls a passion for charging down make shift football fields with motley gangs of boys, resulting in endless cuts and bruises, but states that these were the happiest times of his life. His school work was above average and he abetted his learning with long hours of reading in the public library, to cater to his curiosity about the world. His mother fostered an early interest in literature and often gave dramatic readings in her home and at social gatherings at which young Ronald was badgered into participating. He was taken to the performances of visiting drama companies to see fifth rate versions of famous plays, but this exposure was enough to increase his interest to the people who went on stage and emoted. However, attending plays was less pleasurable than going to the movies and cheering the antics of such renowned celluloid heroes as Douglas Fairbanks, Tom Mix and William S. Hart.

In the summer of 1925, fourteen year old Ronald was forced to relinquish some of the hours he devoted to football to take his first job. The Reagon family income was always uncertain, and it became necessary for the boy to help to common cause, as well as to save money for his own further education. He joined a construction company and went to work with a pick and shovel ten hours a day. By the end of the summer he had been able to save two hundred dollars. The following summer he took a more likable job as a lifeguard at Dixon's Lowell Park, which he continued to work at as a summer job for the next seven years. This position afforded him exercise and fresh air and gave him his first real sense of the nature of human beings, particularly in regard to gratitude. Reagon discovered that people did not enjoy being rescued, and that they invariably did not believe they needed rescuing and that saving their lives in view of others caused them painful embarrassment. But the job was better than digging foundation ditches. One of the people Reagon most admired during his teens was a high school footballer named Garland Waggoner. When Waggoner became a star player at Eureka College, Reagon decided that it would be his school as well. Eureka was a Christian church college similar to Texas Christian University, but a fraction the size. The school was co-educational and had facilities for about 250 students. It was situated about twenty miles from Peorica and was a college with minuscule funds, honourable traditions and high standards. Reagon enrolled in the fall of 1928 and became very fond of the school. He states in his autobiography, "I still think, after years of crisscrossing the United States, that it is one of the loveliest colleges in existence. It seemed to me then, as I walked up the path, to be another home. There were five big main buildings, arranged in a semicircle, built of red American reminiscence of English Georgian architecture. Walls were covered with friendly ivy, and the whole framed with huge elms and rolling green lawns."

Reagan did not have sufficient funds to enroll at Eureka. The tuition was $180 a year and his total savings came to only about twice that amount. But sympathetic school officials, no doubt sensing his desperation and longing, awarded him a scholarship at half tuition costs and a job to enable him to work his way through college. Reagon washed dishes, served as a lifeguard at the college pool and as a coach in sports events. In addition to being a conscientious student, he took advantage of the college standing in the scholastic football league to excel at his favourite sport. Something occurred at Eureka that would reveal a facet of Reagon's nature not previously shown—a propensity of political discussions and debates. The college, always strapped for funds, made the decision to take drastic measures to curb expenditures and revise the management. These plans would have reduced the number of faculty and deprived many students of their studies. The instigating president persuaded the school board to adopt his plans, overlooking the reaction of the student body, which at a school with a strong family environment, was virtually fascistic. The students went on strike and Reagon was foremost among the organizers. He was a representative of the freshman class and was partly responsible for the highly organized, orderly petitions made to the school board. Students and teachers stood united in their cause and soon defeated the plans of the new president. It was during this time that Reagon first stood before an audience and addressed them with his views. He discovered the thrill of holding the attention of a group.

While at Eureka Reagon again became involved in the business of play acting. During a summer vacation in Dixon he had seen the touring company production of 'Journey's End' and reacted to it with curiosity about the job of an actor. Theatrical drama appealed to him, and he joined the school's dramatic society. He had previously preformed in plays at the Dixon High School, but not it seemed an interest worth further consideration. By the time of graduation, young Reagon was undecided about his main pursuit—sports or drama. His passion for both had to do, he admits, with a love of showing off. Either profession seemed an exciting way to live for a boy who had grown up wearing his brother's castoffs, whose father struggled to make fifty dollars a week and whose mother had to work to supplement the family income. The Eureka Dramatic Society won second place in 1931 in the annual play contest staged by Northwestern University, and Ronald Reagon was one of a half dozen student actors awarded an honours trophy. The following year when the initial euphoria of attending Eureka wore off, Reagon decided that he wanted to participate in some form of show business. Hollywood and Broadway were too far removed from reality to consider, but he possessed a talent that could possibly get him into radio broadcasting—the knock of ad-libbing sports commentary.

When Reagon left Eureka with a Bachelor of Arts degree and credits in sociology and economics, he raised eyebrows by claiming that he could earn five thousand dollars a year within five years. It was a boast, but one that actually materialized. In the late summer of 1932, he left for Chicago, at that time, a major centre of American Radio, and went about breaking into business of microphones and airwaves. NBC was his first point of attack, then CBS, then the big independent stations and finally the stations listed in the telephone book. Since he had no money, Reagon made the rounds mostly on foot with refusals at every point, he decided to take a second crack at NBC. It was impossible to see anyone on the managerial level, not to mention get an audition, but a kindly secretary was impressed enough to give him advice. She said there was not a chance of anyone without experience breaking into broadcasting at that level, but that there were many smaller stations always looking for talent. The weary Reagon hitchhiked back to Dixon. His father perked up his spirits with a suggested plan, which was to take the family car and map out a few days of driving within a certain radius to hit all the stations possible. The first hit Reagon made was WOC, Davenport, Iowa, a station which derived its call letters from its parent company, world of Chiropractic, founded by Colonel B.J. Palmer of the Palmer school of Chiropractic. The colonel also owned station WHO, Des Moines, and both stations had a large listening audience. It was unlikely that a newcomer could break into radio even on this level, but that is precisely what Ronald Reagon did.

His mentor in broadcasting was Peter Mac Arthur, a gruff but warm-hearted Scotsman who had come to America as a member of Harry Lauder's troupe of vaudevillians, but who had given up the life of an entertainer when his arthristis reached a crippling degree. Mac Arthur had gone to the Palmer School of Chiropractic seeking relief from his pains, but because of his fine speaking voice and expressive manner he was hired by their radio department. He was programme director of WOC when the eager young Reagon approached him for a job. Mac Arthur explained that he was a week late for the auditions they had been conducting for a new announcer. This infuriating piece of news caused Reagon to storm out of the office, shouting, "How the hell does a guy ever get to be a sports announcer if he cannot get inside a station?" The use of the term 'sports announcer' was responsible for Reagon's start in radio. Mac Arthur called him back and demanded to know if he knew anything about football, and if he did, could he do play-by-play commentary? When Reagon replied affirmatively, Mac Arthur steered him into an empty studio and instructed him to demonstrate. Reagon recalled the exciting fourth quarter of a game Eureka had played opposite Western State University and launched into twenty minutes of frenzied description. Mac Arthur was so impressed that he told Reagon to return in a few days and take a crack at being the announcer for a football broadcast for five dollars and car fare. Reagon's first words on the air were, "How do you do, ladies and gentlemen. We are speaking to you from high atop the Memorial Stadium of the University of Iowa, looking down from the west on the south forty-yard line....". His natural talent for announcer's patter and his enthusiasm and knowledge of football caused him to be hired for a subsequent game broadcast. When an opening at the station became available, he was signed on at WOC at a salary of one hundred dollars a month—a seeming elevation from poverty to wealth.

Despite his skill at sports patter, Reagon was not considered a good announcer in the regular line of work. He had difficulty reading scripts, at getting the words 'off the paper', and this problem stayed with him even as a movie star. First read—throughs of scripts would cause directors and fellow actors in his early Hollywood days to question his screen ability. But once Reagon learned his lines, he always did well. In those first few months at WOC, though, several sponsors complained about the mediocre manner in which their commercials were being read, and on one occasion Reagon was fired by the station. He was rehired when his replacement refused to accept the terms of employment. Reagon put more effort into his work. Peter Mac Arthur again gave Reagon a push in the right career direction. When station WHO in Des Moines needed an announcer for sports events, Mac Arthur sent Reagon, and over the next four years he built a first class reputation in his specialized area of broadcasting. WHO was a 50,000 watt station with a huge audience throughout the mid-west. When it became a part of the NBC network, Reagon was heard coast-to-coast on many top sports broadcasts. He announced dozens of football games form major press boxes in the mid-west and covered hundreds of big league baseball games, track events and swimming meets. He was also occasionally hired to write sports columns in newspapers and to address audiences at banquets. Ronald Reagon found himself well-employed and thoroughly enjoying life.

Reagon's full time employment in radio had begun in January of 1933, when Franklin Delano Roosevelt came to presidential power. To his Democrat family, this seemed like the best of coincidences. His father had happily accepted a position as an official with the works progress administration Jack Reagon was respected for his sympathetic aid to fellow citizens in Dixon, Illinois, and this post also gave his broadcaster son more insight into the world of politics. Sadly, Ronald's father shortly thereafter became afflicted with a heart condition. It was at this time that Ronald Reagon indulged himself in a lifelong hankering to ride horses. This desire might have had its start with the idolized cowboy stars in the movies, but it was also evidence of Reagon's love of sports, the outdoors and being in motion. A fellow announcer was a reserve officer in the cavalry and suggested that Reagon apply for a commission, giving him access to army horses and all the free riding he could want. The idea appealed to Reagon until he learned that eye-sight was of primary importance in the commissioning of a cavalry officer. Reagon at this time wore glasses, and would later wear corneal lenses once they became available. But in 1935 he became a reserve second lieutenant with the 14th cavalry regiment at Des Moines by the simple expedient of cheating. During his medial examination, instead of a piece of cardboard, he held his hands over his deficient eyes and peeped through the slight gaps between his fingers. This had the same effect as punching a pinhole in a cardboard, producing the effect of a corrective lens for a nearsighted person.

As Reagon's fame as a sports announcer grew, he began the first of several annual trips to California's Catalina Island to report on the spring training of the Chicago Cubs. He rarely had an opportunity to get away in the busy summer months, so the trips to the coast allowed a welcome break from the severe Iowa winters. Reagon had not forgotten his idea of breaking into theatrical life. In school and college, and with encouragement from his mother, he enjoyed dramatic performing. Being a sports commentator had satisfied some of that hunger, but during a visit to California in February of 1937, he decided to take measures to get into the movies. The luck and the ease with which Reagon entered radio were repeated in his Hollywood approach. Joy Hodges, a singer Reagon knew in Des Moines, was then singing with Jimmy Grier's Orchestra at the Biltmore Bowl in Los Angeles. When Reagon asked her advice, she arranged for him to meet agent Bill Meiklejohn, who was sufficiently impressed to ask for a screentest at Wanrer Bros for the hopeful. The casting director, Max Arnow, agreed to the test, at which Reagon acted a scene from the Philip Barry play 'Holiday'. When he was asked to wait in Los Angeles for a few days until Jack Warner had a chance to view the test. Reagon replied that he had to return to Des Moines and his job, an independent manner that probably prompted the telegramme from Warners offering a seven year contract and a starting wage of two hundred dollars a week.

Ronald Reagon's Hollywood career began on June 1, 1937. Rumour had it that young contract actors could languish around the studio for weeks and possibly months before being called before the cameras. But Reagon was assigned the lead in a minor picture within days of being on the lot, and was thereafter kept busy by Warners for most of the time he was in their employ, especially during the early years of his contract. He was somewhat surprised at his easy entry into the picture business, assuming that there were multitudes of young men of his kind available. In fact, Warners needed a likeable male actor in his mid-twenties, with typical good American looks—a type that Reagon fitted perfectly. The studio had just lost the actor Ross Alexander (a suicide) and Regan resembled him enough to take his place. They were particularly impressed by Reagon's speaking voice and his bright, enthusiastic personality.

Reagon's debut on the screen was ironic in that the studio cast him as a rather brash radio announcer in 'Love is on the Air'. That same pleasantly eager quality became the keynote of his movie image over the next few years. Reagon found that scooping up the lead in his first film was no guarantee of immediate stardom and that he was strictly a journeyman actor to his employers, whereas other studios might have spent time grooming him as a star. Warner Bros, often described as a working class studio, was run like a well-tooled factory, ever conscious of budgets and rarely sympathetic toward employees. This toughness had, in fact, been largely responsible for the growth of trade unionism in Hollywood. The elation of playing the lead in 'Love is on the Air' was soon lessened by Reagon's receiving an unbilled bit part in his next film, 'Hollywood Hotel,' and by having his small role in 'Submarine D-I' cut from the final print. He hardly had time to dwell on any disappointments, though.

In 1938, he appeared in no fewer than eight movies, ranging from leads in B pictures to small roles in A products. It was a year in which he quickly learned the techniques of acting before cameras, and also that Warners expected total devotion for their wages. Reagon was hired at two hundred dollars a week, which grew to five hundred dollars over the next two years. By the start of filming 'Kings Row' in 1941, he was earning one thousand dollars a week, which was not considered, even at that time, a startlingly good salary for a man who had been a well-known screen figure for four years. However, it was certainly a nice way to make a living and Reagon enjoyed a fine, albeit modest, life style. He indulged in sports such as swimming, riding and golf, and avoided involvement in any scandalous or abnormal activities. He was not noted for being difficult with his employers or untoward in his social behaviour. He enjoyed his good fortune and felt that he was a lucky man. Ronald Reagon had known Jan Wyman since he joined Warners in 1937. She had been put under contract of the studio in 1936, but it was not until they were cast together in 'Brother Rat' in the summer of 1938 that they became seriously interested in one another. Shortly after the completion of the film, they announced their engagement. Wyman made it known that her appetite for nightclubbing had diminished in favour of Reagon's love for sports, particularly football games. After a courtship of just over a year, and much comment about them being the ideal American couple, they were married on January 26, 1940. Louella Parsons had been the first to announce their engagement and had also taken them along on promotional tours. She gave them a wedding reception at her home. At the time of their marriage, the Reagons were film players of about equal rank. They both earned about five hundred dollars a week, which enabled them to live a comfortable life but not one of star magnitude, although neither professed any great desire for glittering lifestyle. Wyman's career continued on the level of a secondary player but Reagon's gradually increased in star status. She claimed considerable pride in this and backed him in his interests. In 1941 they appeared together in a short picture called 'How to Improve your Golf'.

On one occasion, Jane Wyman surprised her fans by announcing that marrying Reagon had changed her personality for the better. She claimed to have previously been an anxious and rather suspicious woman, and that he had helped her to become more at ease with people. "He was such a sunny person. I never felt free to talk to anyone until I met Ronie." Their happiness was increased with the arrival of a daughter, Maureen Elizabeth, on January 27, 1941, which was also Wyman's twenty-seventh birthday. The Reagons adopted a boy in 1945 whom they named Michael Edward. On June 26, 1947, another daughter was born to them, but the child was four months premature and died the following day. Ronald Reagon qualifies as a family man. He claims to have enjoyed his youth in Illinois, despite the hard times, and both his marriages have been traditional domestic relationships. Shortly after his arrival in Hollywood, he brought his parents to live in Los Angeles, which also became the home of his brother Neil, who made a career in the advertising industry. By the time of the move to California, Jack Reagon's heart condition had worsened to the point where the could no longer work, but his actor son gave him the job of handling his fan mail.

Reagon's first four years in the movies were the enjoyable basis for a pleasant lifestyle, but contained few performances that offered dramatic satisfaction. It was not a career which could be listed as important in the film industry. He made an impact with his role as George Gipp in 'Knute Rockne—All American', but mostly Reagon portrayed a pleasing B hero or a solid supporting player to Warner's major stars. In 1941, Warners gave him a lead in 'Kings Row', a somber drama built along epic lines. His performance as a small town playboy brought down by grim circumstances put him into the big film league. His agent, Lew Wasserman, tripled Reagon's salary, bringing him more than three thousand dollars a week. It was the lucky break for which all actors yearn, but it came at a time when it could do him little good. On April 14, 1942 Ronald Reagon was inducted into the United States Army. Because of his commission in the cavalry reserve, Reagon was made a second lieutenant in that branch of the service, but because of his eyesight (he had discarded glasses for contact lenses) he was disqualified from combat duty. Reagon reported at Fort Dixon, San Francisco, and became a liaison officer in charge of loading transports. After a few dull months at Fort Dixon, Reagon was transferred to the rapidly expanding Army Air Corps. Reagon was then sent to the Hal Roach Studios, under Army jurisdiction during the war. The studio was located in Culver City, only ten miles from Warner Bros. enabling Reagon to live at home. The Roach studio soon acquired the Hollywood title of 'Fort Wacky' because of the vast amount of movie talent in uniform stationed there, and also because of the actor's unconventional way of soldiering. It was less formal than most military posts, but most productive. "We would turn out training films and documentaries, and conduct a training school for combat camera units. All of the newsreel material in the theatres of bombings and strafings was the product of these units."

Reagon's years in the army were interrupted a number of times to permit him to appear in Hollywood's contributions to the war. He was relieved from duty for several weeks to make warners'. 'This is the Army', a film which raised millions of dollars for service charities. Aside from his regular duties as a narrator and director of training films, he also appeared in the USO promotional film 'Mr. Gardenia Jones (1942), in which he played a lonely soldier in a strange town; 'Rear Gunner (1944), a film about army Chaplians, with Reagon as a Catholic priest. He also made appearances at events organized to support the war effort. Reagon received his discharge from the army on December 9, 1945, but which time he held the rank of captain. He decided to enjoy a few months of vacation before returning to Warners and resuming his contract. Like many other stars making combacks to the screen, it was not easy to enter the swing of things. New stars has appeared in the meantime, tastes had changed, and, indeed, the world itself had changed. Warners finally found a vehicle which they considered right for Reagon's re-entry into the movie world, 'Stallion Road', but they did not release it until March of 1947. By that time, Reagon had been off the screen for a long while. It was the first of twenty two post-war movies he would be in before retiring from pictures. None of the films, were ever another 'Kings Row'. His salary was star status, resuming at thirty-five hundred dollars and increasing with the years, but it was not simply a matter of money. The films Reagon was making were not of sufficient value to increase his standing as a box office draw. With the making of 'Hellcats of the Navy' in 1957, ten years after his return to the screen, his career was virtually over. But the Hollywood political scene was taking up more of Reagon's time, particularly the running of unions and guilds.

The resultant union demands for labour laws were proportionately severe. During the war, the American Federation of Labour gave the country a no-strike pledge for the duration. The one place where that pledge was not honoured was Hollywood. Toward the end of the war years, strikes rippled through the film industry. They were mostly moves to bring larger salaries and gain better working conditions, but there was evidence of larger political aspects, including talk of communist take over. People began polarizing their position toward the left and right. This was the atmosphere in which Reagon returned to the picture business. He had long been an officer of the screen actors guild and had joined the board in 1938, exhibiting a talent for bargaining and negotiating. Eventually he became a 'rabid union man'. After the war, his involvement grew even wider, and he joined many causes in his belief that the industry and the country were in trouble. Reagon looks back on those years at himself as a liberal of an almost extreme 'bleeding heart' stripe. Aside from SAG, he served on the boards of the American Veterans Committee, and the Hollywood Independent Citizens Committee of arts, Sciences and Professions. He also inadvertently found himself involved in organizations with increasingly leftist sympathies. While maintaining a set of liberal convictions, he began to compaign against communist influence. He was joined by many famous Hollywood figures, but many people in Hollywood disagreed with these views. In October of 1947, Reagon was a witness before the House Committee on Un-American Activities in its investigation of Communism in the film industry. That same year, he was elected President of the Screen Actors Guild. In 1949 he was elected chairman of the Motion Picture Industry Council, representing labour, management and other factions. By that time his skills as an arbitrator were much respected.

In 1950, Ronald Reagon enjoyed a return to Dixon, Illinois, where he was honoured for a week as a local boy who had made good. Not long after, he appeared on his first television show, an episode of CBS 'Airflyte Theatre' unaware at that time how important the medium would later become in his career. Over the next few years, he appeared in a dozen top television dramatic presentations, and in 1954, Reagon accepted an offer to become the host of 'The General Electric Theatre'. This may be regarded as one of the most important decisions in Reagon's life. It was not simply a matter of being the host and, occasionally, an actor on a series which ran eight years, but the opportunity helped to develop his skills as a lecturer and speechmaker. Part of his job was to work with the GE Public Relations Department to promote a company image, which included touring the United States and making personal appearances at GE's one hundred and thirty five plants. He addressed the employees and their families on company policy, the role of business in national life and the dangers of over-government. It is thought by many who know Reagon that his political nature emerged from his role as a GE lecturer. It was, of course, abetted by his involvement in Hollywood union politics. He resigned as president of SAG in 1952, but served on the board of directors until he was again elected president in 1959. In his second term as president, Reagon settled a strike which resulted in increased income and medical benefits for the members, but he resigned a year later when he felt his involvement in a production company would run counter to his union position.

Another major change in Reagon's life occurred on March 4, 1952, when he married actress Nancy Davis. They had met two years prior when Reagon was asked to help clear her of charges of communist leanings. It evolved that there was another woman of the same name in the film industry. During his efforts to help clear up this matter, Reagon discovered a lady who shared his views on politics and supported him in every way. Two years of courting culminated in a wedding in which Reagon's friend William Holden was the best man. The marriage has been described by all who know the couple as ideal, as well as one which further encouraged the actor's political abilities. Nancy Davis was the daughter of Dr. Loyal Davis, a distinguished neurosurgeon and a prominent political conservative. Reagon and his father-in-law no doubt found much in common politically and that the doctor was stimulating to his interests. If Reagon ever felt that he had not been a great Hollywood success before the war and that is postwar movie career was less than he had hoped for, his life after both his marriage and the appointment as a General Electric star spokesman brought him success on a more agreeable level. His income was satisfying, as was his field of work. He also enjoyed the pleasure of creating a second family when on October 22, 1952, Patricia Ann Reagon was born in an emergency Caesarean operation. On May, 20, 1958, Ronald Prescott Reagon arrived, also by Caesarean delivery. In 1954, the Reagons lived in a beautiful home in Pacific Palisades, about a mile from the ocean, and fortune seemed kind to a man who had begun life on the modest side of the tracks.

When the 'General; Electric Theatre' series ended Reagon was out of a job, but not for long. He was hired as the host of the veteran television series 'Death Valley

Days', with its entertaining brief yarns about life in western America. It was a pleasant assignment for Reagon, who occasionally played the lead in the stories, but his days as an actor were drawing to a close. Ronald Reagon finally traded in his Democratic Party membership for the Republican cause in 1962. He had been a Democrat for Eisenhower and a Democrat for Nixon, but throughout the fifties, his political sentiments veered more and more to the right. By the early sixties he was an active campaigner against communism, and in 1964 supported both Barry Goldwater for president and George Murphy in the California senatorial election. A speech he made that year on behalf of Goldwater reportedly drew more contributions than any other in political history. These efforts did not go without notice, and in 1965 a group of California businessmen formed a group called 'The Friends of Ronald Reagon', to support him in running for the office of governor of California.

On November 8, 1966, Ronald Reagon was elected governor with a 57.8 percent of the vote, giving him more than eight hundred thousand votes over Edmund G. Brown. Reagon served two terms and his supporters claim that during those eight years he reduced government spending and rebated millions of dollars to taxpayer. For Californians, the most indelible memory of the Reagon administration was his tough attitude toward the state's academic troubles. He won much admiration for his refusal to tolerate student strikes and demands at the taxpayer's expense. After the completion of his term as governor, Reagon returned to his Pacific Palisades home and devoted his time to writing newspaper columns on political matters and to preparing a daily five-minute broadcast. In the Gallup Poll of January 1975, he was given ninth place among the most admired Americans. By the end of the year, Reagon had decided to enter the contest for the presidency of the United States, but his campaigning met with defeat at

Table 11.1

Ronald Reagan—Star Politico; Reagon's Films of Socio-Political Background in which he acted

S.No.	*Title of the film*	*Year*	*Producer*	*Director*	*Running Time*	*Photographer*	*Other Artistes of the film*
1	*2*	*3*	*4*	*5*	*6*	*7*	*8*
1.	Love is on the Air	1937	Bryn Foy	Nick Grinde	61 minutes	Jame Van Trees	Fddie Acuff, Robert Barrat, Raymond Hatton, Willar Parker
2.	Hollywood Hotel	1938	Hal B. Wallis	Buslry Borkeley	103 minutes	Charles Rosher	Dick Powell, Rosemary Lane, Lola Lane, Ted Healy, Johnnie Davis
3.	Swing Your Lady	1938	Samuel Bischoff	Ray Enright	79 minutes	Arthur Edeson	Hecmphrey Bogart, Frank Mc Hugh, Louise Fajenda
4.	Sergeant Murphy	1938	Bryan Foy	B. Reeves Eeason	57 Minutes	Ted Mc-Cord	Mary Maguire, Donald Crish, Ben Hendicks, Willian Davidson
5.	Accidents Will Happen	1938	Bryan Foy	William Clemens	62 minutes	L. William O'Connell	Gloria Blondell, Dick Purcelh, Sheila Bromley, Addison Richards, Hugh O'Connell Janet Shauv, Elliott Sullivan, Anderson Lawlor, Spec O'Donell, Kenneth Harlan, Don Barclay, Earl Dwire, Max Hoffman, Junior, John Butler
6.	Cowboy from Brooklyn	1938	Lou Edelman	Lloyd Bacon	77 Minutes	Arthur Edeson	Dick Powell, Pat O'Brien, Priscilla Lane, Rosella Towne, Harry Barris, Elisaleth Risdon, Ann, Sheridan, Johnny Davis, Dick Foran, Emma Dunn

(Contd.)

1	2	3	4	5	6	7	8
7.	Boy Meets Girl	1938	George Abbott	Lloyd Bacon	90 minutes	Sol Polito	James Cagney, Pat O'Brien, Marie Wilson, Ralpp Bellamy, Frank Mc Hugh, Dick Foran, Bruce Lester, Paul Clark, James Steppenson, Pierre Watkins, John Ridgely
8.	Girls on Probation	1938	Bryon Foy	Willian Mc Gann	63 minutes	Arthur Todd	Jone Bryan, Anthony Averill, Sheila Bromley, Henry O'Neill, Elisabeth Risdon, Sig Rumann, Dorothy Peterson, Estler Dale, Susan Hayward
9.	Brother Rat	1938	Robert Lord	William Keighley	90 minutes	Ernest Haller	Wayne Morris, Priscilla Lane, Eddie Albert, Jane Wyman, Jane Bryan, Johnny Davis, Henry O'Neill, William Tracy, Larry Williams, Gordon Oliver
10.	Going Places	1939	Hall B. Wallis	Ray Enright	84 minutes	Arthur L. Todd	Dick Powell, Anita Louise, Allen Jenkins, Walter Catlett, Harold Huber, Larry Williams, Thurston Hall, Minna Gombell, Joyce Compton, Robert Warrick
11.	Secret Service of the A	1939	Bryan Foy	Noel Smith	61 minutes	Ted Mc Cord	John Litel, Ila Rhodes, James Steppenson, Rosella Towne, Larry Williams, John Ridgely, Anthony, Averill, Bernard Nedell, Frank M. Thomas
12.	Dark Victory	1939	Hall B. Wallis	Edmund	106 minutes	Ernest Haller	Bette Davis, George Brent, Humphrey Bogart, Geraldine Fitjerland, Henry Travers, cora Witherspoon, Dorothy

(Contd.)

1	2	3	4	5	6	7	8
							Peterson, Virginia Brissac, Charles Richman, Herbert Rawlinson, Leonard Mudie
13.	Code of the Secret Service	1939	Bryan Foy	Noel Smith	58 minutes	Ted Mc Cord	Rosella Towne, Moroni Olsen, Edgar Edwards, Jack Mower, John Gallaudet, Joe King, Steven Darrell, Sol Gorss
14.	Naughty but Nice	1939	Warner Brothers	Ray Enright	90 minutes	Arthur L. Todd	Dick Powell, Gale Page, Ann Sheridan, Helen Broderick, Allen Jenkins, Zasu Pitts, Maxie Rosenbloom, Jerry Colonna, Vera Lewis, Elijabeth Dunne, Luis Alberni, Bill Davidson, Graneville Bates
15.	Hell's Kitchen	1939	Mark Hellinger	Leur's Seiler	81 minutes	Charles Rosher	Billy Halop, Bobby Jordan, Leo Gorcey, Huntj Hall, Gabriel Dell, Bernard Punsley, Frankie Burke, Margaret Lindsay, Stanley Fields, Grant Mitchell, frederic Tojere, Arthur Loft, Vera Lewis, Robert Homans
16.	Angels wash their Faces	1939	Robert Fellows	Ray Enright	76 minutes	Arthur L. Todd	Ann Sheridan, Billy Hallop, Bonita Granville, Frankie Thomas, Bobby Jordan, Bernard Punsley, Leo Gorcey, Huntj Hall, Gabriel Dell, Henry O'neill, Edwardo Ciannelli, Berton churechill, Minor Watson
17.	Smashing the	1939	Bryan Foy	Terry Morse	57 minutes	Jame Van Trees	Margot Stevenson, Joe Downing, Charles D.

(Contd.)

1	2	3	4	5	6	7	8
	Money Ring						Brown, Elliott Sullivan, Don Douglas, Charles Wilson, Joe King, William Davidson, Dick Rich, Max Hoffman, Junior, John Hamilton
18.	Brother Rat and A Baby	1940	Robert Lord	Ray Enright	87 minutes	Charles Rosher	Wayne Morris, Priscilla Lane, Eddie Albert, Jane Wyman, Jane Bryan, Peter B. Good, Larry Williams, Arthur Treacher, Moroni Olsen, Jessie Busley, Paul Harvey, Berton Churchill, Nana Bryant, Mayo Methot, Ed Gargan
19.	An Angel from Texas	1940	Robert Fellows	Ray Enright	69 minutes	Arthur L. Todd	Eddie Albert, Wayne Morris, Rosemary Lane, Jane Wyman, Ruth Terry, John Litel, Hobart Cavanaugh, Ann Shoemaker, Tom Kennedy, Milburn Stone, Elliott Sullivan, Paul Phillips, Enmett Vogan, Ferris Taylor
20.	Murder in the Air	1940	Bryan Foy	Lewis Seiler	55 minutes	Ted Mc Cord	John Litel, James Stephenson, Lya Lys, Robert Warrick, Victor Zimmerman, William Gould, Kenneth Harlan, Frank Wilcox, Owen King, Dick Rich, Charles Brokaw, Helen Lynd, Jeffrey Sayre, Carlyle Moore, Junior; Cliff Clark, Ed Stanley, Selmer Jackson, John Hamilton
21.	Knute Ro Ckne—All American	1940	Hal B. Wallis	Lloyd Bacon	98 minutes	Tony Gaudio	Pat O' Brien, Gale Page, Donald Crisp, Albert Basserman, John Litel, Henry

(Contd.)

1	2	3	4	5	6	7	8
							O'Neill, Owen Devis, Junior; John Qualen, Dorothy Tree, John Sheffield, Nick Lukats, Kane Richmond, William Marshail, William Byrne, John Ridgely
22.	Tugboat Annie Sails Again	1940	Bryan Foy	Leur's Seiler	77 minutes	Arthur Edeson	Marjorie Rambeau, Jane Wyman, Alan Hale, Charles Halton, Clarence Kolb, Paul Hurst, Victor Killian, Chill Wills, Harry Shannon, John Hamilton, Sidney Bracy, Jack Mower, Margaret Hayes, Josephine Whittell, Neil Reagan, George Meander
23.	Santa Fe Trail	1940	Hal B. Wallis	Michael Curtij	110 minutes	Sol Polito	Errol Flynn, Olivia de Havill and, Raymond Massey, Alan Hale, William Lundigan, Van Heflin, Gene Reynolds, Henry O' Neill, Guinn Williams, Alan Baxter, John Litel, Morini Olsen, David Bruce
24.	The Bad Man	1941	J. Walter Ruben	Richard Thorpe	70 minutes	Wells Root	Wallace Beery, Lionel Barrymore, Larrane Day, Henry Travers, Tom Conway, Chill Wills, Nydia Westman, Chris-Pin Martin, Charles Stevens
25.	Million Dollar Baby	1941	Hal B. Wallis	Curtis Bernhardt	102 minutes	Charles Rosher	Priscilla Lane, Jeffrey Lynn, May Robson, Lee Patrick, Helen Westly, Walter Catlett, Richard Carle, George Barbier, John Qualen, Fay Helm, Nan

(Contd.)

1	2	3	4	5	6	7	8
							Wynn, John Ridgely, Maris Wrixon, Johnny Sheffield, George Humbert, James Burke, Greta Meyer, Jean Ames
26.	Nine Lives are not Enough	1941	William Jacobs	A. Edward Sutherland	63 minutes	Ted McCord	Joan Perry, James Gleason, Peter Whitney, Faye Emerson, Howard da Silva, Edward Broppy, Charles Drake, Vera Lewis, Ben Welden, Howard Hickman, tom Stevenson, John Ridgely, Panl Phillips, Cliff Clark, Walter Soderling, Josepp Crehan
27.	International Squadron	1941	Edmund Grainger	Lother Mendes	87 minutes	James Van Trees	James Steppenson, Olympe Bradna, William Lundigan, Joan Perry, Julie Bishop, ToolAndrews, Cliff Edwards, John Ridgely, Selmer Jackson, Addison Richards, Holmes Herbert, Eddy Conrad, Crauford Kent
28.	Kings Row	1942	Hal B. Wallis	Sam Wood	127 minutes	James Wong Howe	Ann Sheridan, Robert Cummings, Charles Coburn, Betty Field, Claude Rains, Judith Anderson, Nancy Coleman, Karen Verne, Maria Ouspensbaya, Harry Davenport, Ernest Cossart, Pat Moriarty, Ilka Grunning, Mary Thomas
29.	Desperate Journey	1942	Hal B. Wallis	Raoul Walsh	107 minutes	Bert Glennon	Errol Flynn, Nancy Coleman, Raymond Massey, Alan Hale, Arthur Kennedy, Ronald Sinclair, Albert Basserman, Sig

(Contd.)

1	2	3	4	5	6	7	8
							Rumann, Patrick O' Moore, Felix Baxh, I lka Gruning, Elsa Basserman, Charles Irwin, Richard Fraser, Robert O' Davis, Henry Victor, Bruce Lester, Kurt Katch
30.	This is the Army	1943	Jack L. Warner	Michael Curtij	121 minutes	Bert Glennon	George Murppy, Joan Leslie, George Tobias, Alan Hale, Charles Butter Worth, Rosemary Decamp, Dolores Costello, Una Merkel, Stanley Ridges, Ruth Donnelly, Dorothi Peterson
31.	Stallion Road	1947	Alex Gottlieb	James V. Kern	97 minutes	Arthur Edeson	Alex is Smith, Zachary Scott, Peggy Knudsen, Patti Brady, Harry Davenport, Angela Greene, Frank Puglia, Ralpp Byrd, Lloyd Corrigan, Fernando Alvarado, Matthew Boulton, Mary Gordon, Nina Campana, Dewey Robinson, Paul Panjer
32.	That Hagen Girl	1947	Alex Gottlieb	Peter Godfrey	83 minutes	Karl Freund	Shirley Temple, Rory Calpoun, Lois maxwell, Dorothi Peterson, Charles Kemper, Conrad Janis, Penny Edwards, Jean Porter, Nella Walker, Harry Davenport, Winifred Harris, Moroni Olsen, Frank Conroy, Kathryn Card, Douglas Kennedy, Barbara Brown
33.	The Voice ot the Turtle	1947	Charles Hoffman	Irving Rapper	103 minutes	Sol Polito	Eleanor Parker, Eve Arden, Wayne Morris, Kent Smith, John Emercy, Erskine Sanford, Joh Holland, Nino Pehitone

(Contd.)

1	2	3	4	5	6	7	8
34.	John Loves Mary	1949	Jerry Wald	David Butler	96 minutes	Peverell Marley	Jack Carson, Patricia Neal, Wayne Morris, Edward Arnold, Virginia Field, Katherine Alexander, Paul Harvey, Ernest Cossart, Irving Bacon, George B. Hickman, Larry Rio
35.	Night Unto Night	1949	Owen Crump	Don Seigel	84 minutes	Peverell Marley	Viveca Lindfors, Broderick Crawford, Rosemary DeCamp, Osa Masen, Art Baker, Craig Stevens, Erskine Sanford, Johnny Mc Govern, Ann Burr, Lillian Yarbo, Ross Ford, Irving Bacon, Almira Sessions
36.	The Girl from Jones Beach	1949	Alex Gottlieb	Peter Godfrey	78 minutes	Carl Guthrie	Virginia Mayo, Eddie Bracken, Dona Drake, Henry Travers, Lois Wilson, Florenc4e Bates, Jerome Cowan, Helen Westcott, Panl Harvey, Lloyd Corrigan, Myrna Dell, Willian Forrest, Gary Gray, Mary Stuart, Lennie Bremen, Buddy Roosevelt
37.	It's A Great Feeling	1949	Alex Gottlieb	David Butler	85 minutes	Wilfred M. Cline	Doris Day, Bill Goodwin, Irving Bacon, Claire Carleton, Harlan Warde, Jacqueline De Witt, Errol Flynn, David Butler, Michael Curtij, King Vidor, Raonl Walsh, Gary Cooper, Joan Goford, Danny Kaye
38.	The Hasty Heart	1950	Howard Lindsay	Vincent Sherman	99 minutes	Wilkie Cooper	Richard Todd, Patricia Neal, Anthony Nicholis, Howard Crawford, John Sherman, Ralpp Michael, Alfred Bass, Orlando Martins

(Contd.)

1	2	3	4	5	6	7	8
39.	Louis	1950	Robert Arthur	Alexander Hall	90 minutes	Maury Gertsman	Charles Coburn, Ruth Hussey, Edmund Gwenn, Spring Byington, Pifer Laurie, Scotty Beckett, Connie Gilchrist, Willard Waterman, Jimmy Hunt, Marjorie Crossland, Terry Frost, Martin Milner, Ann Pearce, Dave Willock
40.	Storm Warning	1951	Jerry Wald	Stuart Heisler	93 minutes	Corl Guthrie	Ginger Rogers, Doris Day, Stove Cochran, Hugh Sanders, Lloyd Gough, Raymond Greenleaf, Ned Glass, Walter Baldurin, Lynne Whitney, Stuart Randall, Sean McClory, Paul Burns, Dave McMahow, Robert Williams
41.	Bedtime for Bonjo	1951	Michel Kraike de Cordova	Federick	84 minutes	Carl Guthrie	Diana Lynn, Walter Slejak, Jesse White, Lucille Barkley, Herbert Heyes, Herbert Vigran, Ed Gargan, Howard Banks, Ed Clark, Joel Franklin, Brad Browne, Harry Tyler, Elijabeth Flournoy, Perc Launders
42.	The Last Outpost	1951	William H. Pine	Lewis R. Foster	88 minutes	Loyal Griggs	Rhonda Fleming, Bruce Bennett, Bill Williams, Peter Honson, Hugh Beaumont, John Ridgely, Lloyd Corrigan, Charles Evans, Noah Beery (Junior)
43.	She's Working Her Way Through College	1952	William Jacobs	H. Bruce Humberstone	101 minutes	Wilfred M. Cline	Virginia Mayo, Gene Nelson, Don De Fore, Phyllis Thaxter, Patrice Wymore,

(Contd.)

1	2	3	4	5	6	7	8
							Ronald Winters, Raymond Greenleaf, Norman Bartold, Amanda Randolph, Henrietta Taylor, Hope Sansbury, George Meander, Eve Miller
44.	The Winning Team	1952	Bryan Foyp	Lewis Seiler	98 minutes	Sid Hichox	Doris Doy, Frank Lovejoy, Eve Miller, James Millican, Russ Tamblyn, Gordon Jones, Hugh Sanders, Frank Fergusan, Walter Baldwin, Dorothy Adams, Bonnie Kay Eddy, James Dodd, Tom Greenway, Rush Clark
45.	Tropic Zone	1953	William H. Pine	Lewis R. Foster	94 minutes	Lionel Lindon	Rhonda Fleming, Estelita, Noah Berry (Junior), Grant Withers, John Wengraf, Argentina Brunetti, Rico Alanej, Maurice Jara, Pilar Del Ray
46.	Law and Order	1953	John W. Rogers	Nathan Juran	80 minutes	Clifford Stine	Dorothi Malone, Alex Nicol, Preston Foster, Ruth Hampton, Russell Johnson, Barry Kelley, Chubby Johnson, Dennis Weaver, Jack Kelly, Valerie Jackson, Don Garner, Tom Browne, Richard Garrick, Tristram Coffin, Gregg Barton, William O'Neal, Wally Cassell
47.	Prisoner of War	1954	Henry Berman	Andrew Marton	80 minutes	Robert Planck	Steve Forrest, Dewey Martin, Oscar Homolka, Robert Horton, Panl Stewart, Harry Morgan, Steppen Bekassy, Leonard Strong, Darryl Hickman

(Contd.)

1	2	3	4	5	6	7	8
48.	Cattle Queen of Montana	1954	Benedict Borgeaus	Allan Dwan	88 minutes	John Alton	Barbara Stanwyck, Gene Evans, Lance Fuller, Fuller, Anthony Caruso, Jack Elam, Yvette Dugay, Morris Ankrum, Chubby Johnson, Myron Healey, Rod Redwing, Paul Birch, Byron Foulger, Burt Mustin
49.	Tennessee's Partner	1955	Bendict Borgeaus	Allan Dwan	86 minutes	John Alter	John Payne, Rhonda Fleming, Coleen Gray, Anthony Caruso, Leo Gorden, Myron Healey, Morris Ankrum, Chubby Johnson, Joe Devlin, John Manfield, Angie Dickinson
50.	The Killers	1964	Don Siegel	Don Siegel	95 minutes	Richard L. Rawlings	Les Marvin, John Cassavetes, Angie Dickinson, Clu Gulager, Claude Akins, Norman Fell, Virginia Christine, Don Haggerty, Robert Phillips, Kathleen O'Malley, Ted Jacques, Irving Moseley, Jimmy Joyce, Scott Hale, Seymour Cassel

Table 11.2

Writers and Musicians of Ronald Reagons Socio-Political Background Films

Sl. No.	*Film*	*Writer*	*Musician*
1	2	3	4
1.	Love is on the Air	Morton Grant	Not Available
2.	Hollywood Hotel	Jerry Wald, Maurice Leo and Richard Macauley	Leo F. Forbestin
3.	Swing Your Lady	Joseph Schrank and Maurice Leo	Adolph Deutsch
4.	Sergeant	William Jocobs	Not Available
5.	Accidents Will Happen	George Bricker and Anthory Coldeway	Not Available
6.	Cowboy from Brooklyn	Earl Baldwin	Not Available
7.	Boy Meets Girl	Sam and Bella Spewack	Leo F. forbastein
8.	Girls on Probation	Crane Wilbur	Not Available
9.	Brother Rat	Richard Macaulay and Jerry Wald	Not Available
10.	Going Places	Jerry Wald, Sig Herjig and Mowrice Leo	Not Available
11.	Secret Service of the Air	Raymond Schrock Not Available	
12.	Dark Victory	Casey Robinson	Max Steiner
13.	Code of the Secret Service	Lee Kitj and Dean Franklin	Not Available
14.	Nanghty But Nice	Jerry Wald and Richard Macaulay	Not Available
15.	Hell Kitchen	Crane Wilber and Fred Nibio, Junior	Not Available
16.	Angels Wash Their Faces	Michael Fessier, Niven Busch and Robert Buckner	Adolph Deutsch
17.	Smashing the Money Ring	Anthony Coldeway and Raymond Schrock	Not Available

1	2	3	4
18.	Brother Rat and A Baby	Jerry Wald and Richard Macaulany	Heing Roemheld
19.	An Angel from Texas	Fred Niblo, Junior and Bertram Millhauser	Howard Jackson
20.	Murder in the Air	Raymond Schrock	Not Available
21.	Knute Rockne—All American	Robert Buckner	Ray Heindorf
22.	Tugboat Annie Sails Again	Walter De Leon	Adolf Deutsch
23.	Santa Fe Trail	Robert Buckner	Max Steiner
24.	The Bad Man	Wells Root	Not Available
25.	Millioıı Dollar Baby	Casey Robioson, Richard Macaulay and Jerry Wald	Frederick Hollander
26.	Nine Lives are not Enough	Fred Niblo, Junior	Not Available
27.	Kings Row Casey Robinson	Erich Wolfgang Korngold	
28.	Desperate Jowmey	Arthur T. Horman	Max Steiner
29.	This is the Army	Casey Robinson and Claude Binyon	Ray Heindorf
30.	Stallion Road	Stephen Longstreet	Frederick Hollander
31.	That Hagen Girl	Charles Hoffman	Fraj Waxman
32.	The Voice of the Turtle	John Van Druten	Max Steiner
33.	John Loves Mary	Phoebe and Hemry Ephron	David Buttolph
34.	Night Unto Night	Kathryn Scola	Fraj Waxman
35.	The Girl from Jones Beach	I.A.L. Diamond	David Buttolph
36.	Its A Great Feeling	Jack Rose and Melville Shavelson	Ray Heindorf
37.	The Hast Heart	Ronald Mac Dougall	Louis Levy
38.	Louisa Stanley Roberts	Frank Skinner	

(Contd.)

1	2	3	4
39.	Storm Warning	Daniel Fuchs and Richard Brooks	Daniele Amfitheatroff
40.	Bedtime for Banjo	Val Barton and Lou Breslow	Frank Skinner
41.	The Last Outpost	Geoffrey Homes, George Worthing Yates and Winston Miller	Lucien Cailliet
42.	She's Working Her Way Through College	Peter Milne	Ray Heindorf
43.	The Winning Team	Ted Sherdeman, Seeleg Lester and Mervin Gerrard	David Buttolph
44.	Tropic Zone Lewis R. Foster	Lucien Cailliet	
45.	Law and Order	John and Owen Bagni and D.D. Beauchamp	Joseph Gershenson
46.	Priso- - of War	Allen Rivkin	Jeff Alexander
47.	Cattle Queen of Montana	Robert Blees and Howard Estabrook	Louis Forbes
48.	Tennessee's Partner	Milton Krims, D.D. Beauchamp, Graham Baker and Taddy Sherman	Louis Forbes
49.	The Killers Richard L. Rawlings	John Williams	
50.	Internation Squadron	Barry Trivers and Kenneth Gamet	Not Available

Filmography of Merchant Ivory Productions

'The Householder' (1963)
Director: James Ivory
Producer: Ismail Merchant
Screenplay: Ruth Prawer
'Shakespearewala' (1965)
Director: James Ivory
Producer: Ismail Merchant
Screenplay: Ruth Prawer
Jhabvala and James Ivory
'The Guru' (1967)
Arcadia Films/Merchant
Ivory Productions for 20th Century Fox
Director: James Ivory
Producer: Ismail Merchant
Screenplay: Ruth Prawer
Jhabvala and James Ivory
'Bombay Talkie' (1970)
Director: James Ivory
Producer: Ismail Merchant
Screenplay: Ruth Prawer
Jhabvala and James Ivory
Adventure of a Brown Man in Search of Civilisation' (1972)
Director: James Ivory
Producer: Ismail Merchant
Screenplay: James Ivory
'Savages' (1972)
Angelika Films in association with
Merchant Ivory Productions
Director: James Ivory
Producer: Ismail Merchant
Screenplay: George Swift and Michael O'Donoghue based on an idea by James Ivory
'Helen, Queen of the Nautch Girls' (1971)
Director: Anthony Korner
Producer: Ismail Merchant
Screenplay: James Ivory
'Mahatma and the Mad Boy' (1972)
Director: Ismail Merchant
Producer: Ismail Merchant
Screenplay: Tanveer Farooqi
'Autobiography of a Princess' (1974)
Director: James Ivory
Producer: Ismail Merchant
Screenplay: Rath Prawer Jhabwela
'The Wild Party' (1974)
Lansbury-Beruh/Merchant
Ivory Productions
(A Samuel Z. Arkoff presentation)
Director: James Ivory
Producer: Ismail Merchant
Screenplay: Walter Marks
'Sweet Sounds' (1976)
Director: Richard Robbins
Producer: Ismail Merchant
Screenplay: Richard Robbins
'Roseland' (1977)
In association with the Oregon Four
Director: James Ivory
Producer: Ismail Merchant
Screenplay: Ruth Prawer
'Hullabaloo Over Georgie and Bonnie's Pictures' (1978)
For London
Weekend Television
Director: James Ivory
Producer: Ismail Merchant
Screenplay: Ruth Prawer Jhabwala
'The Europeans' (1978)
With the National Film Finance Corporation
Director: James Ivory
Producer: Ismail Merchant
Screenplay: Ruth Prawer Jhabvala

(Contd.)

'Jane Austen in
Manhattan' (1980)
In association with Polytel International
Director: James Ivory
Producer: Ismail Merchant
Screenplay: Ruth Prawar Jhabvala
'Quartet' (1980)
With Lyric International (Paris)
Director: James Ivory
Producer: Ismail Merchant and
Jean-Pierre
Mahot de la Querantunnais
Screenplay: Ruth Prawer Jhabvala
'Heat and Dust' (1982)
Director: James Ivory
Producer: Ismail Merchant
Screenplay: Ruth Prawer Jhabvala
'The Bostonians' (1983)
In association with WGBH, Boston,
Redifussion Films, London, and Almi
Entertainment Finance Corporation
Director: James Ivory
Producer: Ismail Merchant
Screenplay: Ruth Prawer Jhabvala
'A Room With a View' (1985)
Director: James Ivory
Producer: Ismail Merchant
Screenplay: Ruth Prawer Jhabvala
Producer: Ismail Merchant
'Maurice' (1987)
Director: James Ivory
Producer: Ismail Merchant
Screenplay: Kit
Hesketh-Harvey and James Ivory
'The Perfect Murder' (1987)
Director: Zafar Hai
Producer: Waheed Chawhan
Executive producer: Ismail Merchant
Screenplay: H.R.F. Keating and Zafar Hai
'The Deceivers' (1988)
Director: Nicholas Meyer
Producer: Ismail Merchant
Screenplay: Michael Hirst
'Slaves of New York' (1988)
For Tri-Star Pictures
Merchant Director: James Ivory
Producers: Ismail
Merchant and Gary Hendler
Screenplay: Tama Janowitz
'Mr. and Mrs. Bridge' (1990)
Merchant Ivory
Productions/Robert
Halmi for Cineplex
Odeon Films
Director: James Ivory
Producer: Ismail Merchant
Screenplay: Ruth
Prawer Jhabvala
'The Ballad of the Sad Cafe' (1990)
Angelika Films Release
Director: Simon Callow
Producer: Ismail Merchant
Screenplay: Michael Hirst
'Howards End' (1991)
Director: James Ivory
Producer: Ismail Merchant
Screenplay: Ruth Prawer Jhabvala
'Jefferson in Paris' (1992)

Some Films of Merchant Ivory Productions are watched by Ronald Reagon also.

the Kansas Republican convention in August of 1976. His party had picked Gerald Ford to contest Jimmy Carter and lost. Political pundits now speculate over what might have happened hac the Republicans chosen Reagon instead of Ford. In 1980, the Republicans selected Ronald Regan as their candidate for President and he was elected as the President of United States of America.

II. GREAT CHARLIE CHAPLIN

Charlie Chaplin (Sir Charls Spencer Chaplin) was a selfmade man who went on to become a creative stylist—more than just an actor or director. His Hollywood films were originally classified as popular entertainment, but were eagerly and whole-heartedly accepted by the art film audience. Serious social questions were often raised through comic stereotypes, common targets were rich snobs, moralistic ladies, preachers and even the police. Chaplin took Hollywood comedy in a new direction combining delicate pathos and hilarity. There was not much to laugh about in Chaplin's early life, however. Born in London on April 16, 1889, to Charles and Hannah Chaplin, performers who taught their son to sing and dance before he could walk, Chaplin first appeared on stage at 8, doing a clog-dancing act in "Lancashire Lads". Since his father died soon after and his mother suffered bouts of insanity, the master filmmaker spent much of his dreary childhood in boarding schools and orphanages with occasional appearances on the stage, often living in the streets. When Chaplin was 17, he joined an English Vaudeville company, till in 1913, Mack Sennett, producer of slapstick films under the Keystone banner noticed Chaplin's talent and signed him on to feature in a one-reeler at 150 dollars a week. He never returned to the stage, or looked back on hard times.

Sennett believed in reducing human beings to little mechanical shots, his primary target was pretention.

Chaplin's Keystone films were a hit, it is in his second one, "Kid Auto Races at Venice", that he hit upon his famous costume. The film made in 1914, was an endearing little improvisation of the troublesome tramp who interferes with a camera team busy taking pictures of the races. Of course, the full pathos and significance of the tramp were only fully realised as the character developed, and Chaplin was a sensation from the start. Soon he was allowed to direct his own films and by the early 1920s, Chaplin's box-office appeal was so great that not many studios could afford him, he started producing his own films. With the advent of sound, his fame scarcely diminished, he did curtail his appearances on the screen, however, and confined himself to directing and producing. Chaplin's salaries soared to break all previous motion picture records from 1,250 dollars a week from Essaney (1915), 10,000 dollars a week plus a 150,000 bonus for signing form Mutual (1916) to 1,000,000 dollars for eight pictures from "First National" the following year."[1]

With the tramp assuming mythic, poetic and sociological meaning, Chaplin began exploring social issues and other serious themes, such as the need for material comfort or human companionship. His earlier films, like "His New Job"—which parodies pretentious films and film stars—and "Night Out", a physical film of drunken brawls and stunts—were still in the Sennett style. But in "The Tramp" (1935) Charlie finally comes into his own. He is the simpleton, the man of nature who sides with the young lady in the film, only to lose her to his city-slicker rival. In "The Bank" (1915), Chaplin plays the janitor who performs heroic deeds a la Walter Mitty, only to awaken from a dream. The growing social commentary in his films was offset by the hilarious use of props and the delicate mime that was to characterise the tramp figure. The superb stylist gained mastery over cinematic technique, realising that his comic style was best suited to the medium shot, the minimum possible cutting was resorted to, so as not to lose out on the mime.

Charlie Chaplin's years at mutual saw an even greater control over the medium. He reached perfection in the short film genre. In "The Rink" (1916), he performs a magnificent roller-skating act to flee from his wealthy enemy and the law. In "The Floor-walker" (1916), he catches a shop thief only to discover to his horror that it is the owner. A consistent motif in Chaplin's films is the boss stealing from his own kitty and Charlie being accused of the crime, because he is shabbily dressed and has no credibility as a poor man. The rich man was a brute, a miser, or a meanie, whereas the tramp was poor but had more value in human terms. The blonde actress played by Edna Purviance in a lot of his films, was the last word in beauty, virtue and gentleness.[2] Some of the later films with this studio were even more serious. In "The Immigrant" (1917), the problems of immigrants to the United States are explored. "Easy Street" (1917) deals with idealistic cliched notions of social progress and human nature. The name of this film is ironic because life with poverty, hunger, drugs and vicious brutality is far from easy on this street, which is really a slum. His best-known film from the First National Years (1918 to 1923) is the story of Scraps, a mongrel (A Dog's Life), where Chaplin compared "the little fellow" (as he liked to call the tramp) to a dog, both desperately struggling for food, shelter and affection. In "The Kid", Chaplin describes genuine familiar love, something he barely experienced himself as opposed to what society expected it to be, with the tramp's relationship with his adopted child (Jackie Coogan). In his last mutual film, "The Pilgrim", the tramp's personal moral framework proves superior to that of both church and state.[3]

Ironic restraint and clever comment became the hallmark of his later films. In "Gold Rush", Chaplin's favourite and perhaps his best, Chaplin prospects for gold in an icy desert, a cold metal in an even colder land. Despite the hilarity, the Callousness and inhumanity of the occupation comes through forcefully. This film also includes the fabulous sequence of the Tramp being stood up on New Year's love by the woman who promises to escort him and the heart-tugging pathos as he stands outside the dance hall where she works, completely alone in the world. Similarly in "The Circus" (1926), the tramp's gentleness and warmth are out of place beside the cruel circus owner and the slimy trapeze artist who romances and steals his girl. Though "City Lights" in 1931 was his first talkie, he preserves silence and mime in "Modern Times" (1936), underscored by clever music that he composed. For his last three films, Chaplin used dialogue, but still maintained much of the wit and ironic iconoclasm of his earlier films. Without studio restrictions, he reached greater cinematic creativity. His "Great Dictator" (1940), contrasted the egomaniacal urges of Hitler to the natural human responses of the tramp-barber; Chaplin played both roles. "Monsieur Verdoux" (1947) acidly and ironically showed murder to be as legitimate a means of making money as any, the autobiographical "Linelight (1952), was a tender, personal recounting of Chaplin's own story.[4] Chaplin's personal life was often tempestuous. He married four times, thrice to his leading ladies, Mildred Harris (1918), Lita Grey (1924), Paulette Godard (1936), and in 1943 to Oona O' Neill, daughter of the celebrated American playwright, Eugene O' Neill. His first two divorces were sensational and made headlines, as did a paternity suit in 1944. His "Monsieur Verdoux" angered the American legion, among others (it was a mordant version of the Blue Beard story) and columnists claimed that he was subversive and a communist.

Charlie Chaplin left the United States in 1952, pressed for back-taxes, and he and his wife and six children settled in Corsier-sur-Vevey in Switzerland. He had his own back on the U.S. authorities by producing in 1957, "A king in New York," released in London, with Caustic Comments on the hypocrisy of the American way of life. The film brought with it further allegations that Chaplin was a Communist, which he categorically refuted. In 1966, he wrote, directed and appeared briefly in "A Countess from Hong Kong", starring Marlon Brando and Sophia Loren. He returned to U.S.A. in 1972 to receive a special award (an Oscar) from the Academy of Motion Pictures Arts and Sciences, Knighted by Queen Elizabeth II in 1975, he died on Christmas Day in 1977, at the grand old age of 88, leaving his indelible stamp on cinema spanning almost an entire century.

References

1. "Apart from illustration Chaplin's stupendous popularity, these unprecedented figures indicated the conversion of the motion picture from cheap novelty to big business, and the advent of the star system, where pictures were judged by the stars they featured, rather than story or plot."

   For much of his tenure at Keystone, Chaplin was the jaunty, gritty, tramp who kicked anybody in the pants and flung dough in people's faces. Chaplin soon realised that life was not one big parody, and that it was more difficult to be able to have a loaf of bread to eat than it was to hurl it in someone's face. Unlike Senett, who turned people into inanimated objects, Chaplin revelled in turning objects into 'live' things. In "Mabel's Married Life", Charlie fights with a boxing dummy, in "His Favourite Pastime", a swinging saloon door becomes his opponent; in "Dough and Dynamite" he turns dough into bracelets and bricks. The Chaplin comic technique was founded on this transposition of objects, like the alarm clock in "The Pawn Shop" which variously turns into a tin of tuna, a sick patient and an infected tooth; in "Gold Rush", a boiled shoe provides an epicurean feast; in "The Great Dictator", he turns the earth into a balloon and a toy ball balanced by a performing seal."

—Sonia Ramaswamy, "The World's most famous Tramp", *Express Magazine,* Weekly, New Delhi, 24 September, 1980, p. 8.

2. *Ibid.*
3. In 1919, Chaplin, together with two of the great film successes of the time. Mary Pickford and Douglas Fairbanks, started United Artists, so that each could produce and distribute their own films independently. After his Mutual contract expired in 1923, the great director/actor only produced for his own company, until he made "A Countess from Hong Kong" in 1966. "A Woman of Paris" (1923) was a daring departure from films at the time, starring Edna Purviance and leaving the tramp character only a tiny, walk on part. It is about a woman who enjoyed the high life as the mistress of a sophisticated Parsian sensualist, and contrasts the purity of provincial life with the temptations of the big bad city, and the lure of materialism as opposed to the need for love. What was extraordinary about Chaplin's statements on love versus prostitution was his refusal to be moralistic about sinfulness in adultery; he asks instead how else the poor woman could enjoy the comforts of wealth."
—*Ibid.*
4. *Ibid.*

Bibliography

Newspapers and Magazines

Hindi Dailies.

Amar Ujala; Agra, Bareilly and Meerut.

Jansatta; New Delhi.

Dainik Jagran; Kanpur and Meerut.

Dainic Navjyoti; Jaipur and Ajmer.

Nyaya; Ajmer.

Punjab Kesari; Delhi and Jallandhar.

Navbharat Times; Delhi.

Rajasthan Patrika; Jaipur.

Hindustan; New Delhi.

Hindi Weeklies, Fortnightlies and Monthlies

Cross Examination; Weekly, Bombay.

Dharamyug; Weekly, Bombai.

Maharashtra Manas; Fortnightly, Bombay.

Madhuri; Fortnightly, Bombay.

Movie Jagat; Weekly, New Delhi.

Saptahik Hindustan; Weekly, New Delhi.

English Dailies, Weeklies, Fortnightlies and Monthlies

Indian Express; Daily, New Delhi.

Times of India, Daily, New Delhi.

Express Magazine; Weekly, New Delhi.

Filmfare; Weekly and Fortnightly, Bombay.

Hindustan Times; Daily, New Delhi.

Screen; Weekly, Bombay.

Indian Today; Fortnightly, New Delhi.

Film Mirror; Monthly, New Delhi.

commonwealth

8819

28-6-99